TITO'S IMPERIAL COMMUNISM

Tito's IMPERIAL COMMUNISM

BY
R. H. MARKHAM

The University of North Carolina Press
Chapel Hill
1947

Copyright, 1947, by
THE UNIVERSITY OF NORTH CAROLINA PRESS

To

All Yugoslav men and women now suffering privations, imprisonment, or exile because of their devotion to human liberty.

Foreword

THIS book is designed to describe some developments that have taken place in Yugoslavia since the beginning of the Second World War. It is not designed to be a textbook in history, nor to serve chiefly as a chronicle, but rather to point out the most salient features of a sad picture. It is an attempt to reveal the pattern in a tragic and extremely complex situation.

The pattern will indicate that the sixteen million South Slavs, inhabiting an area about the size of the state of Oregon, have passed under a ruthless totalitarian dictatorship, exceeding in regimentation and autocracy any regime to which they have been subjected during the last two centuries.

Practically every point treated in this book is controversial and may raise doubts in the mind of the reader. To obtain a clearer understanding of the extremely vital conflicts and trends, one would do well to heed the following admonitions:

First, it is a fatal mistake to believe that B is good because A was bad. Such an error leads one into hopeless confusion.

I believe the Karageorgevitch dynasty had bad kings along with the good. I am convinced that King Alexander I had very serious defects. But that fact in no way justifies the conclusion that Tito is a better ruler than Alexander was. As a matter of fact, Tito is much more lawless, cruel, and despotic than any other Yugoslav ruler has been.

It is also true that the Serbs are ardent, aggressive nationalists. They have often been unreasonable. They have overstressed their Serbian point of view and Serbian interests, thereby estranging other Slav groups. Some Serbs have worked for a "Greater Serbia" and by that act justifiably roused the enmity of Croatians and Slovenes. Serbian hegemony was onerous. But the fact that evils flowed from former Serb domination does not mean that Tito's regime is better. As a matter of fact, Tito's rule has the defects of Serbian hegemony, in a magnified degree. Greater Serbianism was not good, but Tito's Communistic totalitarianism is worse.

It is true there was much "reaction" and governmental favoritism in Yugoslavia, as well as a distressing amount of graft. But the present regime has brought no cure. On the contrary, it is more corrupt. Its very basis is favoritism for the dominant political group.

A second vital admonition one should consider in studying Yugoslavia is that most words used by Tito's Partisans in relation to Yugoslavia are deceptive. They do not clarify but confuse; they do not explain but mislead. They are designed to arouse emotions, incite fanaticism, and stultify thought.

Tito's motto is "Death to Fascism—Freedom to the Nation." But prior to Tito's regime, Fascist totalitarianism never established itself in Yugoslavia. Milan Stoyadinovitch endeavored to become a Yugoslav Mussolini but the nation laughed him to scorn. In Slovenia there was no Duce of any kind. In Croatia the popular leader was Stephan Raditch, a peasant prophet, who much resembled William Jennings Bryan. In Serbia the best loved man for years was the peasant, Nichola Pashitch. He was a political boss, but in most respects unlike Mussolini. He resembled Andrew Jackson somewhat. The first Fuehrer in Yugoslav history is Tito. Yugoslav totalitarianism began with him.

In a similar way Tito's Partisans abuse such words as "freedom," "democracy," "truth," "education," "social justice."

The third thing one should always keep in mind when attempting to understand Tito's Yugoslavia is that there has been no beneficial "social revolution" there, nor anything even approaching it. In no respect is Tito's social or economic program ahead of that of the Croatian peasant leader, Vladimir Machek, or of the Slovene Liberals or the leftist Serb Agrarians. Tito has effected no basic social or economic improvements. All he has done is to make some defenseless citizen get up so that a Partisan could sit down in his place. He has taken a neighbor's house or field and given it to a Partisan. He asks democrats to applaud him for acts on account of which they have always condemned kings.

Tito effected a violent political overturn, nothing more. The common man will have no burdens lifted. On the contrary, burdens are increased and power to bear them diminished.

One who wishes to understand Tito's Yugoslavia must constantly guard against the lure of secular theology. A part of the American intelligentsia has become a victim of leftist scholasticism. These intellectuals are among the world's blindest and most blatant fundamentalists. They appraise all events and especially contemporary events according to Pentecostal formulae. They believe, along with other Holy Rollers, that mankind is sinful, especially the capitalistic bourgeoisie; that there must be an Armageddon, namely a bloody social revolution; and that thereafter we will all live in a millennial paradise, the classless Marxist society. All of this is as much a theological legend as the Old Testament prophecies about the beast with the ten horns. Like contemporary Witnesses of Jehovah, American leftists try to force all events into their rigid prophetic molds, thus hopelessly distorting facts.

One must always keep in mind that leftist "facts about Yugoslavia" are often only Pentecostal "speaking with tongues."

Also, anyone who wants to understand Tito's Yugoslavia must beware of "pie in the sky." There is no current religious yearning which Communist-led American leftists so lustily and hilariously ridicule as the heaven of conservative Baptists "in the Bible Belt." They say they don't want "pie in the sky," but refrigerators here and now. However, they constantly give themselves to ecstatic celestial visions. They see houris in every pink cloud and sing of blessings that surpass the golden streets and angel robes of most gospel hymns. Many of the things they report about Tito's regime resemble the heaven that gleams and glistens when one "gets religion."

Finally, it must be kept in mind that in all the complexity of Yugoslav developments, the main issue is the struggle for and against Communist totalitarianism. Other conflicts and events, though important, are secondary. R. H. M.

Contents

		PAGE
	FOREWORD	vii
CHAPTER		
I.	WHO ARE THE YUGOSLAVS?	3
II.	RELIGIONS IN YUGOSLAVIA	13
III.	MIHAILOVITCH APPEARS	17
IV.	THE WAR COMES TO YUGOSLAVIA	26
V.	SOVIET RUSSIA DEGRADES PROSTRATE YUGOSLAVIA	35
VI.	MIHAILOVITCH ORGANIZES UNDERGROUND RESISTANCE	45
VII.	YUGOSLAVIA'S SOCIAL STRUCTURE	52
VIII.	YUGOSLAV COMMUNISTS	61
IX.	MIHAILOVITCH AND TITO CLASH	72
X.	THE SERBS ARE MASSACRED	80
XI.	MIHAILOVITCH'S ANTI-GERMAN TACTICS	94
XII.	TITO'S ANTI-GERMAN TACTICS	105
XIII.	TITO ORGANIZES A REVOLUTIONARY GOVERNMENT	115

CHAPTER		PAGE
XIV.	Tito's Military Contribution	127
XV.	Collaboration and Accommodation	142
XVI.	Britain Throws Its Support to Tito	155
XVII.	We Plunge Deeper into Yugoslavia's Civil War	170
XVIII.	Tito Is Installed	182
XIX.	Fascists in Tito's Ranks	194
XX.	Balkan Pan-Slavism: Tito's Relations with Bulgaria	205
XXI.	The Role of Macedonia	220
XXII.	Has the Federalization of Yugoslavia Brought Harmony?	231
XXIII.	Tito's Regime and the Yalta Conference	245
XXIV.	What Is Tito Doing to the Common People?	254
XXV.	Tito Menaces Balkan Peace	275

TITO'S IMPERIAL COMMUNISM

CHAPTER ONE

Who Are the Yugoslavs?

THE most dramatic date in recent Yugoslav history is the 27th of March, 1941. On that day or early morning, officers in the Yugoslav Army overthrew the pro-Hitler Yugoslav government and created a new anti-Nazi regime. These army officers took this bold step at a time when Russia was cooperating with Nazi Germany, when the Nazi army was all-triumphant and faced by no active foe, and when Great Britain, crippled and alone, faced the full might of Germany.

Practically all the little nations of Europe had been crushed. Poland had been partitioned between Germany and Russia. France had fallen. Italy had established a base in Albania, at Yugoslavia's rear. Bulgaria had admitted large numbers of crack Nazi troops. In other words, Yugoslavia was utterly isolated and surrounded. England could not give the slightest aid. Russia had shown herself not only unreliable but eager to collaborate with Germany in swallowing up weak nations.

Yet at that moment a group of Yugoslav officers defied Hitler and took a step which could only mean war against Hitler, the master of Europe, the destroyer of nations. And in this rash act the officers received flaming popular support. Peasants and workers wanted the political revolution. City men and women had sought it. Children had feverishly advocated it and wildly applauded it. Grandmas and grandpas had demanded it and gave it their blessing. The Yugoslavs fairly asked for Hitler's bombs and tanks—they asked for death and got it!

Who were these strange rash revolutionists? They were Serbs. Not all Yugoslavs are Serbs. Among them are also Croatians and Slovenes. In the kingdom at that time lived about eight million Serbs, about four million Croatians, one and a quarter million Slovenes. In addition, there were Germans, Hungarians, Albanians, and Rumanians.

The Serbs are divided into several groups or categories. The bulk of them inhabit Serbia, centering around the Serbian heartland, Shumadiya, or "woodland"; about two million are in "Across-the-river," old Austro-Hungarian areas; some are in Macedonia; and three-fourths of a million are in Montenegro.

Some of the Montenegrins do not want to be so completely identified with Serbs as to lose their Montenegrin identity in Serbism, but even these consider themselves Serbs. The Montenegrins have a glorious history, cherish an unquenchable love for freedom, and prize the Montenegrin tradition. In addition, they long had an independent state, with princes and kings. Consequently, some of them have not wanted Montenegro simply to be swallowed up by Serbia, any more than Rhode Island would want to be swallowed up by America. However, in spite of this group of Montenegrin nationalists and separatists, most Montenegrins consider themselves an indissoluble part of the Serbian nation. They are as much a part of the Serbs as Kansans are of the Americans. Many Montenegrins have worn a Serbian emblem on their caps even from ancient times.

Now, who are the "Across-the-river" Serbs, or "Prechani," as they are called? In a narrow sense they are the fairly prosperous Serbs living across the Danube and Sava rivers north of Belgrade, but in a broader sense they are the Eastern Orthodox Slavs scattered throughout the former Austro-Hungarian provinces of southeast Europe. A majority are quite poor. Many are rather primitive. Most live in small towns and villages, inextricably mixed with other types of

Yugoslavs. In some districts, localities, and towns, they constitute a majority; in others a minority. The very fact that they have been cut off from the main body of Serbs has tended to increase their Serbian nationalism. At times their Serbianism was about all they had to live by.

Being under foreign domination for centuries—clear up to 1918—they have always been conscious of forming a minority problem. In a way, they were as Jewish exiles beside the river at Babylon. Serbia was their Jerusalem. But these Prechani-Serbs have not wanted to return to Jerusalem—they have wanted Jerusalem to extend its walls to take them in. Such Serbs fired the shots that caused the First World War. Many of these Serbs have both loved and opposed Belgrade.

There is still another type of Serbs—perhaps the Serbs who aren't Serbs—namely, the Moslems of Bosnia and Herzegovina. They are of Slav origin, speak only the Serbo-Croatian language, and six hundred years ago were an indistinguishable part of the Serb (or at least Christian Slav) family. But they were coercively converted to Mohammedanism and took the side of the Turkish conquerors of Serbia. They scorned Serbdom and the Cross, became as Turks, were called Turks, and served as furious enemies of the Christians. Most of them are quite primitive, rather wild, often fierce mountaineers; they constitute a serious Yugoslav and Serb problem.

The most simple description of the Serbs is involved and complicated. Think, then, how complicated the reality is! Many of the eight million Serbs are not only inextricably mixed up with other peoples, but the various branches of the nation differ among themselves. Their costumes are somewhat varied as are their dialects, their architecture, and their daily greetings. But most—excepting the Serb Moslems—have two traits in common. They are ardently, indomitably nationalistic and they are bellicose. These two traits are really one.

The Serbs are fighters for Serbian freedom. They have spent centuries getting free from the Turks and Hapsburgs and they had to fight to do it. The activity which most Serbs everywhere most highly cherish is fighting for Serb freedom. Their God is a fighter, their priests are fighters, their poets are fighters, their folk songs are epics, their mothers pray fighting prayers and send their sons to battle for freedom, their grandfathers light candles in dim churches to honor dead warriors for freedom, and their grandmothers strew flowers on humble graves to commemorate men who fought for freedom. Such traditions, long cherished and long practiced, make militant nationalists.

However, it would be a grave mistake to picture a Serb as just wandering around shooting people. On the contrary, he is affable, sociable, hospitable, and friendly. Serbs constantly remind me of Texans. Most are tall, all are spirited, a majority are conceited. They believe Serbia is the most beautiful place on earth, that the Serbs are God's favorites, and that God's mother tongue was Serbian in the Shumadiyan dialect.

Serbian women are dark and lithe, vivacious and self-reliant, and among the most attractive in Europe. Serbian men are often handsome, athletic in appearance, with long faces and high foreheads. They are heroic in pose, aggressively friendly, sometimes shallow. They are lavish in entertainment, exhaustive in hospitality, very fond of singing, attached to troubadours, and faithful to tribal standards of honor. They like drinking, outdoor folk dancing, and making love to black-eyed beauties with wavy hair and clever tongues.

All Serb life until very recently has been patriarchal, centering about the family. Most Slavs and especially Serbs have strong, enduring family love. They have lived in very large, rambling houses, often containing twenty or thirty people. Such a family group is called a "zadruga" and includes grandparents, parents, and large numbers of married children. Grandfather runs the show, gives each member his job, puts profits—mostly in kind—into a common pool, and provides everyone with what he needs. Each group owns its own house and land, is master of its tiny kingdom, is proud of its place in the peasant society, and at "Slavas" entertains all neighbors far and near. Girls walk the straight and narrow, boys do as they are told, women openly serve and slyly dominate blustering men; all preserve the family honor and cherish the name of Serbia. None become hired girls or hired men; none are foreign mercenaries. Few Serbs from Serbia proper emigrate to foreign lands. They elevate kings from their own ranks and kill them when they get despotic. They scorn the British and Swedes for importing kings; they believe that Goethe in his productions was inspired by Serbian folk poetry.

The Serbs, first among Balkan peoples, had an independent, autocephalic church of their own. They, chief among the peoples of eastern Europe, transformed their subjugation by the Turks in 1389 at Kossovo into a national epic and centered their whole spiritual life about it. And first among the modern Balkan peoples they rose against the Turks—in 1804.

The Serbs have many serious defects. They tend to be narrow, rather vain, too domineering. But they possess certain spiritual qualities to a degree unsurpassed in Europe. They are brave and very democratic in a patriarchal way. They have placed freedom above all other ideals and consider fighting for it the first duty of every loyal man. This was the people which voluntarily defied Hitler at the moment of his greatest power.

The second largest Slav group in Yugoslavia is that to which Josip Broz-Tito belongs, namely, the Croats. Their language is almost identical with that of the Serbs. It is Serbo-Croatian, a Slav tongue, basically similar to Russian, Bulgarian, Czech, and Polish. A typical Croat from the heart of Croatia speaks a language as similar to that of a typical Serb from the heart of Serbia, as is the tongue of a Chicagoan to that of a Bostonian. When Croats and Serbs live side by side, as they do in hundreds of places, they speak the same dialects.

And as you could hardly tell them apart by ear, you could hardly distinguish them by eye. They look alike. They are both Slavs. Often they belong to the same "racial types." Many of the folk customs of the two groups are similar. Also, most members of both groups are peasants. In most group traits they are nearer together than are the people of Detroit to those of London.

Nevertheless, the Croats and Serbs feel that they are separate nations and want to have the right to give full expression to that feeling. In religion they are decidedly different. Croats are Roman Catholics; Serbs are Eastern Orthodox. Most Croat traditions are Central European; Serb traditions, Balkanese. Practically all Croatians inhabit former Austro-Hungarian provinces. Generations of them were brought up under Hapsburg domination. For hundreds of years up to 1918 they had no state of their own.

They are excellent soldiers, but for a thousand years had no army of their own. Their culture was influenced by Vienna. Their singers, writers, sculptors, tended to crave recognition from Vienna. Their foreign yoke was rather easy; they received some advantages from their masters along with political slavery. Their subjugation was mitigated with some of the appearances and appurtenances of independence. Also, they had a few cities and a commendable culture.

Thus the Serbs were harder, in their age-long fight for liberty, wilder, bolder, cruder, and more successful than the Croatians. They founded a state, created an army, set up their own administration, and eventually helped "free the Croatians." All these differences are causes of rivalry, dissension, bitter hatred, and bloodshed. At times Serbs and Croats get a wild joy in killing each other. Of course, they are not at all unique. Georgians and Ohioans once felt the same way.

The Croats occupy the west central part of Yugoslavia and center about the beautiful city of Zagreb. They also extend south along the Adriatic coast and are scattered through Bosnia and Herzegovina. They likewise extend eastward over the Sava and Danube plains to the very heights of Belgrade itself. Throughout wide areas Croatians and Serbians live side by side, field to field, village to village, even house to house. They are inextricably intermixed. However, there are practically no Croats in Serbia proper, Macedonia, or Montenegro.

The Croats, in my opinion, are a very estimable people. They work hard, both the men and women are sturdy, they esteem liberty, and have much self-respect. They have a sense of beauty and wear costumes that are among the most exquisite in Europe. They love music and nearly all of them sing. They are quite disciplined and loyal and show great attachment to their leaders, as well as much judgment in choosing them. Like the Serbs, they follow no chief blindly.

Croatian national militancy tends to be more passive than aggressive, more defensive than offensive. It has some aspects of Tolstoyism and of moral pressure. This tendency, however, should not be overstressed. The Croats, as a whole, are not pacifists and some of them at times are furiously savage. Their Fascist chief, Ante Pavelitch, who ruled them during the war, was as vicious a savage as was to be found in any Hitler or Mussolini gang. Josip Broz-Tito, a Croatian, is an extreme expansionist. And a brutal one. Greater Croatians abound and are just as obnoxious, unreasonable, and overbearing as Greater Serbs.

However, one may say with a fair degree of accuracy that the two famous Croatian peasant leaders, Stephan Raditch, a martyr, and Vladko Machek, a refugee, are rather typical of the Croatians. They spent their lives amid peasants, working for peasants; they were simple and unpretentious, given to music and song and poetry, and with a high regard for religion—though neither has been clerical. They had extensive and intensive social programs, much resembling those of midwest American Populists and designed to promote cooperative buying and selling, to encourage education from childhood to old age, to establish peasant credit, increase yields per acre, improve distribution, and nourish the longing for national freedom, within the bounds of Yugoslavia.

Machek's motto was that "the Croatians wanted their money in their own pockets, their rifles on their own shoulders, their school books in their own book bags." From the creation of Yugoslavia on December 1, 1918, almost until the beginning of the Second World War the Croats devoted most of their energy not to consolidating Yugoslavia, which at times they bitterly hated, but to resisting Serbian hegemony. Feelings between Yugoslav Croatians and Yugoslav Serbs were very bitter. Many Croatians, including Machek, were put into prison. Raditch, whom most Croatians dearly loved, was assassinated. In turn, the Croatians brought about the assassination of the Serbian King Alexander.

Deep and terrible was the chasm between Croatia and Serbia and it stretched straight across Yugoslavia. Yet the two peoples could not go their ways apart in separate states, because no ethnological border could be drawn. They are all mixed up in many areas, interlocking as the fingers of clasped hands, intermingling as daisies and poppies in a meadow, intertwining as figures on wall paper or rugs.

The fate of Yugoslavia was as sad and tragic as a classic Greek drama. After centuries of struggling and praying for freedom and unity, both the Serbs and Croatians were at last free and united in a new independent state—but they were not happy. They had hallowed every cave and dungeon with their heroic sacrifices. They had made every peak and canyon of their splendid land echo with freedom songs. All their songs now united in a grand chorus from seashore to mountain peak, from bounteous plain to vast dark forest, from sickle-wielding girl harvesters to bearded or shaved priests; yet there was no harmony in the symphony and discord set every ear on edge. Hitler gave the Yugoslavs no time to solve that problem.

The Slovenes are the smallest of the three South Slav groups inhabiting the South Slav kingdom. They number about a million and two-thirds, with somewhat more than a million in pre-war Yugoslavia. The rest were in northeast Italy and southern Austria, mostly in Italy.

The Slovenes are one of the most advanced nationality groups or nations in the world. Their language differs considerably from Serbo-Croatian, perhaps as Portuguese from Spanish. They have developed a very high degree of literacy, maintained schools in every town and village, supported an extensive circulation of good weekly periodicals, and made their little country a model for Central Europe.

They created a creditable Slovene culture, supported a state theater and opera, a university and high schools, choirs and orchestras, and had the noble tradition of building statues to poets. They kept their picturesque little cities attractive and clean, improved their strikingly beautiful, mountain-filled, lake-spangled land by the care they gave it, made its heights and depths echo with the songs of tourists, crowned many a peak with a cozy tourist hut, and bound their ranges together with the best system of roads in southeast Europe.

They developed an extensive industry, worked out a helpful cooperative system, and organized agriculture as well as their uneven land permitted. They were well served by a vigorous daily press. The coffee houses in their cities were as reading rooms in American public libraries, and their churches were well attended. Markets were models of order. The women were neat, few men were ragged, the heaviest weight of toil was relieved by wheels. A self-respecting little people, that prior to 1918 had never been even partially free, moved forward to a distinguished place among the most advanced nations.

Local political life showed a deep cleavage between the priest-led "Peoples' Party," called Clericals, on the one hand, and the Liberals on the other, who were divided among workers, peasants, and intellectuals. By far the largest party was that of the Clericals. On the Serbo-Croatian quarrel the Slovenes were rather neutral. They resented Serb hegemony, but they were unconditionally in favor of preserving Yugoslavia. They tended to favor the Serbs as opposed to the Croatians. They took an active part in Yugoslav politics, often serving to tip the scales between political groups in one way or another, thus acquiring great bargaining power. Their influence, for the most part, was for order and moderate democracy. The Slovenes are in many ways the most constructive element in Yugoslavia.

Such were the main South Slav elements in the state of Yugoslavia, created in 1918. They had never lived together before in all human history. Some had never been free, many hadn't been free for a millennium, the rest had been free for less than a century. The kingdom of Yugoslavia, or as it was officially called at first, "The Kingdom of the Serbs, Croats, and Slovenes," was created to give these South Slavs a chance "to live as people." Along with them were half a million Germans, half a million Hungarians, more than half a million Albanians, a quarter of a million Rumanians, and others.

Of the non-Slavs only the Germans played a role of any importance. And during the last years preceding Hitler's attack on Yugoslavia, their influence was extremely sinister. Moved by Nazi fanaticism, they tried to spread Hitlerism and to accentuate Slav dissensions. They not only sowed seeds of discord, but formed aggressive armed organizations and spread their spies throughout the country.

The new state of Yugoslavia moved toward the greatest conflict in world history, totally unprepared. The King had been assassinated. Leaders of the second largest Slav group had been assassinated. Internal strife raged. Bold native Nazis planted political mines throughout the land. Swastika fires gleamed from mountain tops. A timid, well-intentioned prince, enjoying the confidence of no group, tried to direct that frail, wobbly Yugoslav ship of state into the teeth of the raging tempest. It and he and all the Yugoslav people went down together.

CHAPTER TWO

Religions in Yugoslavia

RELIGION has played and will continue to play a vital role in Yugoslav developments. Attachment to classic old religious bodies is a leading force in the country. It is the most permanent source of Yugoslav social explosions. During the coming years there will be an increase in popular loyalty to organized religion and that trend will radically affect the course of events.

Yugoslavia's three main religions are the Eastern Orthodox church, the Roman Catholic church, and Mohammedanism. Since the first two religious forces are by far the most important, let us rapidly dispose of Mohammedanism first. It is a relic of the five hundred years of Turkish domination in southeast Europe. When the sultans established themselves in what is now Yugoslavia, near the end of the fourteenth century, Islam became a double threat to the nations there. In the first place, Mohammedan tyrants oppressed, exploited, and killed the native peoples, taking the girls for Turkish harems and the boys for Turkish armies. The Mohammedan crescent, the Turkish language, red fezzes, and the slender minarets of mosques became universally detested symbols of brutal tyranny and false religion.

In addition to exercising their oppressive domination, the almighty Moslem masters coerced a number of native Slavs into the faith of Mohammed. Such a group still exists in Bulgaria and an even larger group in Yugoslavia. Naturally, these apostates became more fanatical and more violent defenders of the new faith than the

Turks themselves. They became estranged from the other South Slavs and for centuries carried on war against them. Almost a million of them live in the rather backward mountain regions of Bosnia, Herzegovina, and Montenegro, where they are a cause of constant disunity and occasional violence.

They are an emblem of shame and a sign of national frustration. They are considered a personification of treason and apostasy. They betrayed the Cross, deserted their nation, helped "the enemies of Serbia and of Christ." They added their swords to the swords of the mighty sultans, who were trying to wipe out the Serbian nation. They are considered the classic Quislings of the ages. And there they are in the heart of Serbdom, an indigestible, indomitable, non-assimilable mass. As Serbian church bells call to the worship of Christ, Serbian apostates five times daily mount the minaret and call Serb deserters to pray to a "foreign God" and honor a "foreign prophet." Most of the Slav Moslems are in Bosnia and Herzegovina.

To prevent that apostasy from spreading and to hurl back Turkish oppressors was the chief mission of the Serbian "Holy Eastern Orthodox Church" and of the Serbian nation. This primitive little people of mountain shepherds and pig-raisers felt called by God to play an historic world role. They were defenders of the faith. They were guardians of Europe. They were protectors of the Cross.

That strenuous, dangerous, bloody job lasted more than five hundred years. The Serbs met the Moslem Turks in the first epochal fight in 1389 and finally drove them from all Serbian domains in 1913. During that long period the church and nation were indissolubly united. To be a true Serb and to be a loyal Orthodox Christian were synonymous. The Serbian cross went with the sword; the Serbian sword went with the cross. Every priest was a warrior. Every saint was a hero, every hero a defender of the faith. Many a priest has literally had a cross on his breast and a gun on his hip.

That may all seem crude and crass to modern Americans. And it may be a very poor form of Christianity. But on second thought,

Americans may recall that the old Puritans carried Bibles and rifles, that the pioneers took guns to church, and that even more recently American chaplains have "praised the Lord and passed the ammunition." They may also recall that the good old Protestant champion, Gustavus Adolphus, joined shooting with praying, that an even more famous Protestant, Oliver Cromwell, killed his enemies in the zeal of the Lord, and that devout John Brown prayed both before and after shooting his enemies.

Be all that as it may, aggressive Serbian Christianity and nationalism saved the Serbian people from apostasy and extinction at the hand of Turkish Moslems, and their national church symbolizes the holiest thing in a Serb's life. It embodies Serbianism. A half-subterranean church, partially concealed in the woods, honoring the Cross, scorning the crescent, defying Turkish masters, was the dearest and most heroic emblem a Serb for centuries could think of. Militant Christian hymns in the Serbian language thrilled him. To call his children John and Mary in the Serbian tongue delighted him. To make the sign of the cross with three fingers, from right to left, exalted him as a warrior for Christ and Christendom. It marked his place. He was the man, his was the nation, theirs was the church of the three fingers. They proclaimed it before the world; for it they would live and die.

And they did die, in multitudes. And not only from Moslem Turks or Moslem Slav apostates. Also from Roman Catholics. As though it were not enough for the Serbs to fight Mohammedan invaders, they also fought Roman Catholics. They faced the Moslems in front and the Catholics in the rear. And this second front was no less vital than the first. Nor was it much less bloody.

When the Christian church broke into two sections in the eleventh century, members of the Eastern and Western branches killed one another. They launched crusades against one another. They besieged one another, prepared ambushes against one another, massacred one another in stadiums, dug out one another's eyes. The

Nazis have committed few atrocities which Eastern and Western Christians did not commit against one another.

And the line between these Christians passes squarely across Yugoslavia. The Eastern Orthodox Serbs are on one side and the Roman Catholic Croats on the other—with the Moslems interspersed amid both. That division was and is a line of hate, a trench of battle and of blood. On one side are the people who make the sign of the cross with three fingers; on the other those who make it with five. The first from right to left and the other from left to right. One cross maker is Ivan; the other Jovan. One priest shaves; the other wears a beard. And those little differences are as passwords. They are as battle cries. They mean, "To thy tents, O Israel," that is, "O Serbia," or "O Croatia."

This is all terrible, but let no American raise his hand in pharisaical horror. Do you not remember how Protestant John Huss slaughtered his religious opponents, how British Puritans exterminated Irish Catholics, how Spanish Catholics burned their opponents alive, how American Puritans hanged Quakers in Boston, and how the American Ku Klux Klan has raged, tortured, and killed? Our shortcomings serve as no excuse for Yugoslav religious hatred, but they help us understand it.

Those ecclesiastical emotions, hundreds of years old, yet as new as each blazing noonday's sun, are still terribly potent. Even now in the midst of the twentieth century few passions have moved Orthodox, Catholic, and Moslem Yugoslavs more furiously than the desire to kill one another, which they have done by the thousands. As some Americans have exulted over bombing Japanese women and children en masse, so some Yugoslav Christians have gloated over killing other Yugoslav Christians. The flames have abated somewhat since V-E Day, but the fury of a thousand years is not extinguished. The graceful Moslem minaret, the stately Orthodox dome, the noble Catholic spire, still divide the Yugoslavs.

CHAPTER THREE

Mihailovitch Appears

YUGOSLAVIA faced the approaching cataclysm of World War II, unprepared. Divided by racial, political, and religious strife, the state was in no position to meet a major enemy. The Yugoslavs were in a receptive mood for divisive propaganda, and Axis agents worked on them night and day. Local German Nazis were very active there, more even than in the United States. The boy King had not yet ascended the throne. The Regent, though conscientious, was cautious. The administration was honeycombed with graft. The army was poorly equipped and inadequately organized. Croatia, a major part of the kingdom, had been in almost open revolt. No country on earth needed peace as much as Yugoslavia. It had existed only since late 1918 and had not yet reached equilibrium.

Many Yugoslavs were aware of this perilous situation and had made efforts to remedy it. The principal goal toward which they directed their efforts was a Serbo-Croatian understanding, or reconciliation. Without that Yugoslavia would plainly be broken to pieces by any blow. As long as Croats hated "Serbian hegemony" worse than anything else, they would certainly not risk their lives to preserve Yugoslavia. They would rejoice to see it crash down, as many minority groups had earlier exulted at the collapse of Austria-Hungary. Responsible leaders, working for consolidation, attained partial success and concluded a Serbo-Croatian agreement on August 24, 1939, the first day after the making of the Stalin-Hitler pact.

This arrangement of the Croatian peasant chief, Dr. Vladimir

Machek, and the Yugoslav Premier, Dragisha Tsvetkovitch, who had conferred under the direction and inspiration of Prince Paul, turned Yugoslavia into a federated state and gave the Croatians a very large degree of autonomy. As a result of the concessions, most Croatians became more loyal to the kingdom and were pleased when their leader, Dr. Machek, accepted a leading role in a new Yugoslav government. Croatia, having returned to the Yugoslav fold, assumed a share of responsibility for the future of the state.

This "sporazum" has been bitterly criticized by both Croatians and Serbs, but I thought and still think it was a useful act, even though it did not bring complete confidence or good will. Many Serbians considered its territorial arrangements very unfair to Serbia. Some Croats, on the other hand, thought Machek had made too many concessions. Both sides nursed old grievances. The Croatians had a furious and fanatical nationalistic organization that had killed the Serbian King, while wild Serbian nationalists had killed the Croatians' "uncrowned king," Raditch. Croatian conspirators continued violently to work for secession, and Serbian chauvinists sought to reimpose Serb hegemony and to revise or nullify the "sporazum." Nevertheless, it helped to prepare Yugoslavia to meet the rapidly approaching tempest.

On the whole, the Yugoslav people faced the pest of Naziism as creditably as most other nations, and better than many. The world tone at the time was distressing. The political morality of most nations was deplorable. All powers, throughout the world, big and little, were shivering in their boots, trying to avert a struggle or at least to shove it off onto somebody else. Heroism was rare, pusillanimity and falsehood rampant. France was divided, England was coddling evil, Russia was making dirty deals, America was undecided, and the little nations were terrorized into inactivity. In this global moral crisis, Yugoslavia set no glowing example of high-mindedness, but she was not among the most craven.

After formally establishing internal harmony, the Regent set up a fairly representative and rather democratic government. The cabinet could have been much better, but at least it was better than those it superseded. It allowed much freedom of the press, considerable freedom of meetings, and planned to hold fair elections. The only group it ruthlessly suppressed were the Communists. And for many months it made no deal with Hitler, such as Russia, Hungary, Finland, Rumania, Belgium, and Austria made.

The people as well as the government resisted Axis pressure. The Nazi propagandists made but little progress in most parts of Yugoslavia. The most numerous agents were the half million Volk Germans living there and the most adroit were Germany's business representatives, applying pressure upon a country largely dependent on the Axis. To be sure, there was a Serb Fascist party called "Sbor," led by a vigorous, able, and, strange to say, personally incorruptible Serb called Dimiter Ljotitch. This group had a scattering of members throughout the kingdom, worked in close cooperation with Hitler, and used every totalitarian method of agitation to win the country, but it remained isolated from beginning to end. Most Yugoslavs scorned and spurned any open form of Naziism.

Before Ljotitch began his Nazi crusade, a far more glamorous man, Prime Minister Milan Stoyadinovitch, had vainly tried to lure the Yugoslavs into a popular Fascist movement. As Premier, he had at his disposal much prestige, the whole state administration, the state treasury, the state police, and the state propaganda apparatus, but he attained no appreciable success. The Yugoslavs rejected his Fascist monkeyshines, and when he was removed by a fairly weak prince, not a finger was raised to defend him or his movement. He was ridiculed as a Fascist clown.

In Croatia, also, no Fascist movement throve. The strenuous attempts at establishing Fascism there remained without much success, even though a group of Croatians, led by the notorious conspirator Ante Pavelitch, worked under Mussolini, with the active backing of Fascist Italy and the support of Nazi Germany. Pavelitch's Croatian

Fascists were not only in Mussolini's pay, but at first lived in Italy, received Italian weapons, took Italian courses in conspiratorial activity, and were facilitated by Italy in operations against Yugoslavia. Pavelitch's main slogan, also, was attractive to many Croatians, since he advocated a "Free Croatia," independent of Serbia, even of Yugoslavia, and larger than the Croatians had ever enjoyed. However, even though this flaming, glamorous Croatian Fascist, backed by the Axis, promised the Croatians all they had dreamed of, he won the support of comparatively few of them. The overwhelming majority of the Croatian people remained true to Dr. Machek and the Peasant Party, a decidedly democratic organization. And the powerful anti-Fascist current persisted among the Croatian people even after the war began and the Axis drew all Europe into its claws, with Russian assent and assistance.

In this respect, the record of all Yugoslav groups is good and that of most is excellent; better, I think, than that of Holland, or Belgium, or Denmark, for example.

However, a decided danger from Naziism did exist in Yugoslavia. It came in the first place from the direct intervention of the aggressive German government, which had active, insolent representatives in Belgrade and other Yugoslav cities. The Nazis carried on unceasing propaganda in Yugoslavia and demanded complete freedom for their agents. They also ordered the Yugoslav government to prevent the Yugoslav press from criticizing the Nazis or Germany. And they vociferously demanded complete political freedom for every Volk German in Yugoslavia—all five hundred thousand of them—and even for other Nazis, direct from the Reich, posing as Volk Germans. It was difficult for the timid and rather acquiescent Yugoslav government to resist such pressure.

The Belgrade regime was far from heroic. It didn't want to offend brutal, vicious, powerful Germany. It kept making concessions, in hopes of buying Hitler's good will. In this caution it resembled most other governments throughout the world. That was a dark age in human development. As Europe crashed down before Nazi arms and propaganda, Nazi Germans in Yugoslavia worked to undermine that country, and the Yugoslav government countenanced it so as not to offend Hitler. The government, paid by the Yugoslav people to defend the state, permitted Nazis to work for the destruction of the state. But during those months of cowardice and disintegration, some Yugoslavs boldly upheld the honor of their land and of the human race. One was a thin, hard-working, unselfish, unglamorous Serb colonel in the Yugoslav Army, named Drazha Mihailovitch.

Though well educated, he had not attained very high distinction. He had studied in Yugoslav military schools and in a French officers' academy, where he had made a good record. He had served in a number of Yugoslav garrisons and on the Yugoslav General Staff, and in each post he had won the reputation of being an efficient officer and incorruptible patriot. Because of his schooling, competence, and character he was sent to Sofia and later to Prague as Yugoslav military attaché. These were very important centers in Yugoslavia's system of defense and it was a coveted distinction for a young Yugoslav colonel to be sent there, but such an appointment in no way indicated that the incumbent was a genius. Colonel Mihailovitch was a serious, honest, brave officer with an excellent record in the First World War and warmly devoted to the preservation of his country from Naziism.

His most important anti-Nazi work was not in foreign capitals but in his own land before Hitler attacked it. His self-chosen task was to suppress the activity of Nazi Germans in Yugoslavia. He did this well and at much personal cost. It was loyalty beyond the call of duty.

Native German Nazis worked in Yugoslavia as they were working in the United States and a score of other lands. They had Bunds. They belonged to secret "cells," which made and executed plots against the established order, wore Nazi uniforms, gave the Hitler greeting, sang Nazi songs, paraded, gathered in camps, built bonfires, and lighted huge swastikas on mountain peaks to defile the darkness of Yugoslav nights. They were a belligerent state within a state, actively, implacably at war with Yugoslavia. They followed Adolf Hitler as Nazis found in Berlin or on Polish battlefields. And they were tolerated by the Belgrade government, out of fear of Hitler.

But they were not tolerated by Drazha Mihailovitch and many other private Yugoslavs. Colonel Mihailovitch persistently fought them on his own initiative. It was his private war for the defense of his country.

The supine attitude of the Yugoslav cabinet need not surprise us. Molotov and von Ribbentrop were hobnobbing as friends in Moscow and being photographed in the act of cordially shaking hands. The Soviet government was fulminating against capitalist countries, especially England and France. Isolationism, as expressed by the America Firsters, was rapidly growing in America. France showed many signs of decadence. England had not won a single major victory. Ireland was openly against the enemies of Hitler. Czechoslovakia had succumbed without a blow. Every country bordering Yugoslavia—except noble Greece—was making its peace with Hitler and Hitler's helper, Russia. Was it strange therefore that the Yugoslav government also tried to play safe? When most of the world was without honor, was Yugoslavia, new, confused, distraught, kingless, supposed to display suicidal heroism?

Drazha Mihailovitch, however, did not play safe and he did show heroism.

Removed from the General Staff because of his irreconcilable opposition to Hitler and sent to a provisional garrison near the border of the Reich, he devoted his whole attention to crushing Nazi activity. He became the terror of the Volk German conspirators. He raided camps. He seized Nazis as they were lighting swastikas in the mountains. He and his colleagues beat Volk Germans wearing

MIHAILOVITCH APPEARS

Hitler pins and made it dangerous for boys or men to give the Hitler salute.

In this he defied both his enemies and his superiors. He opposed both Yugoslav traitors and Yugoslav rulers. The native German Nazis complained. The German government intervened. Insolent German representatives shook their fists and swords in Belgrade. The Yugoslav government apologized. They promised to punish the culprit. The obstreperous colonel was humiliated and punished. But he still kept on working against the Nazis of Slovenia.

There was a whole island of Volk Germans in the heart of that beautiful Slav province. They were passionate Nazis, insolent in their certainty of Hitler victory. They showed disdain for Slavs, scorn for Yugoslavia, special arrogance for the Slovenes who had been German vassals for hundreds of years. They were as Hitler in Slovenia—as hundreds and thousands of Hitlers. They imposed an undisguised Nazi regime in their district, raised swastikas upon every available height, made Nazi songs echo through their valleys, and abused any loyal Yugoslav who might dare oppose them.

And what could little Slovenia do? Wedged in between Italy and Germany, it was helpless. Could one million cramped, confined Slovenes defy the weighty Axis? Russia couldn't defy it. Millions upon millions of Americans were trying to avoid a conflict with it. France collapsed at its first blow. Could Slovenia suppress that pestiferous island of German Naziism in its midst? No. It had to tolerate it.

But Colonel Mihailovitch did not tolerate it. He aroused a spirit of resistance among the Slovenes. He gathered brave comrades about him. He and his helpers seized lawless Nazis. They avenged offences to the Yugoslav flag. They stopped some Nazi demonstrations. They laid hands on Nazis who swaggered in Hitlerian regalia through Slovene market places. They placed some of Hitler's ringleaders in provisional confinement.

For that the German Nazis in Slovenia complained to the Reich, whose victorious armies were occupying the capitals of half of Europe. As a result of the complaint agents of the Reich pounded on the table in Belgrade. So Colonel Mihailovitch was again punished. This time he was sent deep into the interior, into the primitive, backward province of Bosnia. There he also found Volk-German Nazis, and there he also fought the traitorous agents of Hitler.

This kind of picayune action was not pleasing to a conscientious and ambitious military man, such as Colonel Drazha Mihailovitch. He had a family, and no father likes to drag his children from province to province. He had an excellent start toward a distinguished career and he didn't like to incur the ever-growing ill will of his superiors. He didn't want constantly to be reprimanded, reproached, and disciplined. He didn't enjoy this kind of demotion and humiliation. And as a regular officer he didn't relish this small-scale, underground, half-conspiratorial way of fighting Nazis. He wanted all Yugoslavia to stand up and heroically oppose the horrible evil.

But Yugoslavia didn't dare; so Drazha Mihailovitch kept on with his little private war. Not many Yugoslavs knew about his activity. He was just a provincial colonel, serving in provincial garrisons. But a great many Yugoslavs—hundreds and thousands and millions—on their own initiative, as a result of their own traditions and convictions, felt exactly as the young colonel and were just as eager as he to do something about it. In the midst of the saddening, paralyzing cowardice settling upon the world, amid the lies blaring from the state radios and the fear stalking up and down Yugoslavia's valleys or over her plains, many Yugoslavs still placed honor, truth, and right above all things, and recalled the glory of Serbia's century-long fight against Moslem despots. These were preparing themselves for action.

Most representative and whole-hearted among them was Mihailovitch. I am not pretending he was a great figure. He had as yet no great conception. He was a simple, honest, fearless man, like thousands of Americans who, prior to Pearl Harbor, tried to arouse our nation against Hitler. He was poor, of humble descent, a typical man of the people. Because of his detestation of Hitler he had jeopardized his career; because of his patriotism he had caused his family acute discomfort. His future looked bleak and dreary. But he kept up his unfaltering fight against Hitler; he was one of the noblest apostles of freedom that those stupendous years brought forth. He was the antithesis of Fascism, the irreconcilable foe of Naziism, the champion of common men and women, the defender of the peasants who owned the little fields which they tilled. He was the chief of men and women who milked cows, fed hogs, and refused to grovel before any tyrant on the face of the earth. Drazha Mihailovitch was as bravely and fearlessly opposed to Nazi tyranny as De Gaulle later showed himself to be.

CHAPTER FOUR

The War Comes to Yugoslavia

THE little private wars which Colonel Drazha Mihailovitch and many other Yugoslavs waged against the Nazis were only harbingers of the great and terrible fight which all Yugoslavia would soon have to accept. Hitler left almost no European country at peace. One by one, they had to make a choice. Russia at first went with Hitler. Poland went against him. Czechoslovakia acquiesced to him. Hungary sprang to his side. Bulgaria was preparing to follow Russia's example and give him assistance. The Hitler Juggernaut implacably approached Yugoslavia and on its bloody banner were emblazoned the words "Decide now."

To hasten the decision Hitler, early in 1941, called representatives of the Yugoslav government to Berchtesgaden and made pre-emptory demands upon them. He wanted a favorable Yugoslav pact that would permit the passage of Nazi troops and arms through the country and would grant economic concessions. During the whole month of February, Hitler pressed his claims and the Yugoslavs stalled. The ministers argued, discussed, disputed, but they wouldn't commit themselves. No responsible Yugoslav statesman could be induced to sign up with Hitler. On March 1, Bulgaria bowed to the Axis and allowed Nazi troops to pour over the Danube into Bulgaria. Nazi armored forces penetrated to the eastern Yugoslav border. Making the most of this additional pressure, Hitler ordered the Prince Regent immediately to meet a Nazi emissary in Slovenia. Paul did so and was handed categorical new demands. Instead of giving an immediate answer, the Yugoslav government ordered partial mobilization and then went into a huddle.

The situation seemed desperate. Europe was prostrate. Nazi submarines appeared to be on the point of paralyzing ocean traffic and isolating England. Great Britain faced Hitler's might alone; her war production was suffering from incessant bombardment, her position in Africa was precarious. Hitler, well established in Bulgaria, might make arrangements to sweep through Turkey and attack Egypt from two sides, thus tearing the British Empire to bits.

And a new Nazi campaign season, after a winter of intense preparations, was at hand. Could anyone believe that weak, unprepared, disunited Yugoslavia would defy Hitler at such a moment and attract to itself the force of his whole war machine? Was Yugoslavia to commit suicide? In contrast with this, if Yugoslavia in a "reasonable" way cooperated with Hitler it would get a long-coveted portion of Greece and extend its borders to the Aegean Sea. That was very tempting, though dishonorable. Still it would be no more dishonorable than the steps other nations were taking, right and left, and still are taking. Had not Britain and France "sold Czechoslovakia down the river" for personal advantages? Had not Stalin made a deal with Hitler? Had not Moscow repeatedly proclaimed that it would make any deal with anyone to weaken its enemies? Would it not have been perfectly in line with contemporary morality for hard-pressed Yugoslavia to jump on "the wave of the future" and make the most of a desperate situation? Would she not have followed eminent examples if she had signed up with Hitler "for the sake of peace," and if she had stabbed her poor ally and neighbor, Greece, in the back for the sake of a reward?

What did she do? The Prince Regent, knowing that the Yugoslavs, especially the Serbs, would be outraged by a deal with Hitler, urged the opposition to join the cabinet and help form an all-national, coalition government, in order to make the most of an irremediable situation. He wanted such a government to accept unavoidable Nazi demands and persuade the nation that the government had acted for Yugoslavia's good. The opposition indignantly refused even to consider such an offer. And not only that, five members of the government itself threatened to resign. They did not want to go into history with the stain of that act upon them.

In this predicament Prince Paul told Hitler he couldn't get his ministers to sign up. By that time Hitler's patience was exhausted. His global plans and the whole 1941 military campaign were being held up by the obstinate Yugoslav corn-growers and pig-raisers. So the mighty Fuehrer, on March 20, delivered to distracted Belgrade an eight-day ultimatum, containing his irreducible demands. They were a non-aggression pact, a friendship declaration, and economic concessions. He no longer demanded the right of passage for his armies. About all he wanted was favorable non-belligerency, for which he guaranteed Yugoslavia's territorial integrity and promised rich territorial acquisitions. What he chiefly demanded was economic and moral support. He wanted Yugoslavia to sell its granary and soul; he wanted it officially to approve Nazi world tyranny. Moscow was showing great deference to the ambassadors of Germany, Italy, and Japan, which had created an anti-Russian world bloc. Pétain was kowtowing to Hitler's new world order. Was Belgrade, within the inexorable vise of German tanks and helpless beneath German planes, to defy Hitler?

No, the Belgrade government was not to be so heroic. The Yugoslav Premier and his Foreign Minister wended their sad way to Vienna and on March 25 signed up. They saved their people from the awful scourge of war, even from the presence of foreign troops of any kind. The government had done as well by Yugoslavia as Sweden was doing. It had created a situation in which the Yugoslav people might make a lot of money as the Swedes were doing and the Americans were doing and the Russians were doing. With very little backing, the Yugoslav government had driven a pretty shrewd bargain. They returned from Hitler's lair bringing their people peace —without honor—as Prime Minister Chamberlain had done three years earlier. And Mr. Chamberlain had been wildly cheered by most Britishers. Were Dragisha Tsvetkovitch and Alexander Cincar-Markovitch cheered by the Yugoslavs?

They were almost lynched. Their reception was one of the most remarkable phenomena in recent history. Their country bordered on the Reich. Every home in the kingdom was exposed. Every Yugoslav mother and child was in mortal danger. There was not the semblance of succor on any horizon. The most ruthless gang of murderers in modern history held machine guns at every Yugoslav's head. And the government had saved the people from that indescribable menace! Did not a wave of relief sweep over Yugoslavia? No. Rather, a fire of indignation.

Amazement, horror, and rage flamed from one end of the land to the other. The people felt defiled. They felt that their history and all their traditions had been polluted, their churches desecrated, their flag violated, their homes contaminated. A moral furore seized the Yugoslavs. They wanted to wipe out the shame that had been placed upon them. They forgot about prospective pain and suffering and starvation and destitution. They just wanted to be clean again. Pupils and students broke up classes to protest. Teachers gathered in groups to express their feelings of outrage. Old men collected in obscure village inns and sent indignant telegrams to Belgrade. Old women came together in peasant yards and sang old funeral songs. Officers all over the country decided to leave their army which had accepted disgrace without striking a blow and planned to make their way alone or in groups to Greece or England or any place where they could fight against Hitler. A few had actually gone. Crowds spontaneously marched through the main cities, crying out against the government that had "betrayed" them.

But the outraged Yugoslavs did not content themselves merely with protests. A group of army officers in Belgrade began to act. Very early on the morning following the second night after the signing of the pro-Nazi pact this band of patriotic conspirators seized all vital public buildings, overthrew the government, arrested the Prince Regent, elevated the young King to the throne and then turned the state over to a new revolutionary government, consisting of representatives of every party in the kingdom, except that of the Communists.

Only one single peaceful night passed between the announcement of that pro-Nazi pact and the overthrow of the government which signed it.

And so completely was the nation in sympathy with the military conspiracy that no body of men anywhere tried to defend the ousted government. The army, the police, the gendarmes, all favored the revolutionists. Nowhere throughout the country was there the slightest resistance to the coup. Every Serbian province, city, town, and village immediately and joyously sprang to the side of the new regime. The Serbian Orthodox church took the lead in urging and supporting the change. Serbian professors applauded, students paraded, pupils milled hilariously through the streets, peasants flocked into cities from neighboring villages to show their approval, workers left shops and factories to join the demonstrations, banks and government offices emptied as clerks and officials took their place in the throngs.

And the crowds showed that they knew what it meant, for they not only sang songs of liberty and honor and right, they not only lauded Serbia and Yugoslavia, the young King and the Allies, but they also denounced Germany, damaged swastikas adorning Nazi officers, and actually attacked Germans. To be sure the revolution had aspects of a carnival. It seemed somewhat like a macabre dance of serenaders before an earthquake. Groups of ecstatic children appeared to be playing ball with time bombs. It was horrible for an outsider to look upon that joyful, shouting, singing, thanksgiving nation and reflect that soon, inevitably, the most terrible war machine in the world would blow them to smithereens, send their king fleeing, and cut their kingdom into half a dozen pieces. But it was not an irresponsible masquerade, created by a few exalted, foolish, and misled officers. The revolution showed a people expressing its will. It was a nation keeping the faith.

And that nation was primarily the Serbs, heartily supported by the Slovenes. Heretofore in this chapter I have spoken of all the Yugoslavs. And I have no desire to belittle the Croatians, of whom I am fond and to whom I am sincerely attached. But the 27th of March was a Serbian act and must be described as such. The Croats were surprised by it and opposed it. The Slovenes hoped for it, unanimously approved it, and unreservedly supported it, but it was the Serbs who effected it. Serbian officers were the actors. A Serbian youth assumed the responsibility of becoming a revolutionary king and risking his whole future in a fight with Adolf Hitler. Leopold, Wilhelmina, Haakon, Lebrun, the Polish President, the Danish King, and Eduard Benes were in exile or captivity. Winston Churchill had publicly suggested that the British rulers might have to flee to Canada. Hitler had made ludicrous wrecks of thrones and presidencies, but there in Belgrade an eighteen-year-old Serbian boy mounted the precarious throne and shook his fist at Hitler.

This Serbian act was in keeping with the grandest moments in Serbian tradition. I am singing no hymn to Peter, the King, but I am stressing that in his defiant act he represented the common men and women of Serbia at their best. He spoke for Serbia's peasant nation. He was a native sovereign, scion of a native dynasty, descended from a family of native pig-raisers. He was the great grandson of peasant Black George, who in 1804 led his fellow peasants against the despotic Turkish lords of Shumadiya, the subjugated Serbian woodland. He was the grandson of Serbian King Peter, who in 1914 defied the German world when Emperor Franz Joseph, backed by Kaiser Wilhelm, tried to deprive little Serbia of its sovereignty. He was a spiritual descendant of Serbian King Lazar, who in 1389 marched to Kossovo to meet the mighty hordes of the all-conquering Turkish sultans.

I, as a fanatical American republican, have no intention to laud kings anywhere at any time. But I have vast admiration for freedom-loving nations, and when King Peter in the early hours of March 27, as a David, stepped out into the darkness to defy Adolf Hitler, Benito Mussolini, and Hirohito, he was speaking for his people. They were thrilled and pledged him their unrestricted allegiance. The boy led them toward blood and tears and death, but they said, amen. I would by no means justify the steps which Peter took during the years following that fateful act. But on that apocalyptic morning, as the thunder of Armageddon was echoing in the distant hills, young Peter stood forth, white and pure, in the brightness of the dawn, as the soul of a heroic nation and as the conscience of mankind. Timid men the world over, who had been struggling in their souls, cringing in their sheepish desires to evade duty, and making dirty deals with their sense of right, applauded the young offspring of Black George, the tyrant-killing pig-raiser.

Yet nobler and grander than the young sovereign were the peasants, workers, clerks, and schoolteachers, the whole Serbian nation, who flocked into their churches to ask God to bless their heroic ruler. They lighted crude homemade candles, watched black-bearded priests swing fragrant censers, made the sign of the cross with three fingers, knelt on cold slab floors, and prayed to the God of Battles and to the "Mother of God" to bless them.

I have no desire unduly to exalt any nation or class or group of men. I loathe men-worshippers and detest the modern craze of turning human masses into idols. That leads only to such blind nationalism as Naziism, to such hideous class war as is seen in Communism. When masses or nations are worshipped, individual men and women are defiled, degraded, and exploited. However, when individuals, groups, or nations that are strong in faith, pure in heart, and unerring in their sense of duty, offer everything on the altar of right, I think they deserve respect and admiration. And among the nations of the world, during the shady months preceding June, 1941, the Serbians deserve a high place for moral heroism.

America didn't fight till attacked, neither did Russia, nor Holland, nor Norway, nor Belgium. France and England didn't act till Hitler had slapped them in the face. Serbians acted even when their government had arranged for them to weather the storm and profit from it. The men who led in that revolutionary act had no political ambitions —they immediately relinquished power to others. And those who thereupon assumed leadership sought no personal advantages. Only exile and death stared them in the face. The Serbian nation rose and moved as resolutely into the face of death as Leonidas, when he led his Spartan band to Thermopylae, or as John Brown, when he went to Harper's Ferry.

Americans rightly honor the handful of New England patriots who defied the oppressive British Empire. Very appropriately they revere the Declaration of Independence and its signers. But no act of our own glorious forefathers outshines in moral grandeur and spiritual splendor the uprising of the Serbian people in the dark morning hours of March 27, 1941, and their stand against world-conquering Naziism. Little men and women, wearing homemade pigskin moccasins and handmade sheepskin caps stood before history and said, "We'll die before we'll accept Adolf Hitler," and they did die. As long as humanity honors right it will cherish that page as one of the brightest in world chronicles.

Now, in a kind of postscript, it must be pointed out that with that heroic act, Josip Broz-Tito and his fellow Communists and his fellow Partisans had nothing whatsoever to do. They were the one and only group in Serbia and Slovenia that had no part in that act. They were outsiders. They were with Soviet Russia, which had a pact with Hitler and at that moment was showing favors to Nazi, Japanese, and Fascist ambassadors in Moscow.

This revolution was the deed of all Serbs, except Tito's, of rich and poor, villagers and city-slickers, army men and civilians, shepherds and factory workers, professors and pig-herds. It was the act of a united nation, taking its stand for freedom, for right, and for world liberation. It was a supreme demonstration of democracy; it was the utter and absolute antithesis of Fascism. Such people are the eternal foe of totalitarianism; they are the ones who in all ages and all lands tend the fires of liberty.

CHAPTER FIVE

Soviet Russia Degrades Prostrate Yugoslavia

THE tempest struck Yugoslavia ten days after the people's revolution against Adolf Hitler. The first Nazi act—of course without formal declaration of war—was a furious early morning air attack on Belgrade, the capital, a defenseless city with a third of a million inhabitants. After that, military events moved very rapidly. The Nazis had carefully invested Yugoslavia on two sides with powerful armored forces, while Italy had armies strewn along a third side. The mighty German Wehrmacht was engaged in no other operation that would distract its attention from Yugoslavia. Its one immediate task was the utter and final annihilation of that new, disunited, unprepared state.

And the task was soon accomplished. Within twelve days Yugoslavia disappeared from the map. For centuries the stream of history had flowed over southeast Europe, showing not so much as a Yugoslav ripple. Then suddenly in December, 1918, a new South Slav state had appeared, the Kingdom of the Serbs, Croats, and Slovenes. It had struggled along for twenty-two years of confusion, barely reached a state of hopeful equilibrium, was struck one hefty blow, and vanished. The irresistible stream of history continued to flow on over Zagreb, Ljubljana, Bihach, Sarajevo, Mostar, Belgrade, Nish, but again showed no sign of a Yugoslavia. One noted a Slovenia, Croatia, Dalmatia, Montenegro, Serbia, Voivodina, the

Sandjak, all dispersed among greater powers, as they had been during the centuries.

The South Slav kingdom was cut into ten pieces. South Slavs were killing South Slavs and helping their most implacable enemies kill them. Not for five hundred years had they been in a worse condition.

The reasons for the collapse are plain and simple. Chief among them was the terrific might of the German Army. Little Yugoslavia could not hope to resist the furious force that had swept away most of Europe and so far had stopped at no land barrier. Yugoslavia simply went the way of France, Poland, Czechoslovakia, and Holland. In addition, the Yugoslav Army was disorganized. I think that no part of that army and no nationality group in it distinguished itself. The twelve war days were a continued, unchecked, military debacle.

A major reason for this confusion and impotence was Croatian defection. Many Croatians lay down on the job; many of them actually helped the Nazis. There is no doubt whatsoever about this. It is as indisputably attested as the entrance of Allied armies into Paris after its liberation. The Nazi troops on April 10 swept into Zagreb, Croatia's capital, and were received by many Croatians not as enemies but as liberators. Croatian men gave them hosannas, shouted welcome. Croatian women strewed flowers before them. After twenty-two years of separation from German and Austrian masters, many Croatians welcomed those masters back to their capital and into their strongholds. As one part of the Nazi Army was killing Yugoslavs in Belgrade, Nish, Skoplje, and Sarajevo, another part was being hailed by Yugoslavs in Croatia.

Not only did this Croatian defection completely derange Yugoslavia's geographical plan of defense, but it demoralized the whole army. There were Croatian soldiers in every division, Croatian officers in every regiment, Croatian groups on every frontier. When they ceased to fight, the army tended to become a sieve with a thousand holes for enemy penetration. Confusion seized every front and every concentration center. A Yugoslav soldier could not distinguish reliable comrades from unreliable, friend from foe. The Serbian or Slovene soldier did not know whether his neighbor wearing the Yugoslav uniform and carrying a Yugoslav rifle would aid him or kill him. As some Yugoslav units, composed of Serbs or Slovenes, retreated from German armies toward interior mountains for a last stand, they met on the congested roads Croatian soldiers moving out of the mountains toward the attacking Germans to surrender. The Yugoslav Army Command disintegrated, leaving every unit, group, and individual to act alone. The government fled, the King fled, and the generals capitulated on April 17.

The most momentous month in the modern history of Serbia ended in utter darkness. On March 25 a Yugoslav government ruling over the tenth largest state in Europe, with the seventh largest population, and with a big army at its disposal, made a deal with Hitler to avert war and preserve the state. The Serbs rejected that arrangement and twenty-three days later the worst fears of the cautious Belgrade government were more than realized. Yugoslavia had vanished. The government had fled. The army had melted away. All the efforts and sacrifices of Serbia during 137 years were nullified. A nation of eight million people was exposed to starvation, exile, and massacre.

For this catastrophe I would not place sole blame upon the Croats. But the tragedy of Yugoslavia cannot be understood without a clear perception of Croatia's part in it. Most Croatians, it must be pointed out, did not go with Germany, but they went against Yugoslavia. Dr. Machek, the peasant leader, became neutral. His peasant followers at that moment fought neither for nor against the Axis. And most of them remained democratic. To the end they rejected Hitler's Naziism.

The attitude of Machek and of his party was basically the same as that of Russia, Great Britain, America, Norway, and most other states, namely, nationalistic; their supreme allegiance was to Croatia. They thought of Croatia first. In the midst of terrific world events over which they could have no control, they wanted to save Croatia's independence regardless of Yugoslavia's fate and of international developments.

Great Britain signed away Czechoslovakia because Mr. Chamberlain thought that would be good for Great Britain. Soviet Russia made a deal with Hitler, thus "selling Europe down the river," because Mr. Stalin thought it would be good for Russia. Norway, at a vital moment, refused all cooperation with Great Britain because its government thought such action good for Norway, even though the British Empire might disappear. Such precisely was Dr. Machek's attitude regarding Croatia and Yugoslavia and Great Britain.

As a member of the pre-revolutionary cabinet, Machek had favored a Yugoslav deal with Hitler, such as Stalin had made. He thought the weak fox should be as wise as the mighty bear. He was against war with Germany and Italy, as were most Croatians.

Machek was not pleased with the action of the 27th of March, which had overthrown the cabinet of which he was a part. One of his close colleagues, Dr. Juraj Shutej, Minister of Finance, joined the new anti-Hitler government only at the point of a gun. The Serb revolutionists forced him to give the appearance of a united front. Machek himself did not join at first. Finally he went in, with a heavy heart, and on condition that the new anti-Nazi regime would do everything possible to avert war with Germany. When that proved impossible and the German Wehrmacht attacked Belgrade, Machek did not flee the country with the other ministers. Instead, he authorized the Croatian leaders Subashitch, Shutej, and Krnevitch to speak for Croatia abroad and he went back to Zagreb to share all future calamities with his people. Machek, because of his loyalty to Croatia and democracy, has often been in prison and more often in danger, but he has rarely separated himself from his nation voluntarily.

He was not among the Zagrebians who welcomed the Nazi soldiers and tanks into the Croatian capital. Neither was a majority of his party. He did not wish Italy or Germany, nor Italian and German agents, to exercise domination over Croatia. Neither did a majority of his party. He saw that Yugoslavia, for the moment, was doomed and he believed that little Croatia could not determine future world events. He believed that mighty empires were settling Yugoslavia's fate far beyond the power of little Croatia to add or detract, and he wanted the Croatians to take a passive attitude, to remain united, and to emerge from the world storm as a compact national unit.

In other words, he did not advocate active resistance to German arms or occupation, though he did not go with Germany or German agents. He tried to preserve his party as an irreducible, intractable political and national entity that could be used by no outside force. Neither Tito, the Nazis, the Italian Fascists, nor the Croatian Quislings were able to use Machek or the bulk of his party. In fact, Machek and some of his party colleagues were very badly treated by the Nazis. Machek himself was in concentration camps, prisons, jails, or house arrest during most of the occupation. He was cajoled, threatened, vituperated by Russia, Germany, Italy, Tito, and Quisling Pavelitch. He felt his task was to preserve Croatia for the grand day when the war was over, when he could lead her intact into a new democratic Yugoslavia, or a new Central European federation, or preserve her as a small, independent state. In any case, he wanted to do for Croatia what Generalissimo Stalin was trying to do for Russia and Premier Chamberlain had tried to do for Great Britain. For Yugoslavia such an attitude was extremely dangerous. Serbs considered it treason.

Such a passive, defensive Fabian leader naturally did not dominate the lightning developments in Croatia. Balkan events moved with the tumultuous velocity of a torrent and another far more dynamic figure tried to steer the Croatian bark through them. He was Dr. Ante Pavelitch, the arch-Fascist and arch-conspirator. He was the unabashed agent of Mussolini and had long been in Italy's pay and service; he now jumped at the chance to accept the job of acting as the Croatian Duce, under his grandiose, imperial master, Benito. He proved to be one of the most sinister figures of modern times.

He had an organization modeled after Hitler's Nazi Party and made up of Ustashas, or Uprisers, who resembled S.S. men. They were hard, tough, brutal, and bloody. Many were criminals, others fanatical totalitarian chauvinists, some cynical opportunists. Many were good soldiers, a majority were greedy, most were brave, all were murderous. They were united by a desire to humiliate Serbia and to establish a great independent Croatia. The Axis chiefs immediately set up an independent Croatia under Dictator Pavelitch, which with German help he maintained about four years. It cannot be denied that most Croatians were pleased by the creation of "Nezavisna Hrvatska" (Independent Croatia). A majority rejoiced that this had come to pass, even though most were against the bloody Poglavnik Pavelitch. It must be kept in mind that the Croatians wanted to be free, just as the Massachusetts colonists wanted to be free in 1776.

Now what was the attitude of Dr. Machek toward Pavelitch and his Independent Croatia? It must be carefully defined. At first Machek did not work with or actively against Pavelitch. The totalitarian Croatian dictator announced over the Zagreb radio even before the total collapse of Yugoslavia that Machek had officially requested all former Croatian officials of every sort to remain at their posts and serve the new state. This has been interpreted as meaning that Machek threw his support, which at that moment was of great importance, to Hitler's agent Pavelitch. A few days earlier Machek had been Vice-Premier of Yugoslavia, and now he seemed suddenly to back a destroyer of the Yugoslav state who was the agent of Yugoslavia's deadly enemies, Mussolini and Hitler. "Thus Machek turned traitor," it is charged.

So far there is no evidence that Machek gave such an order or that he spoke over the radio. However, I believe that alleged order roughly corresponded with Machek's policy, at that fateful hour. He did not want his Croatians to fight Pavelitch's Ustashas. He did not want Croatians to kill Croatians. He did not even want Croatians destroyed in killing the Nazi occupiers. What had happened, had happened. Machek had tried his best to avert it or postpone it or divert it, as Stalin and Chamberlain had tried. But without success. The deluge was there. Machek wanted all the Croatians to stay in their ark together on the wild sea of war. I believe he wanted them to remain at their posts, even under Pavelitch, as civil servants had remained at their posts in Denmark. Let historians and philosophers decide whether or not he was a traitor.

In any case, his inactivity helped the invader and the native dictator. Appeasers usually aid aggressors and handicap the attacked; pacifists usually assist the evildoers and penalize the innocent. The Croats played into the hands of the enemies of Yugoslavia, some actively, others passively. They hastened the destruction of Serbia and the agony of the Serbs. The nation which had dared rise up against Hitler was attacked on every side. Hungarians stormed in from the north. The Bulgarians moved in from the east and south. Italians pressed in from the west. Croatian Pavelitch gloated over the Serbs' discomfiture; Croatian Machek left them to their fate; German tanks rumbled through their cities; Nazi executioners hanged Serb patriots from Serb lampposts by the score.

And at that supreme moment of destruction, as Serbs sank toward their nadir, Soviet Russia added a bitter insult to all the injuries. As Teuton Nazis were crushing Slav Serbs beneath their boots, Russia, the Mother of Slavs, gave encouragement to the Slav-killers. She ordered the Yugoslav representatives out of Moscow, and no Soviet government spokesman even deigned to bid them farewell.

Many sad and tantalizing events led to that tragic break. For two decades the Yugoslav government, under the supreme direction of King Alexander and Prince Paul, had refused to recognize Soviet Russia. However, in spite of that, Yugoslav delegates secretly met Soviet delegates in Turkey early in 1940 and later a Yugoslav trade delegation went to Moscow. A trade treaty was eventually concluded, though it proved quite ineffective, both politically and commercially.

After these first official contacts between Russia and Yugoslavia, the Wehrmacht won resounding military triumphs in western Europe and attained diplomatic successes that greatly enhanced German prestige in the Balkans and Near East. The Nazi government induced most of the Danubian nations to join the Anti-Soviet Three-Power Pact, lavishly entertained a special Japanese envoy, Matsuoka, transferred Southern Dobroudja from Rumania to Bulgaria, stealthily sent troops into Bulgaria, and finally on March 1, 1941, forced Bulgaria to join the German-Italian-Japanese alliance. Russia did nothing effective to counteract this growth of German prestige and power in southeast Europe. It left the little countries to their fate.

To be sure, it uttered a few veiled protests and showed a few signs of disapproval, but it made no commitment of any kind. It urged the Balkan states to stand up against German encroachments but counterbalanced each such plea with resounding concessions to Hitler. Moscow asked the helpless Balkan states to be brave, yet itself was careful to act in an almost abjectly conciliatory manner.

Here are some of the steps Moscow took after January 1, 1941, to please Hitler and appease the Nazis. It concluded a favorable trade agreement with Berlin, according to the terms of which the Nazis were assured large new shipments of grain. Berlin jubilantly called it "the biggest deal in wheat ever recorded." A few months earlier the Soviets had recognized Hitler's puppet state of Slovakia and concluded a trade agreement with it, thereby officially accepting the destruction of Czechoslovakia. Also, after whole companies of German soldiers had infiltrated into Bulgaria, the Bulgarian Communists, undoubtedly on instruction from Moscow, were directed by their leaders not to clash with those Nazi invaders. Generalissimo Stalin made it plain that while he was urging the little nations to defy Hitler he was taking every measure not to provoke him, himself.

The boldest thing that Russia did during these tragic weeks was to conclude a non-aggression pact with Yugoslavia. It was signed at Moscow on April 5, 1941, the day before Germany bombed Belgrade. The ceremony was staged with a good deal of flourish and Generalissimo Stalin himself was photographed in the act of watching Molotov and the Yugoslav, Milan Gavrilovitch, sign the treaty. The agreement obliged both parties to remain friendly to each other, should either be attacked. Plainly, Moscow's intentions were good. The spirit was willing. And there were a few useful acts. Some Yugoslav aviators were allowed to take refuge on Russian soil. Moscow even sent a train to the border for the use of the Yugoslav diplomatic representatives leaving Hungary. However, as Germany advanced, Moscow's friendly attitude changed to coldness and she ruthlessly sacrificed Yugoslavia and other small nations in hopes of diverting Hitler's attention from Russia.

On Easter Day of 1941, the Sunday of the week on which Yugoslavia capitulated, Molotov and Stalin concluded with Japan a treaty of friendly relations, neutrality, and mutual respect of borders, which included the inviolability of Manchuria. The signing which took place in Moscow was accompanied by much splendor and was raised to the rank of a major event. Stalin himself, after ardent toasts and intimate conversation, made the unusual gesture of going to the station to send off Matsuoka, the special Japanese envoy. On parting, the Russian dictator embraced the Japanese three times and said, "We shall be friends." He also shook hands with the German ambassador, saying they too would be friends. Italy's representative, likewise, basked in the brilliance of the great occasion. As Nazi armies rapidly battered Yugoslavia to destruction, Moscow was cordially shaking hands with, and even warmly embracing Hitler's ambassador and the emissaries of Hitler's allies. And Russia was recognizing the inviolability of one of the most notorious thefts of modern times. If Japan was confirmed in seizing Manchuria, would not Germany be confirmed in smashing Yugoslavia? So must have reasoned the desperate Serbs.

A few weeks later, Tass, the official Soviet news agency, announced from Moscow that the Russian government had recognized the pro-Nazi Iraq government which had seized power by a *coup d'état*. This was a pronounced pro-German, anti-British act. About the same time, the Soviet government expelled from Moscow the envoy of the heroic Greek nation, whose state Mussolini and Hitler had just smashed to bits, while a few days earlier it had expelled from the Soviet capital the representatives of Norway and Belgium. The pattern was devastatingly clear. Pro-Nazi, anti-Allied Iraq was honored and its representative welcomed, while pro-Allied, anti-Nazi Greece, Belgium, and Norway were humiliated. Their envoys were sent out to seek refuge in any democratic land that might dare receive them.

And then, to cap the climax, the representatives of heroic Yugoslavia in Moscow were also expelled. Barely had the ink on the Soviet-Yugoslav friendship pact dried, barely had the radiant photographers of pact-signing Stalin, Molotov, and the Serbian Gavrilovitch developed their films, before a minor Russian agent appeared and ordered the homeless diplomats of helpless Yugoslavia to clear out. Out the back door, at that! As Nazis swaggered through every Serbian valley and down every Serbian street, as the stiff, misshapen bodies of Serbian patriots hung grotesquely from Serbian lampposts or slumped in blood-covered piles before Nazi firing squads, as a Nazi ambassador rode with flying swastikas through the boulevards of Moscow, mighty Russia, the Mother of Slavs, sent her own Slav child as a Hagar into the wilderness. Moscow refused all contacts with the exiled Yugoslav government. Not until the month of August, after Russia was overrun by the Nazis, did Stalin again mention the Soviet-Yugoslav pact. He asserted it was still in force. By then, aid even from broken Yugoslavia was welcome to Russia.

CHAPTER SIX

Mihailovitch Organizes Underground Resistance

IN SPITE of the hopeless condition of the Serbs after the capitulation of the Yugoslav Army, they did not lose heart. On the contrary, they began to fight back. Spontaneously and in various parts of the kingdom, groups of Serbian soldiers and officers began to organize resistance to the Nazi occupiers.

Naturally, these underground fighters called themselves "Chetniks." That is an old Balkan term, long held in high repute. A chetnik was literally a "member of a band" or "bandit." But he was a special kind of bandit, a Robin Hood operating against foreign oppressors. Bulgarian and Serb chetniks were outlaws who went to the mountains to fight Turks. They killed Turkish governors, did away with Turkish police officers, robbed rich Turkish beys and distributed their wealth among their own poor. Now and then, also, at propitious moments they led large-scale uprisings.

As was natural, a glowing popular lore came to surround these men. They were considered heroes. Girls lauded them; boys and youths emulated them; mothers sang chetnik lullabies to their boy babies; fathers, instead of calling their sturdy little sons "Butch," gave them chetnik nicknames. And the chetniks themselves created a romantic tradition, connected with guns, campfires, heroism, distant brides, lonely death, Turkish prisons. They wore beards, probably because of the absence of shaving facilities, and also as a symbol of mourning for lost freedom, had special costumes when possible, and took solemn, mysterious oaths. They gave a good deal of glamour to a long period of gray, drab, Serbian servitude.

This is not to say that Balkan chetniks were as admirable or unselfish or noble as depicted in the popular songs. Their business was killing and pillaging; they were constantly under a strain and always in danger of betrayal, so were intolerant and cruel. They sometimes disposed of rivals and comrades in a summary way and occasionally were more interested in serving themselves than their nation. In spite of that, many of them were true heroes; on the whole they were as noble as the guerrillas and minute men of any oppressed nation anywhere. In the popular imagination, theirs was the highest of all callings during the centuries of Turkish domination. And in the abysmally dark days after the destruction of Yugoslavia by Hitler, thousands of Serbs felt uplifted by old chetnik songs and stories. They solemnly dedicated themselves to the perilous calling of revolution and spiritually joined the eternal band, or "cheta," of volunteer warriors which they believed had championed Serbia through the ages. As their forefathers had sallied forth from mountain lairs to kill Turkish despots, the new chetniks prepared to operate against German tyrants.

As might be expected, Colonel Drazha Mihailovitch was among the Serbs who decided to fight as chetniks. He had no official position of leadership and was far from being first in military rank. But he had long been fighting Nazis on his own initiative, regardless of official orders, even in defiance of them, and he merely continued that fight. He gathered bold comrades about him, just as hundreds of other leaders in hundreds of other places did, and, because of his ability, energy, devotion, and high integrity, became the man whom all the others considered chief.

At the time the war broke out Mihailovitch was in Mostar, Herzegovina, and after the collapse he made his way to Serbia. Already at the beginning of May, 1941, in the mountains of Serbia and Bosnia he formed his first "cheta" of volunteers, and solemnly swore in the first guerrillas. Naturally, his authority was limited. He had no way of executing a general order or of enforcing a general command. Communications from one end of Yugoslavia to the other were precarious and an all-over plan of action was entirely lacking. For many weeks, even months, Mihailovitch was merely fighter-in-chief among equally brave Serb irregulars. For a long time there was no such thing as a *Mihailovitchist*, any more than there are Trumanists in the U.S., or Eisenhowerists in our army. Mihailovitch was neither minister, commander, nor party boss. He had no special ideology. He was just Number One among a lot of Serbs trying to hamper Hitler's soldiers in Yugoslavia.

And it is well to emphasize that most of the fighters around Mihailovitch were Serbs. A few were Slovenes. There were practically no Croats. Of course, among the Serbs were many Montenegrins. As a result of a natural and unavoidable tendency, Mihailovitch's resistance movement was more Serbian than Yugoslav. There is no question about that. For a while it was even anti-Yugoslav. Temporarily it assumed aspects of "Greater Serbism." This trend was regrettable, but easy to understand. Yugoslavia, for the moment, was gone. During its twenty-two years of existence it had disappointed many of the Serbs even more than it had the Croatians, and in its collapse, many Croatians had helped the enemy. It would have taken celestial grace to prevent the Serbs, during those first terrible months, from becoming anti-Croatian, and thus anti-Yugoslav. Later, the Mihailovitch movement resumed and stressed the Yugoslav ideal.

The Serbs alone had been responsible for the popular uprising of March 27 against Hitler. They alone had been taken prisoners by the Germans. Only their land was occupied by the enemies. They were compelled to flee in droves from all parts of the kingdom. They were being pillaged and murdered by Croats in a hundred valleys and in a thousand forests. They were forcibly expelled from

Zagreb. Serbia was fairly teeming with helpless, destitute, terror-stricken refugees. And during those days and nights of horror, many Croats in their capital of Zagreb were rejoicing. Their brass bands were playing, their bells were ringing, their flags were gaily snapping from spires and mountain peaks. Many Croatians exulted in the creation of "Independent Croatia" and revelled in the destruction of Yugoslavia, which they considered a "Versailles monstrosity." Some Croatians gloried in the catastrophe that had befallen the Serbs, and even boasted of their aid to Hitler.

The Nazi-controlled Croatian press denounced Serbs, the Axis-serving Croatian radio jeered Serbs, some Croatian clerics reviled Serbs, the dictator of Croatia was creating a double army of Ustasha shock troops and Home Defense forces with which to fight Serbs. Quisling Pavelitch, in full Croatian panoply, marched beside Mussolini and Hitler with Croatian trumpets blaring and Croatian bayonets glistening, to kill Serbs. And as the Serbs thought of their two hundred thousand war prisoners, their destroyed cities, bereaved homes, and the multitudes of destitute refugees pressing upon them, is it strange that they hated Croatians and Yugoslavia, which seemed symbols of the disaster? Would it not have been superhuman for the Serbs to try to reconstruct Yugoslavia at a time when Croatians were exulting in its destruction and trying by force of arms to perpetuate its disappearance? And was it not logical for the Serbs to give their first thoughts to saving themselves? In any case, it is understandable that at such a moment the Serbian undergrounders made Serbia's deliverance their chief aim. That was the main motive of the men around Colonel Mihailovitch and they would have been abnormal if they had had a higher one.

Were they Fascists or were they democrats? The answer is they were a nation fighting for its life. Practically all of them were peasants. A few were army officers, the sons or grandsons of peasants. The Chetnik fighters were poor people, the offspring of men and women living in very humble village houses of their own and

MIHAILOVITCH ORGANIZES UNDERGROUND   49

tending their own small farms. Nearly everyone was a tiller of the soil or a worker. A few were clerks, small officials, and small town storekeepers. A number were schoolteachers and functionaries of cooperatives. Most wore homemade moccasins, home-sewn caps, homespun breeches, home-embroidered shirts. They were pig-raisers and plum-producers and cowherds and potato-hoers. Their sisters harvested wheat on hot hillsides under blazing summer suns with sickles. Their mothers kneaded bread, beat clothes on banks of brooks to wash them, carried babies on their backs, and hung the babies in hammocks in trees as they toiled in field and meadow.

Such were Mihailovitch's Chetniks, members of a one-class, working nation, composed of independent peasants, who chose their own leaders, including kings, and cherished equality of worth above all things except loyalty, freedom, and Christianity. For glib, ill-informed, formula-bound American writers, each receiving ten times more than the wealthiest man among the Serb Chetniks ever received, to call them Fascists or defenders of class privileges is base. If the Pilgrims who settled New England were Fascists, if the minute-men who fought at Bunker Hill or on Lexington Green were Fascists, if the pioneers who went to Nebraska or Oregon in covered wagons were Fascists, then the Serbs who rallied round Mihailovitch to resist Nazi invaders and help the Allies were Fascists.

Actually, it was a nation trying to prevent subjugation. And to the very end, the bulk of the Serb nation was with Mihailovitch. He led no Serb faction or party. He had no new creed or slogan. The movement he headed was not his invention. It was Serbia in action; it was a nation fighting for its life. Almost every Serb became a Mihailovitchist.

Look for a moment at the leaders who were with him! They were the men of March 27. They had shown themselves the most desperately bold anti-Nazis in Europe. They were the only people on earth who overthrew an appeasing government in order that they might defy Adolf Hitler. They represented every political party, every social and spiritual group in Serbia except a tiny Fascist gang with Dimiter Ljotitch and the Communists. These men represented the Peasant Party in all branches, the Radicals, the Democrats, the Socialists, the cooperatives, the schools, the Church.

The last, with practically all its clergy and membership, stuck to Mihailovitch to the end. A few Orthodox priests in Montenegro, Dalmatia, and Bosnia turned against him and one in Serbia. But during the terrible years of massacre, humiliation, and privation, the Serbian church supported Mihailovitch. It may be a good church or a bad church—I shall not discuss that—but it has been the supreme symbol for the Serb nation, for common Serb men and women, for the poor and heavy-laden. Also, its clergy is made up of the sons and nephews of peasants. They are villagers, living in villages. As a hundred times before in Serbian history, they now stuck by their nation and its boldest anti-Hitler leader. It is a grave error, fostered by opinionated secular theologians and scholiasts, to believe that Mihailovitch represented a privileged ruling class, fighting against an upsurging proletariat. He spoke for and fought beside a nation.

To describe his early campaign is not the purpose of this book. Within four months after the capitulation of the Yugoslav Army, the underground movement had gained much force, in both Serbia and Montenegro. The Germans were very eager to move as many divisions as possible to the Russian front, and at first they left comparatively small forces in both Serbia and Greece. Italians held Montenegro; Bulgaria garrisoned much of Macedonia and some of Serbia. This weakening of the garrisons facilitated the work of the resistance forces, so that by the end of August the Chetniks dominated much of Serbia. During that summer also they launched a revolution against the Italians in Montenegro and for a time were very successful.

I do not want to leave the impression that the poorly organized and badly armed guerrillas of Mihailovitch constituted a formidable military obstacle to the German Wehrmacht. In general, the role of

Europe's guerrillas in this war has been overemphasized by propagandists. However, Serbian resistance fighters had attained such power by September that they retarded vital German communications, slackened the flow of German forces toward the Mediterranean and Africa, and compelled the German High Command to send into Serbia large forces that were badly needed elsewhere. Mihailovitch had established his headquarters in the heart of Serbia, had set up a fairly effective system of communications, was able to send messages with considerable impunity to every part of the land, and succeeded in pushing Axis military forces away from the most vital points and communication lines.

The Germans and Bulgarians remained in possession of most Serbian cities, but the underground forces had turned the cities into isolated garrisons, thus making Germany's position uncomfortable. To prevent further underground encroachment, the Wehrmacht decided to strike a terrible blow that would serve as a lesson to the guerrillas once and for all.

In the clash that ensued the Nazis faced two kinds of underground fighters; namely, the forces under Mihailovitch and the Communist-led Partisans. The irregulars were fighting under separate leaderships but both opposed the Germans. Both groups were terribly mauled by the far better armed German detachments which attacked them with tanks and artillery. The victorious Nazis laid whole areas waste, demolished towns and cities, and killed up to seventy thousand Serb civilians. They machine-gunned Serbian patriots in masses and strung the leering corpses of many victims to Serbian lampposts. The second phase of Serb resistance ended disastrously, as had the first. The guerrillas were as badly beaten as the regular army had been. But Mihailovitch with his Chetniks took to the Serbian mountains and kept on fighting. The Partisans left Serbia and undertook to reorganize their shattered ranks in the wilds of Bosnia. They also kept on fighting.

CHAPTER SEVEN

Yugoslavia's Social Structure

IT WAS stated, at the end of the preceding chapter, that another body of guerrillas, besides the Chetniks, was operating in Serbia. They were the Communists, and extremely brave men they were. Their spirit was high; their discipline, excellent; their aims, glowing. They fought as in the zeal of the Lord. Who were those Communists and why were they there?

Before answering that we must take a glance at the social structure of Yugoslavia. The state, which contained 95,557 square miles in 1940 and was about the size of Oregon, is very mountainous. About 46 per cent of the land surface is arable and of that, only 56 per cent is plowed for fields. Nevertheless, 80 per cent of its sixteen million (1940) inhabitants live from the soil. Practically all of these agriculturists are peasants and a majority own the land they work. Most of the Yugoslav villagers are poor, since good, rich, level farmland, similar to that of Ohio or Iowa, is found only in the northeast corner of the kingdom, in the valleys of the Sava, the Danube, and the Tisza. However, taken as a whole, Yugoslavia has a surplus of agricultural products. It exports grain, timber, and meat and imports manufactured articles.

At the beginning of the war Yugoslavia's arable land was quite equitably distributed. There were very few large estates or great landowners. "Feudalism" was nonexistent, and there was no rich "landed class." There was a landed nation, as far as the limited number of fields could be made to go around. The average family holding was thirteen acres. Of the total area under cultivation 92.5 per cent belonged to the peasants cultivating it. Only 7 per cent was in farms of two hundred acres or above, and many of those larger farms were worked by large peasant families. Eighty per cent of the population lived in villages and another 5 per cent in village-like small towns.

Most of Yugoslavia's income came from agriculture. There were no great industrial centers and but few "industrial tycoons." The chief factories were in Slovenia and northern Croatia. In wild Bosnia there were some large private holdings in woods and a fairly extensive private lumber industry, but 60 per cent of all Yugoslav forests were state or community owned. There were private coal mines in Slovenia, private copper and lead mines in Serbia, owned by foreigners. The railroads, telephone and telegraph systems, and arms factories were owned by the state. Public utilities were owned by the cities. Cooperatives were well developed. A State Agrarian Bank provided the peasants with credit. Land taxes were low. Social legislation was advanced. There was extensive free medical help and a vigorous state activity for sanitary improvement. Workers' social insurance institutions were housed in some of the best and finest buildings in the land. The number of rural schools steadily increased and three-fourths of the peasants under twenty years of age were literate.

In all Yugoslavia there were no more than 475,000 industrial and transport workers, a majority of whom were in Slovenia and Croatia. Even now Tito's coercive United Trade Union claims only 622,000 members. Many of the industrial workers were in small family-shops. Wages were low and most Yugoslav workers were poor—very poor. That was largely due to an oversupply of manpower, as is the case in all peasant lands. In Yugoslavia many peasants are so poor that they are happy to work in a factory at almost any wage. The factory work ekes out their farming incomes; farming ekes out the factory incomes. There are surplus workers waiting for employment at every Yugloslav factory.

Thus, most workers and most peasants had a low living standard, but there was no urban proletariat in Yugoslavia; there were few "serfs," deprived of a livelihood because of bad land distribution, and no large class of bloated monopolistic capitalists. A few rural Yugoslavs inhabited rich agricultural areas, and were prosperous; others inhabited barren, unproductive mountainous areas and were permanently in want; most lived on gentle hills or in broad and narrow valleys, yielding their hard-working owners enough bread, peppers, onions, cheese, wine, brandy, pork, and mutton to enable them to retain a sense of self-respect and security.

There was no milk monopoly or flour monopoly or meat monopoly. Peasants took their milk, butter, cheese, poultry, fruit, flowers, potatoes, eggs, and cattle or sheep or pigs direct to market and personally sold them to the consumers. That takes lots of a peasant's time and requires him to walk long, wearying distances from the village to the city, but it does away with an "exploiting merchant class."

Let us look at the country, region by region, and watch the people at work. In the southeast corner, called Macedonia, bordering on Greece and Bulgaria and Albania, we see a primitive, thrifty, frugal peasant nation of Slavs, Albanians, and a few Turks. In the whole region there is but one modern city, Skoplje, and a half-dozen towns, which are beautiful only in the eyes of their loyal inhabitants. All other settlements are villages largely devoid of modern conveniences. Most of the people are busy in gardens, little fields, vineyards, and orchards, or in flower beds and poppy patches, strung along the water courses. The domestic animals are oxen, cows, pigs, sheep, and donkeys. The main implements are simple plows, hoes, scythes, and sickles. Most of the clothes—and they are very picturesque—are homespun and homemade. Pots, kettles, saddles, comforters, tables, boots are made in little shops by the artisan-owners and the owners' apprentices, who in turn hope someday to have little shops of their own. There is no separate working class and, since the expulsion of Turkish masters, very few great beys or landlords. There are schools in the cities and in many villages. A church dome dominates each settlement, sharing eminence, now and then, with a Moslem minaret.

What kind of social revolution would one impose on that Macedonia? Practically all sources of production are already divided. Nobody can horde or hog very much. What Macedonia needs is progress, honest government, good laws, security, and more productive methods. But you wouldn't improve the lot of peasant Ivan in Deep-George village one iota by hanging the "Liberal Party" mayor Dimiter-with-the-big-ears and putting his Marxian brother Dimiter-with-the-big-mouth in his place. In each case the same sun would shine over the same bare hills and narrow valleys, the same little streams would flow, the same hens lay, the same girls sickle the rye, wearing bright orange aprons and singing sad songs about stern mothers-in-law. What the Macedonians want is a government that takes no graft, exercises no political or economic terror, and gives good service to all. That would be as a gift from heaven. That, not social upheaval, is what the Macedonians need.

Look next at Serbia. You see a pleasant land of wooded hills, patched with green or yellowing fields and dotted with patriarchal homes. Among the hills are fertile valleys and a few wide, rolling plains. Serbia has one city of more than one hundred thousand inhabitants, another of more than fifty thousand, and two-score provincial, patriarchal towns. All the other settlements are villages. The tall, lithe inhabitants wear natty moccasins with jaunty upturned toes in front and fancy latticework on top. The girls swish about in embroidered, homemade skirts; the men swagger around in tight-fitting trousers, making even civilians resemble glamorous soldiers. Of the Serbs, 85 per cent are peasants with land holdings of about twenty acres per family.

There are no great landlords, very few big factories, no entrenched "ruling class." The people are ferociously equalitarian with aggressive family pride. Everyone is as good as every neighbor and a little better. The daughters never go out as servants; the sons rarely as "hired men." The Serbs raise solid, buff-colored oxen, plant corn on the hillsides, tend vineyards on the sunny slopes, raise great quantities of blue plums for prunes and brandy, dance hilariously in village squares on holidays, entertain lavishly on family name days, make fun of the priest on week days and go to his church on Sundays. Most of the boys and many of the girls attend school.

All Serbs sing epic songs of Serbia. They prepare cheese for the year, salt down pork, string red peppers to dry over the walls of their white houses, and hang myriad ears of corn, bound in pairs, from the rafters. They preserve very sweet marmalade or jam (sladko) to serve guests, giving each a spoonful, as mutual good wishes are exchanged. Sons stand in the presence of the elders, brothers defend the honor of sisters. Serbs are proud of ownership, conscious of their place in the Balkans, nationalistic, self-reliant, hard, and sentimental.

I am not attempting to praise, but to describe, the Serbian social system. The Serbians have plenty of faults. On hot days they smell of B.O., in season they spread the aroma of garlic, their houses may abound in fleas, and they drink too much brandy to suit me. But there they are, sturdy tillers of the farms they own, with a society as near Tom Jefferson's economic ideal as has existed and nearer the ancient vision of each man "under his own vine and fig [plum] tree," than is realized by any western nation.

Montenegro presents a grander, barer, simpler picture. As its name implies it is a land of black mountains. It contains no large city and before the war only two towns with as many as ten thousand inhabitants each. It is practically devoid of railroads, large market centers, and industrial plants. Its peasants work meager fields on steep hillsides near rapid streams; its artisans make clothes, hats, and utensils in small shops; its merchants, presiding over simple counters, sell a few store goods to the more pretentious town people. There is no proletariat, no feudalism, no blood-sucking industrial magnate class. Most of the Montenegrins are tall, slender, robust, and picturesque. The men are handsome, gallant, pretentious, and a bit cantankerous; the women are beautiful, self-reliant, resourceful, and diligent.

Montenegro has an astounding tradition of freedom and glories in its age-old defense of the Cross. The people possess much literary ability and intellectual acumen. Since their land is barren and majestic, thus inspiring longings and offering no possibility of their fulfillment, the Montenegrins are notoriously restless. The leading people in Montenegro are priests, army officers, lawyers, and state officials. A few storekeepers and an occasional money-lender exert some influence. Even they live humbly, but the poorer envy them. Barriers between groups or classes are absent.

Any Montenegrin with vigor, eloquence, persistence, and nerve can become first in his little land. All aspire to attain that place. Failing, they denounce those who succeed. They are classically, fervently Russophile. Montenegrin revolutions are not social. They merely consist in the efforts of one group to seize the few government plums enjoyed by another group. John kicks Matthew out and the rooters for his team cheer, as life for the people goes on unchanged. Political parties are instruments for getting jobs.

In Croatia, whose geographical boundaries are vague and which includes Dalmatia, Slavonia, and other former Austro-Hungarian areas, there are semblances of class differentiation. European feudalism did exist there for centuries, creating a class of "gentlemen," who scorned the peasants. Most Croatians have been considered serfs by Austrians, Hungarians, and their own lords. That period of "upper class domination," however, passed with the creation of Yugoslavia in 1918, and during the intervening years the peasants became the dominant political and social factor.

Most Croatians are peasants, living meagerly from the rather unproductive soil. The land is well distributed and most holdings are small. There are more factories than in most other parts of Yugoslavia and a number of industrial workers, but few large plants. One detects the semblance of a proletariat and notes a small urban "ruling class" rather snobbish in attitude and affecting European "culture." The biggest banks of the Balkans were found in Zagreb, along with an opera, a theater, museums, and art galleries. A few people lived well in fine houses, traveled extensively and spoke foreign languages.

There has been bitter "class" strife for three decades in Croatia, but it was not primarily between workers and the "capitalistic blood-suckers"; it was between the peasants and city slickers. In this long fight, the peasants, organized in a strong party, won the victories. They took the lead and set the pace. They became Croatia's banner carriers and culture bearers. Croatia was the classic peasant land, with 85 per cent of the people voting the peasant ticket, and the whole nation centering its loyalty around peasant chiefs.

The Peasant Party was both democratic and practical and turned its attention to markets, housing, health, culture, singing, costumes, adult education, and patriotism. It organized peasant markets, taught better agricultural methods, trained wives in domestic economy, arranged singing contests, gave prizes for stock raising, yearly published peasant songs and stories, promoted peasant art, encouraged child care, and above all aroused peasant pride and loyalty.

Peasants were "it" in Croatia. They swallowed up Croatia. They waved its flags, beat its drums, sang its songs, formed its parades, and said its prayers. Steadily they increased their own power as well as that of Croatia.

Most lived poorly in very beautiful regions. Their little houses were strung thickly along the road in every fertile valley or scattered at long intervals through woods or stuck on bare mountains. Croatians often traveled far to find work, even to North and South America. At home they tended vineyards, planted corn on the hillsides, harvested little patches of wheat, raised pigs, and carried milk, butter, eggs, potatoes to city markets on their heads. With sighs, songs, tears, and many prayers, they eked out pretty plain existences, ever envying the city clerks and salaried state officials. Their lot was far from enviable. But through their Party they dominated their land. Their peasant chief was Croatia's "uncrowned king."

It is not necessary to describe Yugoslavia's social and economic structure in further detail. The general picture must be clear. It was a variegated land with European Slovenia in the northwest, differing greatly from "Turkish Macedonia" in the southeast. But it showed certain general characteristics. It was a peasant country, with the fields well distributed, with no titled class, no entrenched "Junkers," no dominant industry or extensive "finance capital," and only an embryonic proletariat. The peasants, producing most of the wealth of the country, sold most that they didn't use direct to the ultimate consumer; and through political organizations, peasants tended to dominate the politics of the state. Society in most places was patriarchal and classless.

Now, this does not mean that Yugoslavia had no social problems. It fairly rocked with problems, most of which centered about political control. The supreme source of wealth and position and power in Yugoslavia, as in many states, was not land or mines or factories or banks, but the state itself. The government represented a cluster of political feudal estates; it furnished political mines, political oil wells, political golden vestments, shining medals, and fine houses. Control of the state machine is what the Yugoslav Cortezes have fought for.

Every bold Yugoslav adventurer turned himself into a political knight, mounted his party steed, seized the long, vicious lance of police intimidation or administrative discrimination and rode forth to storm the citadel of state power. That was the hope and aim of most Yugoslav politicians, of the good and bad knights, jousting for authority and using it for graft, discrimination, favoritism, corruption, terrorization, and also for service to the people.

There was no fixed "ruling class" in Yugoslavia, no "submerged proletariat," no exploitation of one social stratum by another, but just political "ins" and political "outs."

There were about sixteen million common, hard-working men and women, mostly peasants, among whom were small groups and cliques and gangs of strong men, good and bad, struggling to decoy peasant votes in order to seize and maintain state power. These masters, who were peasants or the sons of peasants, used power partly for their own advantages and partly for the good of the people. As the state grew stronger and richer the might of these knights became greater and their takings vaster. In the same proportion the struggle of the outsiders to get inside increased in ferocity.

I do not mean to condemn all Yugoslav politicians. They were like politicians in many other lands. Among them were good men who tried to serve the people and did serve the people. But I want to emphasize that the reports of a "classic class struggle" in Yugoslavia are largely a myth. The main struggle was and is for state power. What Tito and his Communists wanted, acquired, and are determined to hold is state power. Every other aspect of the new regime is of minor importance.

CHAPTER EIGHT

Yugoslav Communists

DURING the period between the First and Second World Wars, Communism made considerable headway in three Balkan lands, Bulgaria, Greece, and Yugoslavia. In the first, it became strongest and was driven underground, by the various Sofia governments, with great brutality. The Greek Communist movement was vigorous in the shipping center of Piraeus and in the Macedonian tobacco area. Yugoslav Communists were scattered throughout the country but in small numbers. From the beginning, the Party was outlawed there and active Communists were cruelly persecuted.

A casual observer may wonder why Communism, whose appeal is supposed to be to an urban proletariat, throve in such peasant countries as Bulgaria and Yugoslavia which have no distinct proletariat, only a very small working class, practically no powerful industrialists, and most of whose larger enterprises were state owned. The answer is that Communism in the Slav Balkan lands was a secular religion. It inspired idealism. It was also a political conspiracy. It was a revolt of impatient high-school or college graduates against the universe.

Communism was a cult through which restless intellectuals obtained spiritual satisfaction. It was a furious, fanatical idolatry enabling yearners to feel they were a part of a higher world and associated with a chosen fellowship that was redeeming humanity. Along with this, it was a plot for taking possession of state power. It closely resembled early Mohammedanism. Almost all of its leaders were doctrinaire and its chief support came from the "intelligentsia." It was an extremely dynamic form of worship with a beautiful and terrible theology, with both grand and abominable aims. It inspired astounding sacrifices and provoked the basest crimes.

To understand Balkan Communism one must make an emotional map of the Balkans. That is a drab, grim part of Europe with age-old traditions of foreign oppression and with a mystic awe for revolutionists. The land has strikingly beautiful aspects, but also extensive "passive areas," that are bare, gray, and sterile. The towns are pretty squalid, the villages are dirty, rather disorderly, and terribly isolated. Life is dull, stereotyped, cramped. It is tedious, monotonous, and obscure.

Within the last fifty to one hundred years that peasant, patriarchal area has been brought into touch with the modern world. Young men and women learn of store clothes and automobiles, wonderful theaters and beautiful houses, of freedom, fame, wealth, and justice. Young people study about those things at school. They read of them in books and papers, they hear of them over the radio. And they yearn to enjoy them. It all sounds like "The Arabian Nights." The Balkanese feel like Cinderellas, with princes disporting just beyond the horizons. They imagine distant Utopias. They entertain visions of beauty and fame, of marble halls and silken gowns. But what they daily come in contact with are cows and pigs, illiterate mamas and antediluvian, dictatorial grandpas, with baggy pants and boxes of snuff. So the youth rebel. They go on a spiritual rampage for that bright world. They hate banal reality. In their revolt they frantically embrace revolutionary, world-transforming, apocalyptic Communism as a golden chariot taking them to heaven. They love it all the more because it comes from legendary Mother Russia, their idol, their shrine, and their champion.

If you want to feel the lure of Balkan Communism, just attend a rousing Pentecostal meeting in a big American tabernacle, with a gifted evangelist calling people down the sawdust trail. Picture the drab jobs and homes of the listeners and their meager future; then behold the grand vista which the preacher opens up—the second coming, Jesus appearing on the clouds, all the evil people being punished and all the converted being caught up to ride to heaven in effulgent band wagons. The listeners climb onto those celestial band wagons! So do Balkan youth mount Lenin's shining chariot to ride to paradise.

And they really ride that chariot! The cult or sect of Communism does transform its Balkan devotees. It lifts them out of the dust and mud and flies and cow manure and makes Marxian heroes of them. It gives them Marxian wings. They join the invisible host of the saved. They are transfigured, as the early Christians. I am not making this up; I'm describing people I have intimately known.

Slav Communists become well read and copiously informed. They have all the answers. They learn by heart the revealed Communist theology, that solves all riddles and opens doors to the whole future. They feel superior and happy and strong. Everyone else appears ignorant, uninitiated, stupid, lost. The Communists know history, geography, literature, and economics. They reel off the past till you're dizzy and the future till you're dazed. They pick up all the nations and classes in their hands and spread before you the panorama of the ages. You see Armageddon and the great upheaval; then the endless Utopia and the blessed, classless society where everyone loves everyone and all evil is swept away. The Twenty-third Psalm pales and Isaiah's bright vision fades beside the glory of the glowing new order.

For this vision boys and girls willingly die. They despise the bourgeois world, meaning cow stables and pigpens. They welcome chains and dungeons. They have found a higher pleasure and consecrated themselves to what they consider a nobler cause. How revolting to such revolutionists is the sputtering of candles in "superstition-bound Orthodox churches," and how dull the crooning of old ladies in stereotyped prayer meetings or the "Latin mumblings of shaved priests at mass!" The Communists have found the hotter, fiercer gospel that satisfies.

And they thrill to its imperious demands. They glory in its categorical imperatives. They spring to the fulfillment of its stupendous *Thou Shalts,* ringing out from the Moscow Sinai, sanctified and beatified by the most high Lenin, who loved all mankind, hated every evil, and gave his life for the world. These boys and girls are soldiers of the precious scarlet banner, marching hand in hand through all the lands to slay the bourgeois dragon.

Of course they hate father and mother for that doctrine. They despise the existing order and all its banal trappings. They gladly leave home and family. They reject pinchpenny bourgeois morality. They leap from the chains of such enslaving obligations as right, truth, loyalty, fidelity, and the keeping of promises. They have a new loyalty, a different morality, a "higher" Marxian ethics. They lie and steal and destroy and kill for the cause. To deceive a heretical bourgeois is a virtue. They are rude, arrogant, insolent, brutal, for in that way they show their superiority over the capitalistic riffraff.

They nourish themselves in hate. They hate churches, hate courts, hate laws, hate duties. They hate formal paintings, normal statues, poetry that rhymes, and logic that commands. They hate marriage and washing diapers and supporting children. They hate charity and kindness and pity and good will. Their basic doctrine is "the worse it is, the better it is." What they most love are signs of approaching cataclysms. They strain their ears to hear the rumbles of coming explosions.

They are taught that they can win only in times of disorder and upheavals and especially war. They like strikes, disasters, international strife, because when norms are swept away and men and women mill about as frightened, angry cattle, Communists can win followers and make gains. They are especially eager to do away with "pillars of society," with people who inspire love or respect or fear or righteousness on the part of the weak and less fortunate.

They try to eliminate priests, substantial merchants, morality-observing teachers, and all those community leaders who through the ages have been called "the elders," who give counsel and create stability. Communists call such persons "the enemies of the people."

Their policy in relation to other groups, as expressed by Lenin himself, is, "It is necessary, in order to be able to counteract all of these methods [of "reactionary" trade union leaders], to be prepared to resort to every possible sort of subterfuge, trick, illegal device calculated to conceal the truth and prevent its becoming known—in order to penetrate into the trade unions, to remain in them and, at any cost, to carry on Communist activity." *

The Communists show disregard for people as individuals, both for comrades and class enemies. What is one man or woman in comparison with the "holy Communist cause"? Every individual is an expendable. What is a village! What, even, is a nation! They are as dust in the balance, yea, as fine dust in the eyes of the god of Communism and on the scales of world revolution. Therefore, Communists are cruel and hard and ruthless. They are as priests offering up their own children. They consider mercy a weakness and romantic love a vice. With the glory of the bloody Communist dawn dazzling their eyes, how can they see a little thing like John or Mary! May Lenin preserve them from such weakness!

And when they are out of power, what to them is a fatherland! Their only fatherland is the world revolution. Their unique and only capital, which alone commands their loyalty, is Moscow. They live only for that new Jerusalem. For Moscow, the citadel of world revolution and the guarantor of a redeemed humanity, they scorn king and government, laws and oaths, national interests and state security. For them, when out of power, patriotism in relation to their own country is treason and fidelity to homeland a crime. They offer it all on the altar of Russia's interests and of the world revolution.

* From "Left-Wing Communism and Infantile Disorder," Vol. 25 of the *Collected Works of Lenin*, German edition, page 240.

Such were the ideals, ideas, and practices of the Yugoslav Communists.

Immediately after the First World War they attained some success. In fact, they elected fifty-seven members to the first Constituent Assembly. Though many of these deputies were little more than representatives of national minorities protesting against the dominant parties and groups, that number did reveal a strong Russian influence in Yugoslavia. Lenin plainly was accepted as protector by some weary and heavy-laden Yugoslavs. Marx's thunderous appeals to the world's workers to unite and throw off their chains affected the inhabitants of not a few little Yugoslav towns that had endured frustration for centuries. Some Yugoslavs heard the great Slav Mother and gave heed. They voted for the millennium.

But, they didn't get it. The Yugoslav government took measures. It suppressed Communism. On most other matters most Yugoslavs disagreed with one another. Government succeeded government with great rapidity. Every group called every other group bad names. But they all agreed on outlawing Communism. And all favored the use of cruelty in doing it. Therefore, most Yugoslav Communist leaders spent much of their time in exile or in jail.

Nevertheless, the movement persisted, consolidated itself, and even spread a little, though at a very slow pace. It never became a major factor or played a leading role. It was always on the fringe, in the dusk, a threatening specter, not a determinative reality. Still, this specter was more than a fantasy. A Communist movement existed. Communists were active in schools, labor unions, literary and art clubs. They circulated considerable literature, even had meetings. They advocated wonderful ideas, made beautiful promises.

Not a few Yugoslavs wrote Communist poems and stories and plays. They painted pictures inciting to revolt. They defied conventions, advocated moral mutiny, extolled absolute freedom. They were not in the mountains or caves, but rather in the coffee houses and theaters. They murdered the old bourgeois reactionaries in satires and poems and dramas, for profit and applause.

Communist protests against wrong were the most sweeping and furious, and so aroused enthusiasm. There were a million things to criticize in Yugoslavia—and the Communists did it best. They ridiculed moderation, rejected partial reforms, scorned palliatives. They called everybody else a crook or idiot, arousing admiration for their boldness and "profundity." In contrast with all this they offered the perfect new order, the complete upheaval, the apocalyptic joys of a new heaven and new earth.

Some youth fell for it. In Belgrade most Serbian University and many high-school students tended toward Communism. No informed observer would deny this. In a few of the Serbian provincial high schools, also, Communism had taken root. One Serbian priest even went "red," and he was a forceful man. Some poets, journalists, artists, novelists, lawyers, and teachers went very red. Indisputably, Communism was an ideological and conspiratorial force among Serbian youth. They had no economic or social plan for Serbia. But they were tired of political graft, party immorality, violence, and frustration. They wanted a new order and were eager to fight or go to jail for it, at any rate to shout about it.

The actual number of Serbian Communists would be difficult to estimate—perhaps 5 per cent of all the people, though the organized Communists were not half of one per cent. In Montenegro the proportion was greater. Among the young people of the Black Mountains I believe 25 per cent were Communists. Even some Montenegrin student-priests or theological students were red. Of course, the actual number of Communists was small, because the total number of Montenegrins is very small. But that little state was the main nest of Yugoslav Marxism.

What an astounding commentary that was on Karl Marx! These barren rocks with no workers, no cities, no factories, no banker making one thousand dollars a month and with "industrialists" happy to make one hundred dollars a month—these provided the spring of Yugoslavia's "social revolution." The rebels were simply insurgents against the gods—all existing gods. They went to school, got diplomas, prepared for the good life, and found themselves stymied in wretched villages with nothing but fresh air and scenery.

They wanted jobs and money and power and fame. They detested the chicken dung, cow manure, and all-consuming obscurity. Also, they hated bad government. They tied it all up with every respectable man in the country, the priest, the lawyer, the storekeeper, the neighbor with six beehives, the old retired major, the elderly schoolteacher who flunked some boys and told the girls to preserve their virtue. They wanted to blow the whole machine sky high and turn little Montenegro into a paradise like Mother Russia. Such Montenegrin Communists were stationed all over the kingdom and became a political factor of some importance.

In Slovenia, the Communists were very few but very able. In the whole province of a million inhabitants there were barely one thousand active Communists. But they were extremely active. They were educated, trained, traveled, skilled. Of course, all worked underground. They were completely international. Their fatherland was Russia and there the leaders got their training. They spent time in Vienna, Rome, Paris, and Spain. The world was their stage, Stalin their master, Slovenia their sector of the world front. They proselyted among workers, peasants, students, soldiers. And on the whole without much success.

On Slovene politics they had almost no influence. They did their most effective work on the fringe or margin of the intelligentsia, among the "pinkos." They managed to introduce a little stream of rebellion, revolt, and hatred through art, literature, the theater, and journalism. However, "Liberalism," Clericalism, Agrarianism, and Nationalism were so strong in Slovenia that the Communists were a negligible factor, except as secret agents preparing for the apocalypse. That was their task. They performed it masterfully. The apocalypse came in 1941.

Zagreb, the capital of Croatia, was a Communist center. I do not mean to say that many of the people there were Communists. But taken as a whole, there were more influential, recognized Communists in Zagreb than in any other city. For example, the leading literary figure of Zagreb was a Communist. He was not in jail much of the time and he was not a conspirator or party agitator, but he made Communism speak from most of his writings. Other writers, journalists, artists, and even some workers openly professed adherence to Communism. They formed a circle of revolt and were accepted by many intellectuals as heroes, crusaders, and heralds of a grand new order.

Zagreb for many years was a labyrinth of intertwined, overlapping, mutually hostile revolts. The Ustasha Fascists were subversive, the Clericals were raging against Orthodox Serbia, the Peasant Party was conspiring both openly and secretly to overthrow Serb domination, and the Communists worked for their millennium. Among these groups the Peasants were by far the strongest and the Communists by far the weakest. This means they were not a formidable political factor, but they were an appreciable force slowly increasing in power.

South of Zagreb, in the Adriatic coastal cities, Communism had a foothold. A good many crusaders were also to be found throughout the mountains of Bosnia. There was no city in the whole land without a Communist cell and no region in which the restless youth had not heard the message of Communist revolutionists.

From the very beginning of the Second World War the Yugoslav Communists were especially active, just as they were in America and everywhere else. They saw that the world cataclysm was here. Armageddon was being fought. The grand and awful day of trouble had dawned, when empires would crash, established norms would be swept away, hunger and want stalk through the land.

This would cause confusion and chaos, in the midst of which little groups of bold, organized Communist conspirators would be able to impose their will.

So, from the day Stalin and Hitler signed their pact in 1939, the Yugoslav Communists sprang into activity. Of course they were not against Germany. And naturally, they were not with England or France. Neither were they for Yugoslav unity. They were for the universal upheaval, following the guiding star of Russia and nothing else, serving Russia and no other power. They denounced the Allies in furious terms. They portrayed the war as exclusively a fight between bloodthirsty empires. They excoriated the whole capitalistic order and joyfully predicted its imminent collapse. They poured out streams of invectives against the Yugoslav government and Regent and army.

And they formed cells. They pushed their organizational activity to the uttermost limit. When free, they shouted their doctrines from the housetops. When imprisoned, they disseminated them through a dozen secret channels with the aura of martyrdom surrounding them. The great "day of the Lord" was upon them and they worked incessantly to be prepared. They devised plans of action. They set up a secret military organization. They gave every member of their party his or her place for future action. They established a romantic, thrilling, sinister shadow state within the official state. They marked the prospective victims who were to be eliminated.

They spread their net over the army and navy. They had agents in the courts, the secret service, and the whole communication apparatus. They had representatives in printing offices, at switchboards, in the telegraph stations.

Naturally, many were arrested. War raged between the real and the invisible state. The government opened concentration camps for Communists. Scores were confined; some were beaten. The hard-pressed Yugoslav government had to maintain a new front against a group of its own citizen-traitors. Germany was pressing, Italy was pressing, Bulgaria was pressing, native German Nazis were conspiring, and in the midst of all these difficulties the Yugoslav Communists, from one end of the kingdom to the other, were doing everything possible to hasten the collapse of the state and bring about a chaos of which they could take advantage.

As 1938 passed and 1940 passed and 1941 came, making the world situation more dangerous, the Communists stood, taut and tense, by day and by night, as racers waiting for the pistol shot. Their ears were strained to hear the signal-giver, Moscow.

When March 27 came, with all Serbians defying Hitler, the Communists at first ignored it as a futile bourgeois act, and then on March 28 attempted a futile counter-revolution. But their great moment had not yet come. Their conspiratorial network was not created for the banal task of saving the "fatherland," Yugoslavia. They had seven more weeks to wait for the clock of destiny to strike. Then Hitler attacked Russia. The detestable war between capitalist empires was transformed into a holy crusade. The day had dawned in preparation for which the Yugoslav Communists had spent their lives. They began their epochal role with a heroism and fanaticism rarely equalled in the heroic, fanatical Balkans.

CHAPTER NINE

Mihailovitch and Tito Clash

BY LATE summer, 1941, five months after Hitler had launched his attack on Belgrade, two underground forces were fighting the Nazi occupiers of Serbia, the Chetniks under Colonel Drazha Mihailovitch and the Communists under Josip Broz-Tito, an able and forceful Croatian Communist. Mihailovitch's fighters in those operations were exclusively Serbian; Tito's guerrillas were of various nationalities, but the majority were Serbs and Montenegrins.

The rapidity with which Tito launched his underground campaign and the vigor with which he executed it show how well the Communists were organized. Within a month after Hitler attacked Russia, the Yugoslav Communists were effectively fighting in Serbia. They had been informed during previous months that Hitler was transferring troops from Germany toward Russia. They themselves had observed how German units were moving out of Greece and Yugoslavia through Hungary and Rumania toward the northeast, and had been instructed, with much precision, how to operate.

For months they had anxiously followed Hitler's penetration into southeast Europe toward Turkey and had learned from the press and radio, as well as through direct channels, that Russia was worried. Also, they had been taught, as the most fundamental point in their whole system of Communistic theology, that sooner or later Soviet Russia would fight the rest of the world. Since many of the Yugoslav Communist leaders had been in Russia, they knew that the Soviet regime was making all its plans with that prospective war in view. They had personally seen that Russia's five-year plans, her industry, her collective farms, her financial system, her education, and her propaganda were designed to prepare Russia for the "inevitable clash." To aid Mother Russia in that hour and help her through to final victory, which would guarantee the triumph of the world revolution, was considered the supreme duty of every Yugoslav Comrade.

The breaking out of that struggle would be as the "coming of the bridegroom"; for it every bridesmaid kept her lamp burning and filled with oil. That was as basic in the faith of Yugoslav Communists as the Resurrection and Easter Day were in the faith of their Christian brothers. Many special signs had indicated that "the hour" was approaching, and for it the Yugoslav Communists had put their conspiratorial machine in readiness. Couriers were on their toes to dash away with messages to every part of the kingdom. Communist officers in the Yugoslav Army were designated for certain key positions in the revolutionary army and leading civilian Communists were prepared to fill other military posts. The chief commissars were appointed, definite campaign plans had been agreed upon, methods for getting weapons had been worked out, local "cells" in vital points of operation were on the alert. The Communist underground machine was as an armored locomotive resting on a hidden track under full steam. When "the great day" of June 22 came, the whistle blew and the locomotive sped to the attack.

The objective had been carefully defined. The Communists, whose leadership consisted principally of Serbs and Montenegrins, along with a few Macedonians, Slovenes, and Hungarians, all under the supreme direction of Communist Tito, were to seize accessible places in western Serbia, raise red flags, and set up local Soviet republics. A new sector of the global Soviet front was to be established in Serbia.

That aim was momentarily realized. Yugoslav Communists did seize towns and villages. Red flags proudly snapped over some town halls. The "cells" appeared in the open, as little soviets. Communist secret police instantly went into action and summarily disposed of the main local opponents of Communism. Active bourgeois leadership in the "freed" areas was eliminated. All necessary goods were requisitioned, youth was mobilized for the new Communist army and the new order was inaugurated. In the initial stage of this action, the principal victims of the Communist attack were Serbs themselves. Most of the places taken were of secondary strategic importance to the Germans and but lightly garrisoned. Tito's forces did not have to overcome many Germans. They overcame Serbs.

The forces of Mihailovitch operated in a different manner. In the first place they launched no revolution, since they considered their activity a function of the long-existing state and a continuation of the official anti-Hitler fight which was begun on March 27. They flew the Yugoslav flag and regular regimental banners, re-established local Serbian authorities, sought to revive Serbian faith and courage, reassembled units of the Serbian Army, urged Serbs not to serve Germans, tried to prevent the Germans from confiscating Serbian stocks of food, restricted the movement of Germans, blew up vital military installations and killed German agents.

Mihailovitch and his Chetniks did not care to waste their forces in trying to take large cities in open battles. They preferred to avoid head-on clashes. They wanted to reorganize their shattered nation and prepare it for long, effective, wise resistance.

Since these forces of Mihailovitch and Tito were fighting in a fairly small area, they soon found themselves in contact. And to avert clashes the leaders met. Mihailovitch and Tito conferred. They sought a plan for common action, but failed in their efforts. Tito wanted a separate revolutionary command for his forces; Mihailovitch demanded that all forces comprise a single army under one command, his own. So they disagreed, separated, and fought. Their soldiers began to kill each other; Yugoslavs shot Yugoslavs, as the German invaders cheered.

Each reader may form his own opinion as to who was right and who was wrong in this clash. Tito was willing to have his army do its part in fighting the common foe, if his army were allowed to act with complete independence. Mihailovitch categorically rejected that offer. He did not approve of a state within a state. He hoped all efforts would be directed against Germans, not against Germans and Yugoslavs.

The Communists, by no means a new and unknown force in Serbia, were in the service of Russia. Tito even spoke to Mihailovitch as an emissary of Russia. He had a Russian wife, had spent years in Russia, and had recruited Yugoslavs to go to Spain and fight for Russia. Some of the men about him had also been in Russia.

Tito's Communists had seemed to put Russia's interests ahead of Yugoslavia's and had not fought against Germany until after Russia was attacked. When Yugoslavia was attacked and was being smashed, Tito's Communists did not resist the Germans. They began their offensive for the sake of Russia, not for their own country. More than that, as the Yugoslav Army was desperately fighting Hitler's Wehrmacht whose tanks were rolling ruthlessly through Yugoslav towns, Tito's Communists actually tried to prevent the Yugoslav Army from fighting. Communist orators appeared before hard-pressed army units and urged them not to resist Germans, not to lose their lives fighting for "bloody British capitalists," not to sacrifice themselves in a foreign war between predatory empires. And not only did Yugoslav Communists make such oral appeals to the Yugoslav Army, but they splashed them across walls on posters.

Mihailovitch knew this and his Chetnik advisers knew it. As he sat with Tito, who spoke as a Russian, Mihailovitch was aware that he was dealing with a man who had worked to destroy the Yugoslav state, who wanted to eliminate the monarchy and had actually aided in the destruction of the Yugoslav Army during its most tragic days. Mihailovitch was convinced that Tito and his Communists were taking advantage of Yugoslavia's terrible plight to impose their regime and that Tito's foremost aim was not to fight Germans but to conquer Serbs and take possession of their land. In this view, Mihailovitch was right. He was dealing with some of the most fanatical Communists on earth, for whom Serbia was a mere instrument serving in the attainment of greater aims. Consequently, he refused to authorize them to maintain an independent army in Serbia.

If an American wants to understand the position in Yugoslavia at that catastrophic moment, he can best do it by imagining the state of Massachusetts in 1943, faced with the demand that in the interests of America's war effort it accept an independent Communist army, led by Earl Browder or William Z. Foster, with the prospects that red flags would fly over the state house, as well as over most Massachusetts cities, including Boston, and that eventually Communists would control all the schools, the press, and the whole economic life of Massachusetts. One must also presuppose that, in facing this prospect, the Massachusetts leaders knew the Communists had already massacred many of the more substantial citizens, both Protestant and Catholic, in a dozen Massachusetts cities. Would responsible Massachusettsans, if faced by such a dilemma, have accepted? Would not 98 per cent of them have rejected it? Would they not have rejected it indeed with the same patriotic ardor with which Massachusetts heroes once assembled at Bunker Hill?

That was the predicament in which Mihailovitch was placed. And when he rejected Tito's demands he made no arbitrary, capricious, or selfish decision, based on personal ambitions. He spoke in the name of and on behalf of the common men and women of Serbia. He expressed the will and desire of 90 per cent of the Serbian people. Serbia, not merely Mihailovitch, spurned that Communist offer. Serbians, not merely Chetniks, despised it. Serbians detested as traitors that group of Yugoslav citizens who, on finding their land prostrate and occupied by an implacable enemy, took advantage of the calamity to murder Serbs and impose a dictatorial regime.

And what had Tito's Communists to offer the Serbs? Was he

bringing "redemption and relief"? Was he coming with emancipation, social liberation, freedom from want and oppression? Was he presenting Serbia with a new social order? There was not so much as a slight ephemeral tinge of a beneficial social revolution.

Was he wiping out a Serbian land-owning class? Serbian land had long been divided among the Serbian people. Tito's followers weren't redistributing land to the peasants; they were grabbing land from the peasants. Were they smashing a Serbian Junker army? Why, all Serbian officers were the grandsons—or sons—of peasants. Theirs was a peasant army. Almost nowhere on earth was an officer so close to the privates. Serbian officers rode third class with peasants! The gap between an officer and a private in the Serbian Army was far narrower than that in Russia or in Tito's army. Tito was not crushing military rule in Serbia; he was trying to impose it upon Serbia. He was bringing Junkerism.

Was Tito bringing state ownership of essential economic facilities to the Serbian people? Already for years whenever a Serb rode on a train, it was on the state railway. When he phoned, it was on a state telephone; when he wired, it was by means of a state telegraph system. When he made airplanes or munitions, it was in state factories. He studied in state schools, was healed from sickness in municipal hospitals, prayed in a state church, rode in municipal street cars, drank municipal water, got credit from a state bank, smoked cigarettes sold by a state organization, and used gasoline distributed by a state agency.

Was Tito bringing schools to Serbia? Already the nation had set up three universities, a high school in every city, elementary schools in every town and most villages. I am not praising Serbian education. There was decided room for improvement, as there is in the American cities of Boston and Birmingham, but the Serbians had made great progress, and certainly Tito had no schools in his knapsack.

Was he bringing civil liberties? Just the opposite; he was wiping them out. Was he bringing a perfect new jurisprudence? On the contrary, he was subverting all justice. Was he bringing deep, fine, humane consideration of ordinary Mrs. Jovanovitch and ordinary Mr. Dimitriyevitch? Oh, no, he was jamming Mr. Dimitriyevitch into a conscripted, revolutionary army and throwing Mrs. Jovanovitch into jail as a Fascist and "enemy of the people," because she protested against Communist commissars taking her last hog.

Was Tito leading a land of exploited Serbian workers and peasants, an outraged and exploited proletariat which had at last arisen against its oppressors, to demand justice before God and history? Were the Serbian masses rising under Tito's leadership to throw off a capitalistic yoke? Not 5 per cent of Tito's followers were Serbian factory workers. His army was in no respect a Serbian proletariat. It was a band of intellectual rebels. It was a political conspiracy. It was a secular cult on the war path, resembling the Mohammedans who had swept up those very valleys five hundred years earlier.

The Serbian people knew that this was a conspiracy against them and out of their long experience summoned up courage to reject it. Mihailovitch spoke their word for them. It is unfortunate and erroneous for an American to consider this a feud between an individual called Mihailovitch and another called Tito. It was no more that, than another conflict was a feud between a man called Abe (Lincoln) and another called Jeff (Davis). It was, rather, one of the most basic issues in human history. The Serbian peasants and artisans, after struggling long decades for freedom from the Turks, and after heroically rejecting Hitler's yoke, now spurned another bondage, brought from abroad.

Twenty-four years before, as the Germans pressed into Russia, Nikolai Lenin had taken advantage of the distress and confusion to impose his dictatorship upon Russia. In 1941 Tito was trying to do the same in Serbia. Lenin's conspiracy had much to justify it, because the Russian people were victims of terrible social wrongs. Tito's plot had no such justification. He brought no basic reforms.

He resembled the neighbor of a man whose house was burning and who moved in with a gun to make himself master. But the Serbian nation, although battered, had moral strength to resist him.

Of course, that meant civil war. Tito after long preparation had pulled a Fort Sumter. From the end of the summer of 1941, civil war raged in Yugoslavia, along with the war between Yugoslavs and Germans. The main struggle in Yugoslavia, after Tito's fateful invasion of Serbia, was the civil struggle between the Communists and anti-Communists. There were many dramatic secondary fights—indeed Yugoslav developments were as a labyrinth containing a dozen spots of intense interest—but the supreme struggle dominating all others, giving meaning to all others, providing an unchanging pattern in the chaos, was the fight between Communist totalitarianism and its opponents.

Naturally, the civil war which Tito provoked in Serbia facilitated the work of the Germans. During the early fall of 1941 new Nazi divisions crushed both Serbian resistance forces with terrible cruelty, left towns and villages smoking ruins, and massacred civilians by the scores of thousands.

CHAPTER TEN

The Serbs Are Massacred

MANY Serbians who were in the country at the time have stated that no fewer than six hundred thousand Serbs had been killed by the end of 1941. Within nine months after the Serbs spontaneously arose to defy Hitler and take the side of Great Britain, about 8 per cent of the nation was said to be dead.

As to the accuracy of the number I cannot vouch. Long experience in the Balkans has taught me that most numbers are exaggerated. Extreme sadness and furious hatred create an emotional aura in which numbers seem bigger than they are. However, I do know, from personal contact with large numbers of relatives of the victims and with persons who had escaped attacks, that masses of Serbs were killed in all parts of Yugoslavia by Axis agents and by Partisans. Bulgarians, Germans, Italians, Hungarians, Croatians, Moslems, and Communists all killed Serbs.

The Serbs, from the Bulgarian border to the Adriatic coast, and from the Hungarian frontier to that of Albania, were pot shots for almost everyone with a gun—and everyone had a gun. I am sure that hundreds of thousands of Serbs were killed. I am convinced that the Serbs have had far greater losses in *killed*, in this war, than the British Empire, and more than twice as many killed as the American nation. There were about as many Serbs in Yugoslavia as there are Australians in Australia. Both were in this war against the Axis. Australia was in extremely grave danger, as was Serbia. Both fought bravely, but Serbian losses in killed were fully thirty times greater than Australia's. That is 3000 per cent.

To list these fearful losses would be tedious. Astounding as it may seem, there is nothing so banal as hearing of atrocities. When one's brother gets shot or drowned or smashed in a machine it is deeply exciting, but constant killing day after day, or mass killing, is boring. It comes to be no more interesting than the activity in a slaughterhouse, which is as dull as threshing wheat or ginning cotton.

Therefore, I shall not attempt to report Serbian losses in detail, even though they are one of the most significant and important facts of this war. I know from long personal observation that nothing affects an individual or family or clan or class or nation as much as killing. A feuding Kentuckian or Albanian never forgets the shedding of blood. Our little "Boston Massacre" goes resounding down the centuries with thunderous reverberations, though it took fewer victims than many an auto accident. The shooting of laborers by cops is never forgotten by laborers. Blood leaves an indelible mark, influencing every new generation. Consequently, the massacring of thousands upon thousands of Serbs is a colossal, ineradicable act that will long affect Balkan developments. Every planner of the future must bear that in mind.

As an example of how real it all was and is, I will tell of an individual case. I got the story personally from Dimitrina Jovanovitch. She is a twenty-two-year-old, unmarried Serbian girl from a village in western Yugoslavia near the frontier between the provinces of Kordun and Lika. Most of the houses in her settlement belonged to Serbs who according to the tradition had lived there for centuries. They had an Orthodox church, served by a vigorous, auburn-bearded priest, who read mass in old Slavic, taught his flock about Serbian history and traditions and about the "Serbian mission," prayed each Sunday for the young Yugoslav King, and in a customary sectarian way, no more inflammatory than one finds in the columns of the *Christian Century* or the Bostonian *Christian Register*, urged his parishioners to beware of Roman Catholics. He shared the views of many American Protestants that Rome is "the harlot of Babylon," and occasionally said so. Cloistered on the edge of the village were a few Croatian Catholic families who had lived in peace but not intimacy with the Serbs and who weekly went to a Roman Catholic church in a neighboring village, where a shaved, auburn-haired priest read mass in Latin and urged his flock to remain ardently faithful to the true church of Christ, outside of which there is no salvation.

Practically all the inhabitants of this village were peasants. The surface of the district was far from level, the soil thin, the fields small, the people poor. However, the community managed to support an elementary school, giving a seven-year course. Dimitrina had finished six grades and her three brothers, all seven grades. The two younger girls were still in school. All six children dwelt with their parents in a plain, rather bare ancestral house, living mostly on vegetables and bread, with occasional mutton, eggs now and then, and a little white cheese in season. Dimitrina and her sisters wore rather striking hand-embroidered costumes and they and their mother had worked colored figures on the boys' shirts. The whole family wore moccasins, hand-knit stockings or socks, and the boys jauntily cocked soft caps on the sides of their heads. These were called "shaikaches," and served as an unmistakable sign of Serbianism. Dimitrina and her two sisters didn't have much to look forward to except marriage, living with unromantic mothers-in-law, raising children, tending fields, lighting candles in the church, and finally joining their ancestors in the graveyard, visited yearly through all the generations on All-Souls day and other special occasions.

It was not a glowing prospect, but lyric and epic songs, folk dances, lavishly adorned church walls, gorgeous aprons, grand scenery, intense family love, and the fierce joy of being Serbs, somewhat relieved the gray days and dark nights. Each monotonous year was broken into fairly short intervals by church holidays, giving everyone a little something to anticipate. Two of the boys were planning to escape from this thwarting peasant drudgery, one by becoming a mechanic in the county seat, the other by going to a school for officers.

One Friday in the summer of 1941, when Hitler was absolute master of Dimitrina's land and his furious ally, the Croatian Fuehrer or Poglavnik, Ante Pavelitch, was terrorizing towns and villages with cruelty surpassing even that of a Herod, an order came to Dimitrina's village that all the Serbs were to appear in the Orthodox church on the following Sunday. Every family was seized with deep foreboding, for reports of incredible atrocities were spreading over the country.

It was known that all the Serbs had been expelled from Zagreb and that most of their property had been confiscated. It was known, too, that terrible pressure had been imposed upon the Orthodox Serbs to make them leave their church and that many Orthodox priests had been imprisoned and killed. Startling eyewitness stories had come to Dimitrina's neighbors about Dictator Pavelitch's Croatian Ustashas or revolutionary soldiers, robbing, torturing, and murdering Serbs. These accounts were accepted as authentic, because every Serb knew that the Poglavnik's leading passion had long been hatred of Serbs and that he had trained the most licentious and vicious elements he could find in the art of killing Serbs. These storm-troopers had been given long and thorough education in the bloodiest torture techniques and in the best ways to cause terror and suffering.

Such reports about Pavelitch's methods and plans, coupled with the strange official order obliging all Serbs in Dimitrina's village to attend church on the following Sunday, made the day seem as night and each night seem sheer perdition. Every child and adult had often seen mosques in neighboring towns and more than once had heard Moslem priests or "hodjas" from the top of minarets call the faithful to prayer, and they had shuddered to recall how Turkish armies, following all-conquering sultans, had once moved through these very villages, overwhelming the Christians, killing women and children. Crescent banners had once glowered over the land as heralds and symbols of horror. Now a similar horror held Dimitrina's village in its grasp.

The peasants secretly consulted among themselves as to what they should do. Should they flee into the woods leaving homes and fields and animals? That would only bring starvation, and even in the woods, how could they hide from armed pursuers? Would the babies survive rain and wind with no sustenance and no clean swaddling clothes? Could little boys and girls wander for days unfed and without shelter, ever fleeing from wild phantoms and shaking before every whispering leaf? Should grandpas and grandmas force their bent and tottering frames along hopeless, bloodstained trails that had no end and brought no surcease, either by night or day?

No, the village would not flee. It would choose the unknown evil rather than certain catastrophe. Perhaps one of Pavelitch's men would order them to separate their church from the national Serbian Patriarchate and join some new, phony Orthodox Union of "Free Croatia." Well, then they could decide what to do. In any case, they would go to church, as ordered.

Some of the villagers advised the priest, Father Nicolai, to stay away, since he would be a special object of attack, but he boldly answered that he would not desert his flock or his church. If they were to flee, he would flee with them; if they were to fight, he would fight with them; if they were to perish, he would perish with them. On the appointed Sunday at the appointed hour, the Serbs of Dimitrina's village filled the place of worship. Even the reluctant ones went, for fierce, heavily-armed, bare-bayoneted Croatian Ustasha troopers appeared throughout the village and visited all Serbian houses, fairly driving the people to the service. Only the most aged and infirm remained at home.

But Dimitrina was not there. Neither was her eldest brother,

Teodor. He had stolen to the hills the night before, vaguely resolved to join the invisible band of Serbian Chetniks who on numerous occasions, through the ages, had devoted their life to the protection of Serbia. Dimitrina herself, strange as it may seem, was hiding with a Croatian neighbor. Human relations are sometimes stronger than nationality or class or religious hatred, and the preceding Saturday, a Croatian girl of Dimitrina's age had urged Dimitrina to spend Sunday morning in her house.

Perhaps this companion had a premonition, perhaps she had been told of the nefarious plot. In any case she tried to save Dimitrina and succeeded. As the Serbian sexton, that Sunday morning, rang his church bell for the last time, unwittingly sending a dirge over the village, calling his neighbors to the other world rather than to a sermon about the other world, Dimitrina by a stealthy ruse made her way to the home of her Catholic friend and hid in the stable. That is how she survived to tell me what happened.

When the Serbians were all assembled in church, a Ustasha chief, more vicious appearing than most of the others, ordered the congregation to await a high official of the new government of "Independent Croatia," who would soon come to make an announcement. He then withdrew and closed the door, after which the priest began to read mass. Almost instantly a cordon of armed Croatian Ustasha men surrounded the church, while machine gun companies appeared and took up posts covering every door and window.

After that, groups of very agile men hastily and copiously sprayed the church, especially the doors and windows, with gasoline. They had barely finished before lighted pitch torches were thrown onto the gasoline. The church, crowded with Serbian worshippers, was engulfed in flames, and through the conflagration into the building rattled a barrage of machine gun bullets. Of course, there was a panic and the imprisoned people tried to flee. As they endeavored to plunge through burning windows and through the sheet of fire that filled the entrance, they were met with a hail of lead. Of those who, here and there, evaded both fire and machine guns, most were finished by cold steel.

Quickly, the church, built largely of wood, burned down. Before long the cries of agony subsided. Charred bodies lay in a reeking mass one upon the other. Corpses sprawled thick about the ruins as though death had fallen upon bathers lolling on a beach or as though human ten-pins had been knocked down by bowlers. The stench of roasted meat filled the air. Grimacing faces stared, fixed, toward the heavens; open eyes and mouths were pressed hard into the dust. An hour earlier all those had been people, loved by friends and relations. Among them were the remains of what had been Dimitrina's sisters and her mama and her papa. Now they were as refuse. There lay a butchered village, the massacred vanguard of a nation, a murdered priest with a cross molten on the ashes of his breast.

The Ustashas and some local Croatian peasants, after taking whatever jewelry and ornaments they could find on their massacred neighbors, dug a huge ditch, dragged into it the dead, as hogs that had just died of cholera, with hunks of men, women, and children, all indiscriminately interlocking, and threw earth over them.

The Ustashas built not a pyre; they dug a ditch, a Yama, and for years to come, for centuries, "Yama" will be among the most odious words in the Serbian tongue. Every Serb family will long talk of relatives buried in Yamas; the nation will pray for the souls of brothers, sisters, cousins shovelled warm and bleeding into Yamas; and one generation will transmit to another the terrible story of the Yamas, that lined every Serbian roadside in Croatia, marked half the Serbian villages in western Yugoslavia, and became objects of horror and of reverence in every home upon the globe where burned a Serbian candle beneath a Serbian eikon.

In that immense, freshly-dug village Yama in which the unnamed bodies of Dimitrina's neighbors intertwined with one another, lay almost everyone whom she had loved, while every object she cherished was being plundered. All Serbian houses in the village were unguarded, all stock was left unowned, all Serbian fields were unprotected. The creators of Independent Croatia divided this booty among themselves; murderers revelled in the wine and cheese and sweet preserves of the murdered. And Dimitrina, in the darkness of the night, sneaked toward the mountains with nothing except a loaf of bread that the Croatian friend had given her, with the sorrow of the ages clutching at her throat and every man's hand apparently against her.

It seemed to her that Serbia had fought its way through the centuries in vain. The state was gone, the army was dissipated, the government had fled, the churches were being burned, the priests were hunted as quail, the picture of the King in her humble home was at that moment being desecrated by ribald murderers, on whose hands was the blood of her papa and mama; and she was fleeing in the darkness, she knew not whither, seeking she knew not whom. In the darkness of every succeeding night, month after month, Serbian survivors fled through every valley and gorge of western Yugoslavia trying to find refuge from death and a basis for resistance.

Another Serbian survivor, with whom I have had many conversations during the past year, was very different from Dimitrina. He was a newspaper editor in Sarajevo, later the leader of a Serbian nationalist organization in Belgrade and one of the original supporters of Mihailovitch. When Hitler attacked Belgrade, this nationalistic "Across-the-river" Serb, Alexander, was in that city. He remained in Serbia during the collapse and capitulation of Yugoslavia and later made his way into the western provinces, arriving in Mostar, the chief city of Herzegovina, at the beginning of 1942.

That austere provincial capital, situated on the heights of a bare, gaunt, rock-filled district, had long been a noted center of religious and nationality strife. In it had met cross and crescent, Orthodox and Catholic, Hapsburg and sultan. Some of the most vital frontiers of the ages crossed and crisscrossed in its streets. A Roman spire, a Byzantine dome, an Arabic minaret faced each other above the modest houses. Bearded, high-hatted Orthodox clergymen; shaved, skull-capped Catholic clergymen; red-fezzed, scarf-swathed Moslem clergymen passed each other on the sidewalks, as they performed their ministrations. They personified rivalry as old as the Crusades, as new as each Sabbath or each Friday morn.

The rather bleak, rock-bound city of twenty-one thousand inhabitants contained, in almost equal numbers, Orthodox Serbs, Catholic Croats, and Moslems, the latter of which were popularly called "Turks"—though they were of the purest South Slav blood and spoke only the Serbo-Croatian tongue. When Alexander, after wandering through the confusion and disorder of most of Yugoslavia and after cautiously making his way past hostile German, Ustasha, Partisan, and Italian forces, entered the Serbian quarter of Mostar he found a dismal sight.

There was not an adult male Serb left in town. He was the only Serbian man that had been on the streets for months. Every Serbian store, workshop, lawyer's office, or place of business had been destroyed, closed, or taken over by a Croatian or a "Turk." Every Orthodox priest had vanished. All Orthodox churches were closed. The surviving Serbian women and children clung timidly to their houses, hardly daring to be seen on the streets.

When this newly-arrived Serbian nationalist called on the terror-stricken Serbian families, he seemed to them an apparition. They looked upon him as a spirit from another realm. They were startled to see a live Serbian man appear boldly at their doors. With trepidation they received him and told him stories that passed belief.

Every priest but one had vanished without a trace. For days, Croat Ustashas, aided by local Moslems, had conducted a war of extermination against the Serbs. They had seized Serbs in their homes, grabbed them in their stores, surrounded them in the streets, ambushed them in their fields. Many they had shot at sight; most they had collected in prisons, schools, and barracks to be led away in groups, machine-gunned en masse and buried in unmarked ditches, or Yamas.

Most of the women and small children were spared, and as they cowered in their humble houses through the days of terror and the nights of death, hearing the tramping of heavy feet, the crack of rifles, the rattling of machine guns, and the awful cries of death, they envisioned fathers, brothers, and sons, being stabbed, tortured, mutilated, killed, and then crammed still warm into ditches. In anguish they recalled last words, the last meals together, the last holidays; they revived happy recollections of weddings, betrothals, confirmations, school honors; they looked again into family albums, secretly lighted candles under hidden eikons, and softly sang the epic songs of Kossovo, about Turkish conquerors who temporarily destroyed Serbia but could not destroy the Serbs.

The visitor from Belgrade who was determined to do what he could to revive the Serbian spirit in Mostar and Herzegovina asked his terrorized countrymen if they knew of any Orthodox priest who had survived the holocaust. It was reported that an old man was hiding in a distant woods, and the bold Serbian nationalist went off to seek him. His search was successful, the priest was persuaded to return to Mostar, and word was passed among the Serbian women and children that there would be a service in the main Orthodox church.

When the day and hour came the priest was present in his impressive vestments, candles flared again, once more boys reverently carried the sacred banners, and the fragrance of incense filled the building. The visitor from Belgrade helped, as a layman, in singing mass, as accords with the liturgy. One lone and aged priest, one visitor from afar—those were the only representatives of Serbian manhood in the church.

It was the most moving service the worshippers had ever attended. It was as a resurrection, as an Easter morning, as the dawn after an apocalypse. God seemed to have come back. The widowed mothers placed their defenceless children in His hands. They considered the service a funeral for their massacred loved ones. In it also they rejoined the invisible heroes, saints, and martyrs of their race and found strength in them. When the priest in his tremulous voice read the gospel, he succumbed to emotion and cried without restraint. Having come out of a cave where he had been hunted as a beast, he was now in a church again, reading the Bible again, praying to God again, acting as a man again. His feelings of relief were more than he could master.

The widows thought of their husbands who had so often been with them in the church but were now tangled corpses in rain-soaked ditches, and they cried too. The mothers thought of their sons, the children thought of their fathers, and they all cried. The mass gave way to a collective dirge, the liturgy from books acceded to the liturgy from hearts. That service became a sad and holy lamentation of people who had nothing left but God and memories. Distant was the King, inaccessible the government, gone the army. Sinister seemed the call to prayer sounding from the minaret near by; menacing were the strokes of the bell which had called Ustasha murderers to worship in the Catholic church across the street. Cruel and hard and hateful seemed the stony mountain wastes, stretching endlessly away. Bereft Serbian mothers appealed to God alone and felt some comfort.

That evening as the visitor from Belgrade, who was trying to revive Serbianism in Mostar, entered the yard of a humble Serbian house in which he had a room, two Moslems hit him over the head with an ax and a club and left him for dead. But he didn't die and later I often saw him. Scores of thousands of others whom the "Turks" of Bosnia and Herzegovina left for dead will never be seen again and no one will know in which ditch their bones lie buried.

The Nazi massacre in Serbia's third largest city, Kraguevats, has often been reported. It took place on October 22, 1941. Thousands of Serbians were executed, among them nearly two hundred high school youths. Many Serbs have told me of it. I remember especially the case of Constantine, whose brother reported how he died. Constantine was in the next to the last gymnasium class, which corresponds perhaps to the freshman class in an American college. He was eighteen years old and the son of a Serbian peasant. He was hoping to be a doctor. In the summer he helped in the paternal fields and gardens, tending pigs, hoeing corn, scything hay, and pruning vineyards or gathering grapes. He worked beside his mother and his sisters. Though dearly attached to his family, which made great sacrifices and endured onerous privations to put him through school, he was quite critical of patriarchal ways. He criticized the King, excoriated the governments, felt resentful of slick city people, who he felt exploited the villagers. He tried to organize his fellow students in an aggressive, radical, peasant movement, inspired by a former University professor named Dragoleub Jovanovitch.

Constantine lived in a very modest room in Kraguevats, which he shared with another young peasant. Much of his food he got from home, in the form of cheese, black bread, stewed beans, salt pork. His frugal, Spartanic life caused no comment among his fellows because many others lived in the same way. That was the way poor boys got ahead, the way they could dream of becoming doctors and serving their nation and making Serbian villages modern. Since he was a student, his military service was postponed and he had not served in the army.

The Germans occupied his vital little city in which a state arsenal was situated and he often saw hateful Nazi soldiers patrolling the streets. Some of the students, town people, and workers had insulted the occupiers and on more than one occasion had been arrested. The atmosphere was electric. The Germans posted big posters on the streets threatening dire punishments and stating that one hundred Serbians would be executed in revenge for every German that was killed. Also, men were arrested as hostages. Yet in spite of all this ten German soldiers were suddenly killed in ambush and twenty-six wounded. There were not enough hostages on hand to pay the penalty; so German military authorities decided to choose indiscriminately new victims for shooting. Among others they selected the students in the highest gymnasium or high-school class.

A company of German soldiers appeared at the school and ordered all the students into the assembly room. A German officer standing amid bare bayonets and tommy guns ready for action then told the assembly the soldiers were going to execute all the senior boys. Surprisingly there was no appeal for mercy, no disavowal of guilt for killing the German soldiers, and no visible manifestation of fright. Instead of that, a senior arose and defiantly said they would be glad to die for Serbia, after which the whole room applauded.

Thereupon Constantine, under the inspiration of the terrible drama, arose and said, "Kill us all if you wish, but German despots can never conquer us free Serbs." "That's right" burst from almost every voice in the room and instantly the whole school was singing patriotic Serbian songs. The enraged Germans marched nearly two hundred of those boys to the place of execution and shot them, as the boys shouted, "Long live Serbia, long live King Peter." Constantine was among them. Blood gushed from his mouth; his arms and legs twisted in grotesque contortions; his glassy eyes pressed stark upon the stones.

Before that day ended, at least four thousand dead Serbians lay sprawled or heaped in Kraguevats. The mayor said 60 per cent of the men had perished. The surviving citizens tearfully dug their graves and sorrowfully threw cold earth upon them, who had paid far more than a hundredfold for every German life.

Thus from the fateful April day when the German army attacked Yugoslavia, Serbs were daily tortured, shot, hanged, and cut in pieces by strangers and by neighbors, by Latins, Slavs, and Teutons. Unknown individual graves filled the land, while shallowly covered, mass graves emitted stench beside a hundred highways. Dogs ate half-buried corpses, whole villages were levelled to the ground, broad areas remained uninhabited, the shells of gutted churches lifted piteous walls toward heaven, hundreds of thousands of "Across-the-river" Serbian refugees poured from north and west and south into prostrate Serbia. One Serb out of every ten or twelve was reported dead. And through most of 1942 the Germans continued to triumph everywhere.

CHAPTER ELEVEN

Mihailovitch's Anti-German Tactics

BY THE beginning of 1942 the supreme problem of Mihailovitch and of every other responsible Serb was how to aid the Allied nations in the global fight against Germany, without wiping out their own nation. This meant very frankly that the Serbs could not continue to kill Germans at the cost of one hundred dead Serbs for every dead German.

Rarely do Americans or Britishers in considering Serbia's case put themselves in the place of the Serbs. It is accepted, as an axiom, that every American mother wants to save her own baby, her home, and her nation if possible. But some Americans allow themselves to imagine that Serbian mothers felt differently about their babies, and should have acted differently.

There are very few normal Americans who would say that Americans in fighting Hitler should make one hundred times greater sacrifices proportionally than England or Canada. No conscientious American father or mother would urge our government to sacrifice civilian lives blindly and unrestrainedly, without regard for the results attained. Yet, some Americans have let themselves think the Serbs should have done that. Some Americans have vituperated Mihailovitch for not causing the death of Serbian babies uselessly. It seems to me immoral for an American father to sit safely in an utterly secure home, with his baby cooing in his arms, and call Mihailovitch a traitor because Mihailovitch dared refuse to have Serbian families wiped out by the thousands, without bringing any appreciable aid to the Allied cause.

American newspapers abound in stories of American soldier or sailor fathers who were rushed across oceans in airplanes to get a last look at their babies who had been doomed by some sickness. Our nation glories in such acts of kindness on the part of our army, navy, and government. Our army even sent an officer home from Germany to see his wife who was held in prison for shooting a man, after far from exemplary conduct on her own part. Americans give their blood without stint to help some ailing child. We lavish presents on a nine-year-old Italian boy, coming to our land as a stowaway, and pass a special law to facilitate his living happily as an American. Kindness to "kids" is a beautiful American trait. Yet many Americans have excoriated the Serbs for presuming to think of their children.

Every American, regardless of his political affiliation, honors and applauds the American government for refusing needlessly to risk the lives of American soldiers. We consider the sparing of American lives one of the most basic elements in our method of waging war. Before we send our sons and brothers into battle, we give them the best guns, ships, airplanes, tanks, and munitions that American genius can create. If necessary, we blast an enemy position for days and weeks before sending our boys against it. We "soften" the enemy with fire and explosives for months before an invasion. We even use atomic bombs.

Because of this regard for American life, we refused to open "the second front" a single day before we were ready. Russia was constantly crying for a second front, and with reason, because she was hard pressed. The war was going badly. The whole global situation was critical. Germany was steadily winning successes. Yet we refused to risk the lives of our soldiers in a second front until we had implements and explosives to protect them.

And when we did launch an overseas front, we first attacked not where the opposition was stiffest, but where it was weakest. We struck at the "soft" underbelly—or at least we thought the place of attack was soft. We adopted that strategy partly in order to save American lives. And after landing in Africa, for what we hoped would be an easy victory, we waited almost twenty full months before we opened a front in western Europe. We waited for the completion of stupendous and magnificent preparations. We kept some American soldiers waiting in England more than a year, while we got ready. And the whole nation praises General MacArthur for sparing the lives of his soldiers in the Far East.

History through all future generations will applaud America for this method of sparing the lives of its sons even in the most critical days of the most awful war. And tactics which American leaders considered vital for their numerous and powerful nation, Serbian leaders considered vital for their small, weak, and terribly exposed nation. If responsible Americans deemed it necessary to save our man power, was it not equally essential for responsible Serbians to preserve the man power and woman power and baby power of a little nation which even before America began to fight had lost many more in killed than America eventually was to lose during the whole war against the Axis?

Would it not have been basely immoral for mighty America to urge a weak ally to throw away its mothers and children—for nothing—after that ally had already lost more in killed than the British Empire? During the Communist and Chetnik campaign against Germans in the summer and fall of 1941, there were more people killed in Serbia alone than the fatal casualties in all American armies during the first year of the war.

And how does the situation of Serbia look from the vantage point of Great Britain? Every informed American recalls that during the most awful days of the "blitz" against London and other British cities, the Britishers sent women and children to the U.S.A. for protection. We Americans welcomed those British seeking safety, and honored Mr. Churchill and his government for trying to preserve them. But is there any conceivable logic which makes it honorable for a Britisher to send his wife across the ocean to safety yet treasonable for a Serb to refuse to have his wife and baby blown to smithereens —for nothing? What is the moral and spiritual law that makes a British baby worth so much more than a Serb baby?

I have an intimate English friend who, after sending his own two daughters away to fairly secure places, appealed to the Serbs almost daily over the radio to take action that would cause the loss of scores of thousands of Serbian girls—for nothing. And because Mihailovitch refused to sacrifice Serbian girls, at the command of the fathers of fairly safe English girls, this Englishman vituperated Mihailovitch as a traitor. At a moment when the Serbians had far more men, women, and children killed than the British Empire, some British were almost hourly calling the Serbians traitors.

As Mihailovitch and his companions, toward the end of 1941 and the beginning of 1942, worked out their policy of resistance to the invaders, they daily received the most terrifying news from every part of the country about the execution of Serbs. The enemy was executing Serbians in their homes and shops, digging out their eyes, cutting off their ears, hacking off their limbs. The enemy was throwing Serbians into furnaces, skinning them alive, hurling them into rivers. Those stories came from eyewitnesses and were not doubted. Foes from a dozen sources seemed to be chopping, burning, stabbing, shooting, and freezing the Serbian nation to extinction.

In view of that, Mihailovitch adopted a policy of restrained or indirect or partial resistance. In the first place, he usually avoided frontal, open attacks. Practically no guerrilla force in an occupied land, during this war, has been able to take and hold a city, or communication center, or port, that was vital to the enemy during his period of maximum strength. Such attempts of guerrillas have not only been largely futile, but have resulted in terrible loss of civilian life. Mihailovitch decided to refrain from raids against German posts in Serbian civilian centers. He considered that would result in useless baby killing.

In contrast with this, he tried to organize the nation in every sort of non-lethal resistance, such as withholding supplies, hiding farm products, refusing to work in enterprises helping Germans, delaying transportation, opposing forced labor, stealing enemy supplies and money, sabotaging the state regime that was in the service of the Nazis. He set up or confirmed patriotic governing bodies in Serbian communities. He executed Serbians who opposed such patriotic action. He established an underground network of communications throughout the kingdom.

He did everything possible to strengthen the Serbian spirit. He worked with the schoolteachers and especially with the priests. He worked with mayors, post-office officials, telephone and telegraph operators, railroad men, bus drivers, policemen. To a large extent, he was an invisible master of the state administration, of communal governments, of the churches and schools, of city markets, and of food distribution.

I am not pretending that he managed all that efficiently, for even in normal times Serbian governments showed many defects, and Mihailovitch was no genius. Also, he didn't control any of the larger Serbian cities, and that greatly hampered his work. In addition, his headquarters were inconveniently located in rather isolated mountains. Outside of Serbia, in the new provinces, his organization was still less effective. But the vast majority of all the Serbs of Serbia definitely and consciously cooperated with Mihailovitch. They shared his patriotism, cherished his aims, and approved his tactics. Most Serbs of Serbia were as much united behind him as the Americans were behind President Roosevelt and renewed their faith through him.

The reader may condemn the Serbs of Serbia for that, if he wishes. The Serbian nation was as good and as bad as Mihailovitch.

They hated the Germans, they loved the Americans, they were inspired by Russian heroism. In spite of our terrible bombing of their cities they were *all* extremely kind to American aviators who fell in Yugoslavia. If an American in an American uniform appeared anywhere in Serbia—outside of the bigger cities—he was protected and cared for, though not knowing a word of Serbian. A peasant would go into town and call a doctor for him. A state police, ostensibly in the service of the German-dominated Serbian government, would help hide him. A telegraph agent would immediately notify underground guards to take him to a safe place. The mayor, town clerk, teacher, priest, sheriff, and telephone operator could all know about the American and not one would tell a German or Bulgarian garrison. The chief saloon keeper could throw a party for the American, inviting many guests, and no Serb for any reward would report to the occupier. Practically all Serbians instinctively and without special instructions worked for the Allies and against Germany.

But, one may object, they didn't accomplish very much. I personally believe that is true. They were "cunctators." They had delivered a very grave blow to Germany, they had suffered and were suffering cruelly for it, and now they were following a policy of helping the Allies without provoking massacres.

And most decidedly the people in Serbia were not engaged in a revolution. They wanted to preserve, not overturn. They were giving all their energy and making every sacrifice, short of being massacred, to save their Serbia. City dweller and villager, the man with store pants and the man with peasant breeches, the teacher and the blacksmith, the old mayor, the old priest and the young workers, the tax-gatherer and the disgruntled pig-raiser had King Peter's picture in their houses. They looked upon themselves as continuing Serbia's role. They rejoiced in Serbian history, with all its faults. They dreamed of the time when traditional Serbia would be given an honorable place among the democratic nations in the hour of triumph over Hitler. They did not imagine themselves creating a completely new world, but defending and improving the old. This ideal of *preservation* influenced Mihailovitch's tactics.

And Mihailovitch, in addition to organizing this general resistance of the whole civilian population, which stopped short of provoking massacres, also maintained an army which he called and considered the regular Yugoslav Army. In fact, in December, 1941, he was promoted to the rank of General and made War Minister by the exiled Yugoslav government. He used his underground army to intimidate, harass, and embarrass enemy forces, to protect Serbs, and to hinder movements of German armies into and out of Greece or toward North Africa.

The activity of this army has been a subject of furious disputes. Some Communists and Communist supporters have denied that it ever fought Germans. But Tito in his own early secret communications to his associates reported "joint activity" with Mihailovitch against Germans. Milan Neditch, the head of the Serbian "Pétain-like" government serving the Nazi invaders, constantly appealed to Mihailovitch to cease action. Nothing could be more revealing than these appeals. Neditch knew what he was talking about, for he was at the head of the state apparatus and knew that Germans and especially German agents were being killed. In addition, the German commander in Serbia publicly offered a very large reward for the capture or assassination of Mihailovitch. The reason must have been that the Serbians under Mihailovitch were fighting Germans. During the last half of 1941, Mihailovitch's armed forces carried on vigorous activity against Germans.

And after 1941, the Chetniks continued to fight, outside of Serbia. Many of these attacks took place in Bosnia, and were directed against Croatian Ustashas and Germans—both Axis forces. Even the most casual reading of Pavelitch's newspapers during 1942 and 1943 shows the Ustashas' fear of Mihailovitch. In fact, Pavelitch kept repeating in his press and over the radio that Tito's Partisans were merely carrying on Mihailovitch's anti-Ustasha war. The Chetniks were exalted by Pavelitch as his most terrible enemies.

Also, late in 1943 the Germans undertook a long and bitter campaign against the Chetniks, which shows that the German General Staff, even at a moment when it desperately needed soldiers elsewhere, considered Mihailovitch enough of a menace to require the sending of new forces against him. The German military leaders believed that in case of an Allied Balkan offensive, Mihailovitch would give the liberating armies formidable support. The Germans knew that Mihailovitch and the Serbs were bitter enemies of the Reich.

One of Tito's main associates, and one of the foremost Serbian Partisans, the fiery Serbian priest, Vlada Zechevitch, has emphatically, even vehemently, assured me that Mihailovitch never opposed the Germans. He said he would be willing to have in his body all the bullets Mihailovitch ever shot at Germans. But a large amount of evidence from enemy sources shows that Zechevitch was wrong. Mihailovitch and his followers killed many Germans.

But it is equally true that they later adopted the policy of refraining from killing many Germans, unless attacked. Mihailovitch's armed Chetniks, of which there were scores of thousands, did not engage in many pitched battles with the German occupiers of Serbia after 1942. But they did damage military railroads there and elsewhere. However, I should be careful not to overestimate even this activity. I have personally learned, from participants, of important cases of transportation demolition carried out by Mihailovitch's forces. Allied military leaders attest that the Serbs appreciably helped retard the activity of the Wehrmacht at an extremely vital moment in the war. According to official British and American military reports, from the very highest sources, they made significant contributions to Allied successes in North Africa. Nevertheless, Mihailovitch's bridge-destroying activity was restricted.

There were two main reasons. First, Great Britain was exceedingly inept in supplying Mihailovitch with suitable explosive material. It sent liaison officers to train and direct sabotage groups and naturally these officers were equipped with instruments for communicating with the British base. Thus the British in Africa talked with Britishers in Mihailovitch's camps. Arrangements were made for dropping specific material at specific places for specific tasks. But the plans were execrably executed by the British. The material came with long delays and after the Serbs had gone night after night, in snow and rain, to distant mountain tops to receive it. When dropped, it often landed miles—even scores of miles—from the designated places, and when found it frequently proved unsuitable or with vital parts missing.

In other words, the British kept pressing the Serbs to blow up bridges and promised them aid, yet as a rule didn't deliver the promised materials in an adequate way. Relations grew strained. Mihailovitch resented the arrogance of the chief liaison officer, Colonel S. W. Bailey. The Serbians have long been a sovereign nation and are pretty arrogant themselves. They have an excellent record as fighters. They don't like to be shoved around or scolded or given lessons in heroism and they are outraged at being treated as colonists or inferiors. They have even handled kings and emperors pretty roughly. Yet, Bailey kept lecturing Mihailovitch, ordering him around, accusing him of bad faith, cowardice, false reporting, and inefficiency. The Serbian Mihailovitch felt he was being treated as an African retainer.

The two men had altercations and exchanged offensive epithets. The British accused Serbia of lying down on the job; the Serbs accused Great Britain of wanting to use Serbians as cannon fodder. More and more, Britain appeared to the Serbs as a heartless exploiter, ruthlessly consuming small nations for imperial interests. Mihailovitch saw that Britain, in a flash, would turn to some other Serbian leader, if it could find one who would blow up a bridge, even at the cost of five hundred Serb civilians.

Mihailovitch had come to feel that a bridge wasn't worth that price. It was usually restored in twenty-four or forty-eight hours. Even the highest, longest bridge could be repaired within a week and trains would be going again. But, in revenge, the Germans would execute scores of hostages, burn every village in the vicinity and destroy every habitation within ten miles of the track on both sides. Thus, for a relatively unimportant act of demolition, causing the enemy little inconvenience, the Serbians would sacrifice hundreds of human lives that could never be restored. They paid for bridges with babies. London papers would boast of demolition in Serbia and Serbian babies would be killed. The fathers and brothers of those victims were not enthusiastic.

And finally, the Serbs of Serbia wanted to save their army and their arms for fighting the Communists. A civil war was on, which *Tito and his revolutionary Communists had started.* The Partisans had hoisted the red flag. Their forces were led by men who had long been trained in Russia, had served the red international for years, were adherents of the Comintern, and had consecrated themselves to a global upheaval. Their political movement was well known throughout Serbia. They had once had nearly sixty deputies in the Belgrade Parliament. They had recruited Serbians for the fight in Spain. Yugoslav Communists had long fought for a world cause and now those very same Communists were fighting in Serbia for a world ideal and for political power, not primarily for the Serbian people. They considered Serbs mere instruments. Mihailovitch and most Serbs were opposed to such masters and were determined to resist them at all costs. Tito's civil war had disrupted Yugoslav unity and destroyed the common front against Hitler.

The acts of every nation in a great world conflict are open to the appraisal of each generation and each land. Mihailovitch and his nation, acting in general accord, stand before the court of world opinion. The courage and passion and loyalty with which the Serbs had first fought Naziism were unequalled among the United Nations. The sacrifices the Serbs made were unsurpassed. Their persistent attitude continued to be unconditionally anti-German and pro-Ally. But after 1941 the method of opposition was less aggressive resistance, more consideration for the physical preservation of the nation, and preparation for participation in a grand, general, final offensive.

I believe those were British and American tactics, too. I think it is regrettable for an American to call a Serb a traitor for not wanting to have his house uselessly destroyed and his family massacred in vain and that it is immoral for an American to consider a Serbian life less precious than an American. I do not believe an honorable American, whose nation of one hundred and forty million had lost in killed only two hundred and seventy-five thousand by V-J Day can reproach a nation of eight million which for the same cause had lost up to a million and was still resisting.

But that is just my opinion—the facts are there; let each American judge for himself!

CHAPTER TWELVE

Tito's Anti-German Tactics

AFTER the crushing defeats of Tito and his troops in Serbia and Montenegro, during the summer and autumn of 1941, the Communist chief changed his methods and tactics. In both of those offensives, the Communists had carried red flags and sought to establish Soviet regimes, but they saw that was a mistake.

In spite of all their heroism, the Communists had failed in their first campaigns. They had lost all the towns which they had taken and been driven from all the places over which their flags had flown. Even more important, the common people had not flocked to their red banners. The Serbs of Serbia had showed that they didn't want Communism. A majority of the Montenegrins also had remained aloof. The Communists had suffered not only military but also political defeat and in addition had lost many of their most fanatical fighters. Consequently, they saw they must broaden their front, raise the Yugoslav flag over the red flag, and extol democracy rather than Marxism. From the end of 1941, Tito preached about a liberated democratic, bourgeois Yugoslavia rather than about a Communist paradise, and his banner was the regular Yugoslav red-white-and-blue, altered only by the addition of a red star.

At the same time, Tito kept up the tempo of his fighting. That was the foremost element in his activity. At first the Partisans, as Tito called his colleagues, fought by day and night, by summer and winter, in rain and drought, in snows and consuming heat. Fighting was a main plank in their platform, a principal source of Partisan lure. They presented themselves as heroes, champions, defenders, waging the people's battles. They claimed to fight Fascists, Pavelitch's Quislings, Neditch's Quislings, Chetniks, reaction, poverty, ignorance, discrimination. They opened a front against all the evils of the world and for that front gave their blood. They erected a global barricade. They divided humanity into the good and bad, the evil and just, and staked their lives on that division. Naturally everybody with them was "good," everybody against them "bad." The division was easy to grasp, the tommy guns and bombs with which it was proclaimed were eloquent. Gradually Tito won new followers.

Who were they? Were they Serbs? Yes, at the beginning most were Serbs and to the end Serbs formed a fairly large proportion of Tito's following. But most were not Serbs from Serbia; they were Montenegrins and "Across-the-river" Serbs, from Bosnia, Herzegovina, Croatia, Slavonia, Srem. Eventually, there were many Croats also and not a few Slovenes. There were a few Bulgarians, Albanians, Germans, Hungarians.

Tito's followers may be divided into the following categories: First were the convinced, fanatical Communists. They provided the political and military leadership. They were as hard, bold, and compelling a group of rebels as were to be found in any land. They could talk and write and fight. They had long worked in and on their organizations. They had placed members in every branch of the Yugoslav state administration and army, and at the collapse of Yugoslavia, which they had accelerated, they collected supplies of arms, in the use of which they were experienced, since they had had a "general rehearsal" in Spain. They were equally practiced in gaining and in organizing recruits. They were versed in courier activity, spying, and subversion. These old-line, fanatical Communists constituted an excellent revolutionary framework or system of conspiratorial "cadres" and were called "activists."

There was another category of Partisans who were not actual Communists but had grown tired of Yugoslav political parties and considered all the old organizations corrupt and inefficient. Yugoslavia had been a new and terribly confused state. From the beginning it had faced enormous difficulties. It was a collection of mutually hostile groups and elements, every one of which had a grouch. Yet, in spite of that, it had made progress. Naturally, however, it had also made mistakes. And in consequence, the old parties had come to seem pretty drab and weak to most Yugoslav citizens. The very word "old" was distasteful to many. Russia, too, exerted a powerful lure and the Russian system, being untried and untarnished in Yugoslavia, seemed worth consideration. Also the fanatical men and women who advocated that new order—the Communists—were unusually forceful and brave. So the Communist-led Partisan movement made a strong appeal to Yugoslavs who cared nothing for Marx but wanted a better deal.

It must be added, too, that its slogans were very attractive. They promised "applied Christianity," plus every good thing everyone wanted. The Partisans offered something good for the poor, good for the rich, good for the simple, good for the ambitious; good for Croats, Slovenes, and Serbs; good for infidels and believers, for Christians and Moslems. Restless, superficial, sincere people, tired of old defects, longing for reforms, enamored of Slav Russians, were attracted by Partisan promises.

Then comes another great and terrible group, which, together with the old-line Communists, dominate Yugoslavia. They are the new proletariat, the homeless, landless, and penniless that were forced into the woods by the ruthless invaders. They were the survivors of the massacres. In this category fell most of Tito's "Across-the-river" Serbian Partisans. This is a comparatively new kind of people in Europe—that is, for the twentieth century. I have described in preceding chapters, how Ustashas, Italians, Moslems, and Nazis murdered the Serbs of western Yugoslavia and destroyed their villages. Some Serbs escaped from these ferocious attacks and fled to the woods. Now, what would you have done if you had been one of them? In the first place, you'd have tried to find a place where you could sleep and get something to eat. After that you would have sought companions, and then you would have endeavored to take vengeance on your persecutors. You would have sought action, and in your bitter sorrow you would have relished words of encouragement that restored your self-respect. Well, Tito gave those things.

Try to picture those sad, wretched, hungry people, fleeing in terror to the woods. They were mostly young or in early middle age. Many babies and children had already died of exposure. The aged had perished from shock and exhaustion. Only the fleetest and cleverest and strongest had won the race with death. And all they had was their bare, empty hands. They were as outlaws among outlaws, with a triumphant world of killers against them. Their past had been blotted out in a red tempest of fire and blood; their future depended on meeting violence with violence. Their first need was bare subsistence. They had no homes, no children, no fathers or mothers. They had no property, no school diplomas, no birth certificates, no jobs. As they wandered from region to region, they saw only ruined houses, destroyed churches, schools in flames, gutted shops. They had nothing to go back to, no surviving social group to count on. They had to start anew, amid horror and flames. They had become true soldiers of fortune. And they immediately had to begin carving out their fortune—or die. Did a revolutionary leader ever find better material? And Tito was not unprepared for it.

He had expected it. He had based his life plans on its advent. Communist revolution is an art, science, and profession. Just as much as war. It has an international general staff. Able men and women have long studied the best ways and means and methods for conducting it. No one knew all that science better than Tito and his comrades. It was their poetry, their religion, their philosophy, their trade. It gave meaning to their lives, made their sacrifices light. Communists count on upheavals and are prepared to use them. Communists know just what to do with uprooted, hard-muscled, bitter-hearted refugees gathering in the mountains.

It was for them Tito had prepared his network. He had cells in every county, receiving stations in every province, and actual recruiting agents in every forest recess. When the distracted, terror-filled refugees arrived, they were welcomed. It was as though deacons were standing at the church doors, ushering newcomers into the fold. The desperate wanderer in the Yugoslav woods felt the warmth of a campfire and the strength of comradeship. He was given some black bread, perhaps cheese, occasionally even a piece of roast sheep or goat. And he was invited to join a group.

He also found a network of defense—or attack. He learned of friendly villages, secret paths, caves containing supplies. He was told of political leaders and military chiefs, of companies and brigades and regiments. And behind it all, he was informed, was Russia. Russia, he was assured, was approaching the borders of Yugoslavia, bringing freedom.

In view of all that, hundreds and thousands of these refugees joined Tito's Partisans. Naturally, one asks: Why didn't they join Mihailovitch? Since most of these poor refugees were Serbs, and patriotic Serbs at that, why did they join a Communist-led organization, headed by a Croat? Wasn't that strange, since it was Croats who were massacring the Serbs? The answer is that although some did join Mihailovitch and the Chetnik forces, most found Tito's Communists better prepared, more elastic, more effectively organized, more revolutionary, and with a better lure for cold, hungry men in a mountain. The Communists were on the spot, with more alert ushers and better gospel songs. Also, the people in these "Across-the-river" areas, including many of the staunchest Serbs, had been ill-disposed toward Belgrade for years. The two strongest "Across-the-river" Serbian parties had joined with the Croatian

Peasant Party in opposing the Belgrade regimes. That rather deeply-fixed, oppositional set of mind made many "Across-the-river" Serbs amenable to Tito's promises and he drew them into his ranks.

Having gotten them there, he subjected them to incessant and masterful propaganda, simple as a handclasp, tangible as a lamb roast, sharp as lightning, and powerful as a camp meeting. This propaganda was living, burning Leninism in its most effective form, with adaptations to local needs and current semantics.

In its essence it was: We're Anti-Fascists. Everyone who is not with us is a Fascist. We're going to lick the Fascists, and then we'll live happily ever after. "Death to Fascism, freedom to the people!" was their wonderful slogan. It was short, thunderous, heart-lifting, and truth-obscuring, as are all the mighty slogans of all murderous crusaders. Joshua declared he was "serving Jehovah," as he plunged into Palestine to kill all the inhabitants, even the cattle. "In the sign of the cross," shouted Constantine, as he led his hordes to battle. "One God, one Prophet," cried the Moslems, as they overturned empires and swept toward the heart of Europe. "One Reich, one people, one leader," shrieked the Nazis as they massacred their fellows. "Death to Fascism" aroused sad, embittered Yugoslavs as Peter the Hermit had aroused Christians centuries earlier with cries of "Death to infidels." In each case the cry incited the same fighting emotions.

To understand the effectiveness of Tito's appeal, which came straight from Russia, it may be well to recall the doctrine with which Lenin turned Russia upside down. It has been summarized, as follows, by John Hargrove in *Words Win Wars:*

"The world revolution is at hand.—
"Comrade Workers, take the factories.—
"Comrade Peasants, take the land.—
"Destroy your enemies."
To these Tito added: "Win freedom!
"Set up a people's government."

I am not intimating that his appeal was Marxism. I am saying merely that it was total revolution. It was unlimited violence against every opponent. It was an attempt to explode every restraining force, every established institution that might be a stumbling block. It was:

Away with the Yugoslav Army.
Away with the administration.
Away with the old cops and courts.
Away with the existing agricultural setup.
Away with the industrial setup.
Away with the King.
Away with the old parties.
Away with everything you don't like.
Up with a new People's Order.

This meant complete destruction of the old and supplanting it with something new and good.

Many conscientious Americans tried to persuade themselves that the Yugoslav Communists were not like the classic Russian Communist revolutionists of thirty years ago. That view is wrong. They are exactly like the Russian revolutionary Communists in their passions, their fanaticisms, their utter narrowness, their complete rejection of the old regime as evil, their authoritarianism, their totalitarianism, their use of violence, their courage, and their determination to establish their own regime. For Americans to believe otherwise means self-deception.

Tito will maintain his regime at any cost, just as Lenin did. He will call it a people's regime of pure democracy and will dub every opponent a "treacherous Fascist," as Lenin called his opponents "the bloody bourgeoisie."

To attain his aims Tito wanted to create a large Yugoslav Partisan proletariat. He wished the number of desperate refugees in the hills to increase. He was not averse to having towns burn and homes crash down, because that strengthened his Partisan army. It brought him recruits. The more carnage and the greater the destruction in Yugoslavia, the better it was for Tito's cause.

From these facts, we see why Tito and his Partisans for a time fought Germans, Italians, and Ustashas at almost any cost. His main aim was not to serve or save Yugoslavs, but to establish a regime. He was not interested in individual lives.

What was the death of individual Russians to Lenin or of individual Yugoslavs to Tito? What was the loss of whole Russian provinces or of whole Yugoslav villages? What was famine and forced labor? What if homeless children roamed the land in droves? That was all a part of the process. That was the cost of the new order. The true warrior for a new age or new millennium or new Reich doesn't shrink from the death of his fellows. That is cowardice and infidelity. To weaken the grand movement for the sake of saving a village is as unworthy as for a true believer to defile his faith by saving a heretic. Tito and his comrades were helping establish a blessed new City of Man, and if people got killed in the undertaking, that only made it seem more precious. One can't take Jerusalem without carnage!

The very carnage in Yugoslavia increased Tito's power. He has often written that after every German offensive against him and his Partisans, the number of his followers increased. That is completely true. When a village was destroyed, new refugees fled to the mountains and joined him. When a town was devastated new recruits gathered around him. What else could they do? When a valley was ravaged by Nazi soldiers and bereft of homes, provisions, shelter, the able-bodied survivors fled to Tito's camps.

The surviving civilian population, that was too old or too young or too weak to fight, was kept in the woods or sent to Italy and Egypt, but it was always subjected to constant indoctrination. And those who rejected indoctrination were eliminated.

And not only did Tito win recruits in this blood and fire, but the foundations of the old order were consumed. All the old pillars of society were knocked down, the old institutions swept away, the old standards submerged. There was no longer rich and poor, saints and sinners, proper and improper, moral and immoral, legal and illegal. Everyone now started from scratch, authority was created anew. All was improvised. The last could become first. The strong, ruthless, clever man with self-reliance and a quick trigger finger became master, lawmaker, and judge.

Thus a new society was created in the wreckage, and a new hierarchy established amid the debris. A new vested interest was set up, a new test for success exalted, and a new social aim formed. The future of the new men in power depended on the permanency of the revolution. They had invested everything in Partisanry and its failure would completely ruin them. Inevitably they abhorred the past, the old values and the old relations. The more old things went up in flames, the securer was the new order in which the new leaders or the new proletariat would be the chief beneficiaries.

So the Partisans made raids, attacked enemy garrisons and momentarily seized towns or villages. The Nazis and Ustashas soon sent reinforcements, put the raiding Partisans to flight, the settlements to flames, and many inhabitants to the sword. Shrieks filled the air, corpses strewed the ground, the old and very young perished, a few of the stalwart survived and began life anew as a hungry, destitute, rabid proletariat. They were as dependent on Tito and his comrades as an army of mercenaries. These are the new Janissaries of the Balkans, whose place in life is as closely connected with the new state as was the prosperity of the medieval Janissaries with their Moslem sultans.

Thus Tito, like most modern revolutionists, based his regime on death and ashes. The war was the grand occasion for which he had waited and prepared. The collapse of Yugoslavia was the first condition of his success. A glorious subsidiary cause, such as fighting invading Germans, was essential as a motive and an appeal. Physically freeing the people from foreign oppression offered the chance which he had long wanted. The perfect revolutionary situation had arrived. The grand Allies gave assistance. The freedom-loving world applauded. The fight of the Yugoslav Communists seemed part of a global struggle for liberty. The fighting against Germans won adoration from without and strengthened Tito's revolution from within. So Tito and his comrades fought with vehemence, persistence, and bravery.

However, they did not always or even usually fight Germans. They, by no means, expended their main energy in fighting Germans. Nor was their chief aim to fight Germans. Their aim was to establish a new regime in Yugoslavia, to destroy all Yugoslav resistance to such a regime, and to wipe out the basis for future opposition. Within the folds of the grand anti-Nazi banner which the world saw, was hidden the Communists' more precious banner of political revolution. To initiated Partisan chiefs the splendid slogan "Death to Fascism" simply meant the setting up of a coercive, totalitarian regime.

It is true that Tito fought long and hard. He and his comrades were brave. But they fought chiefly for power in a new Balkan setup that was to be part of a new world setup. When Yugoslav villages crashed down in fire, they lighted a new revolutionary dawn for Tito. When Yugoslav men and women were massacred because of Partisan raids, that was part of Tito's revolutionary Armageddon. When shrieks of Yugoslav mothers and children filled the dark and bloody nights, that was as the thunderous chorus of the morning stars of revolution, and when valleys and plains were laid waste, that was the destruction of the old in preparation for the new—for the World Soviet and Communist domination.

CHAPTER THIRTEEN

Tito Organizes a Revolutionary Government

THE main motive of Tito and his Communist comrades in fighting the Germans was their hope that through such fighting they would obtain control of the Yugoslav state. Their chief aim was political power. And Tito did not delay taking steps toward forming a country-wide political organization that would develop into a reorganization of the state. In fact, he and the other leading Communists began taking such steps long before the war broke out. As we retrace their activity we see that they moved toward their goal with great steadfastness and skill.

A true Communist resembles a fireman. His whole training is in preparation for a fire. Nothing else is of vital importance to him. To fulfill his function he must yearn for that which other people abhor. Only a conflagration brings him medals and promotion. But, unlike a fireman, a Communist does not strive primarily to put out the fire. He tries to use the fire as a means of getting into the burning house and taking possession of it. The art of pulling off a successful revolution is the art of getting into a burning house, while everyone is in a panic, and of staying in. Naturally, if the proprietor is burned up, so much the better.

Tito and his fellow revolutionists first tried to take advantage of Yugoslavia's conflagration by setting up soviets in western Serbia in the summer of 1941. But that proved premature; so after another year's activity, Tito set up an embryonic Yugoslav government in the west-central city of Bihach. It took the form of a National Council called "AVNOJ" (the Anti-Fascist Council of National Liberation of Yugoslavia), and along with it was formed an Army of Liberation and a Central Committee or Presidium. These rested on what was designed to be a broad geographical and nationality basis and adopted a moderate political program. Furthermore, the composition of the National Council was decidedly eclectic and included representatives of various groups.

This Bihach meeting in November, 1942, was one of the major events in the history of Tito's Liberation Movement. It was decidedly dramatic and thrilled the world when news of it was finally disseminated. At that time, Hitler was almost at the peak of his power.

He was master of Bulgaria, Greece, Albania, and Yugoslavia. America had by no means developed a maximum of strength. Japan held all of its vast acquisitions and a European Second Front was still a dream. But even at such a dark moment, a fairly large number of Yugoslav men and women, in defiance of the occupiers, gathered from various parts of the country and held a meeting of several sessions in a good-sized town. What their work amounted to was the setting up of an incipient new state organization. That showed their confidence in themselves, in Yugoslavia, and in the final Allied victory. It also showed that they no longer recognized the former state. That meeting was a declaration of war against the old Yugoslav state. It was the forming of a confederate rebel government.

The people who participated in the Bihach meeting tended to arouse hope within Yugoslavia and especially outside. The President of the National Council himself, Ivan Ribar, was inoffensive and even reassuring. He was not a Communist or a furious Partisan, not even a professional revolutionist. For years he had been out of politics. He was a Croat from Belgrade, a goodhearted, well-meaning lawyer, disliking Serb hegemony and desiring to help his country. In the Council, also, were Slovenes, Montenegrins, members of the Croat Peasant Party, Bosnians, Macedonians, and Serbs. There were Orthodox Christians, Catholics, Moslems, and Jews. To one who viewed the Bihach meeting from afar, it might appear as a Yugoslav Pentecost. In a land of such terrible hatred, where one group of citizens was furiously killing members of other groups, that interracial, interreligious and interpolitical harmony seemed wonderful. The lion was lying down with the lamb, the Communist with the bourgeois. The Serb was fraternizing with the Croat and both with the Macedonians.

A distraught world, eager for a sign, applauded. Tito, whose identity was still unknown, was acclaimed as a new prophet, while fluent men and women bitterly chided hard-boiled, "oversuspicious" doubters who persisted in seeing red. Communism was merely an evanescent "bogey," as unreal as witches, they said. Wasn't Tito showing that Communists were really arch democrats? And as the outside world cheered, some sincere Yugoslavs, too, were encouraged. They began to feel that AVNOJ and the Liberation Army might solve Yugoslavia's problems.

The program of the Bihach meeting tended to strengthen this belief. It had six simple points: pure democracy, the inviolability of private property, no revolutionary social changes, no coercion, good jobs for good fighters, and national rights for all the peoples of Yugoslavia.

Most of those things had been said a million times. They are as platitudinous as the multiplication tables. Most of them are in the election platforms of all political parties. No Yugoslav politician had so much as run for mayor who hadn't promised most of these blessings. And in fact two of the six points were purely negative. Most of them had no substance and were as fuzzy as the points in Hitler's first program. But if Germans fell for fuzzy Nazi points, why shouldn't Yugoslavs fall for Tito's? Some of them did. They had been deceived a hundred times before by politicians, but they hoped this time the promises would stick. To a starving man even a crust seems sweet.

The most attractive point in the program was the sixth, namely, national rights. In most lands the relation of the provinces to the central government is very important. We Americans fought a terrible war on that question. It has been a major issue at one time or another in Great Britain, France, Italy, and Germany, and is a chief cause of conflict in Yugoslavia. Tito's promise at Bihach, that every nationality would be free, sounded like a true Declaration of Independence to many Yugoslavs. A number of Slovenes, Croatians, Bosnians, Montenegrins, and Macedonians felt drawn to such an ideal. That hope inspired Partisans in their greatest privations and most terrible sufferings.

The creation of AVNOJ gave new impetus to Partisan activity. And when another November came, one hundred and forty delegates of AVNOJ again assembled from many parts of Yugoslavia in the Yugoslav town of Jaice and took another step on the road toward political power. It was a long step. At Jaice, the Partisans were far more aggressive than they had been at Bihach. The year had brought them fame, applause, and Allied support and had hastened their march toward political domination. At their new conference they conducted themselves as already the masters of Yugoslavia.

During the intervening year they had been engaged in very bitter fighting, primarily in internecine fighting. They had been waging a furious civil war, and we might say that Tito had advanced from a Bull Run to a Gettysburg. He was now ready to announce his emancipation proclamation. At Bihach the Partisans had merely set up a token government; at Jaice they tried to make the government a reality.

Anyone wishing to understand the situation in Yugoslavia must constantly keep in mind that although Yugoslavia had an official government, of which Mihailovitch was an official member, Tito, from the very beginning, both secretly and openly, had worked to replace it. He had perpetrated a Fort Sumter and after that had formed a government of his own, just as definitely and defiantly as Jefferson Davis did. But with this difference, Davis and his generals wanted to dominate only part of the U.S.A. They were willing to leave something to Lincoln. Tito was striving to be complete master of all of Yugoslavia. He left nothing to the old government. He and the Partisans had created a situation where either he or Mihailovitch had to lose. They could not both win any more than could both Cromwell and King Charles.

At the Jaice meeting in November, 1943, Tito was made Marshal of Yugoslavia, which was a new South Slav military title, above all that had ever existed. That self-appointed meeting made Tito head of all Yugoslavia's armed forces. In effect, it formally proclaimed the dissolution of the Yugoslav Army, which act was a basic part of Tito's program. It also set up a national administration, thus formally signifying that it considered the whole state machine dissolved. The delegates also expressed bitter opposition to King Peter, poured out their scorn on his government, and with vociferous unanimity branded Mihailovitch a traitor. The political revolution was moving toward a climax. In a little more than thirty-two months after Hitler attacked Belgrade, Tito and his fellow Communists had formally set up a new state. That was their chief aim in all their fighting.

From one point of view, conditions had been very favorable, inasmuch as the old state machine had broken down. Yugoslavia was cut up into six main pieces under foreign masters and all former Yugoslav ties had been destroyed. Effectively the Yugoslav Army was gone, the Yugoslav state police was gone, the Yugoslav administration was gone. The vacuum, such as every revolutionist craves, was there. All Tito had to do was fill it. Toward that end he and his followers directed their chief energies. For that he set up the Jaice government. Everything else in Tito's activity was secondary.

Also in Tito's favor were the facts that young King Peter was not providing strong moral and political leadership, that the government in exile had been hopelessly divided on all questions, thus making a spectacle of itself, and that Mihailovitch's forces at first had been anti-Yugoslav. For a time Tito actually was the principal bearer of the banner of a reintegrated Yugoslavia.

Now we must ask how Tito's state functioned. He and his able Partisan propagandists have filled the world with rosy stories about its administrative miracles but, sad to say, the stories are myths. Wars always bring torrents of deception and one of the greatest in this war was the stream of idyllic propaganda pouring from Partisan Yugoslavia. The Allied world was in a mood to hear it and lapped it up. Millions of men and women wanted to be deceived and the Partisans accommodated them. When one recalls what Americans have believed about the Partisans, he sadly realizes that in certain moods people will temporarily give credence to anything.

Here is an example. Reputable correspondents reported to reputable newspapers in America, and it was printed for intelligent readers, that Tito had opened schools in the "liberated areas" and wiped out illiteracy, which had held no fewer than 65 per cent of the people in darkness.

Try to picture the import of such a statement. In the first place, the Yugoslav Communists seemed to be aping Russian propaganda. They tried to paint Yugoslavia "before taking," that is, prior to Bihach (November, 1942), as very black, and "after taking," as very white. The fact is, that in Slovenia the percentage of literacy and the distribution of good periodical literature were higher than in any state of the U.S.A. Also, in Croatia, Slavonia, and Voivodina most people could read and write, and in Serbia literacy was steadily increasing. Already by 1941, 85 per cent of the Serbian army recruits could read and write.

In addition, a number of Yugoslav organizations, notably the Croatian Peasant Party, had made long, vigorous, widespread and well-organized efforts under favorable conditions to raise the Croatian standard of literacy. This was one of the most inspiring of the many inspiring activities of the Raditch-Machek Party. However, the Yugoslav Partisans trumpeted to the world that 65 per cent of the Yugoslavs were illiterate and that they had wiped out that darkness in a year! And what a year!

It is true that in some Bosnian areas many mountaineers were illiterate, perhaps 75 per cent. Did Tito wipe that out in a year?

Most of the most illiterate Bosnians were Moslems, only 5 per cent of whom followed Tito. He wasn't enlightening most Moslems. Many of the illiterate were anti-Tito Croatians; others, anti-Tito Orthodox Serbs. He wasn't enlightening them; he was killing them. So he couldn't have worked on even half of the illiterate, if he had wished.

But look at the situation. There were half a dozen fierce Nazi offensives, Tito himself says. Armies were constantly moving up and down all the valleys and gorges, massacring, burning, plundering, and destroying. Remember, also, that Tito securely held not a single city of any size. He held only mountain areas and occupied only towns or villages, most of which were constantly in danger.

As Tito himself says, the people were hungry, wounded, poorly clad, sick, without adequate shelter. They were in such terrible condition that he had to send about one hundred thousand out of the country for subsistence. They had no slates, few blackboards, fewer pencils, very little paper, and no schools. Yet, in the midst of all that, Tito's propagandists picture 65 per cent of Yugoslavia's men, women, and children sitting under trees, winter and summer, all learning to write with nothing, on nothing; and after twelve months all are literate! As Nazis massacre these people, they sit calmly writing in the snow! And Americans swallow that!

Actually, most education in Yugoslavia was suspended for three years. In Partisan territories both teaching and schools were lacking. Education didn't advance, but went into a terrible slump. And the fact that Partisans with straight faces could picture themselves to

Americans as wiping out illiteracy in Slovenia, which is already more advanced in literacy than Massachusetts or Utah, shows the nature of their propaganda. What they said about hungry old men avidly learning to write under the trees as their children were being killed and their homes burned, is of a piece with what they said about their elections, their finances, their recruiting, and their armies.

Partisans constantly told of their elections—their free elections—and many Americans believed them. We know that Partisans carried guns and freely used them; we know they lived amid carnage, that they were flaming with hatred, that they called all non-Partisans "Fascists" and treated them as mortal enemies. Everyone who has had any contact with Partisans knows they inordinately boast of their killings; yet amid such scenes, with such passions, we are led to believe they held free elections. They themselves have described such elections. Nine-tenths of the voting was open and public. In a room or in a public square, people raised their hands as men with tommy guns counted them.

All the voters had seen killing. Nazis, Partisans, Ustashas, Chetniks had passed through their villages leaving corpses and ruins behind. After armed Partisans swept in to hold elections, does anyone believe that the inhabitants would agitate and vote against the occupiers or "liberators"? If there were such people, they certainly wouldn't vote against the Partisans more than once! Can serious Americans talk of free elections, in the presence of gallows, ruins, and bomb throwers? An American doesn't consider an election free if a factory boss even distributes literature to an employee, much less if a boss threatens to fire an employee for the way he votes. Yet some people thought a Yugoslav election could be free, even though all the voters feared for their very lives!

The Partisans had committees in many parts of the country to raise funds and food. Such food collecting was all said to be voluntary. That, also, was a pretty Partisan fable. The areas held by Partisans were mostly passive or arid areas, in which the population even in normal times was short of food. In addition, those areas were all devastated. Supplies had been seized, the stock had been taken, transportation was in ruins. Yet we are told that in such areas Partisan committees received enough food in voluntary gifts to feed a quarter of a million fighters and a great number of refugees. In every other country on earth, including America, black markets raged, but in the poorest areas of a poor, horribly ravaged land, people were said to pour out food for Partisan armies. And American journalists have written black on white that under those awful conditions the peasants produced more than formerly!

As a matter of fact, the Partisans lived on requisitioning. They simply took what they needed where they could find it. They and all other Yugoslav armed bands were hated by the peasants of most villages, as hungry irregulars always are hated by peasants. Anyone who knows anything of the activity of revolutionary bands in Greece, Macedonia, Bulgaria, Serbia, or Albania is aware that the bands have to live from plunder and that they are the terror of villages and villagers.

One of the most scintillating of all Partisan fables is the story of the Partisan loan. I have had a good deal of experience with revolutionary loans. They are extortion and blackmail. Yugoslavia had six different kinds of currency, all inflated. Every citizen knew that the future was uncertain and that there would be a revaluation. Every rich man knew that if he gave the Partisans a million dollars or kunas or dinars or liras, he would later be branded as a Fascist war profiteer and his war bonds cancelled. The Balkanese are frightfully suspicious about such things. In addition, the Partisans had control only of very poor areas. And, in the enemy-occupied cities, would the rich, even if sympathizing with Partisans, want to have Partisan bonds lying about in the closet for the Gestapo to find? Gifts there were, some voluntary, most forced, but the loan is as mythical as the story of millions of old grandmas studying writing under the winter trees.

And one of the saddest aspects of the Tito movement was the People's Courts. They were the subversion of justice. They were vehicles for vengeance, devices for eliminating or incapacitating political opponents.

Before a People's Court the accused had no more chance for fair treatment than a heretic before fanatical true believers or than an "infidel" before a group of ardent crusaders. The law was improvised, the judges were chosen by self-chosen committees, the procedure was improvised, the public was violently Partisan, the execution swift.

And the recruiting of soldiers by Partisans was as much obligatory as voluntary. It is true that many destitute, unrooted men and women voluntarily joined Partisan ranks because they had no place else to go. It is also true that many joined from a desire to fight German invaders and create a brave new world. But it is equally true that whenever the Partisans won control over an area they mobilized the available fighters. Partisan drafting was inexorable.

The revolutionary Partisan state, set up in November, 1943, to replace the official state, was as coercive as any that has ever been created. It set up an administration that was subject to the central oligarchy, seized provisions, forcibly collected funds, drafted soldiers, used obligatory labor, maintained a large implacable body of commissars, organized a ruthless state police, formed its own courts, and created an army. It had its own radio, operating via Russia, and issued a fairly extensive periodical press.

It pretended to do all this in the name of a broad democracy. And the composition of the Anti-Fascist Council, AVNOJ, strengthened that appearance. But the impression was deceptive. From the first day to the present moment the Partisan movement has been in the hands of a strong, capable, self-imposed Communist oligarchy. American journalists have written of "a sprinkling of Communists," and intimated that they were of no more importance than a sprinkling of Congregationalists among Methodists and Baptists. In this they misled the American people. The sprinkling of Communists in Partisanry is as large as the Communist sprinkling in Russia. The sprinkling of Communists in the Partisan Army of Liberation is as large as the Communist sprinkling in the Russian Army. And as significant.

Every non-Communist holding a post in Tito's regime is a person of secondary importance or less. Most are figureheads. None is a policy maker. Ivan Ribar, President of AVNOJ, was little more than a front for fooling Americans who wanted to be fooled. The Slovene Partisan leadership was almost exclusively Communist and is of great importance for the whole regime. The Montenegrin leadership was fanatically Communist and influenced every aspect and branch of the revolutionary movement. The Croatian leadership was rabidly Communist. So was the Macedonian—indeed it was ecstatically Communist. The army was led by Communists. The Partisan Gestapo was Communist. Practically all the commissars were Communists. The proportion of Communists in vital positions in AVNOJ was larger than the proportion of Nazis in the first Hitler cabinet. And month by month those Yugoslav Communists increased their domination over the movement.

They and their associates in AVNOJ represented only a small minority of Yugoslavia. Geographically and by nationality the new government rested on a very narrow basis. In it were no authentic representatives of Serbia. It was a government largely without Serbia and against Serbia. It had won the support of but a small part of the Croatian Peasant Party and was opposed by most of the members of most Slovene parties.

In addition, it was not supported by any large group of Yugoslav clergymen. It was bitterly opposed by practically the whole Church in Serbia. Indeed, it had not been able to win the support of so much as half a dozen priests from there, and of not a single one with a high church position. A few "Across-the-river" Orthodox priests supported Tito, and a small number of Catholic priests accepted him. Half a dozen Catholic priests even backed him; one, Monsignor Rittig, was among his leading propagandists. That same Catholic prelate had earlier supported King Alexander's and Ante Pavelitch's dictatorships. The regime which Tito established in November, 1943, had a smaller basis than any regime since the creation of the Yugoslav state. Opposed by the peasant parties, actively supported by almost no workers, scorned by the clergy, hated by the Serbians of Serbia, it set out to impose itself by force. It used the war for that purpose.

I would not like to leave the impression that I belittle the heroism and devotion of many of the Partisans. Some were among the bravest warriors in this whole war. Many of the young Partisans also showed great idealism. They made the streets of Italy, the sands of Egypt, and the mountains of Yugoslavia echo with their songs. They inspired enthusiasm among Britishers and Americans. They ran risks and made sacrifices. But in spite of all this, until the very end of the war, they were only a small, Communist-led Yugoslav minority, trying to seize power over a majority. Always claiming to speak for the people, they tried to suppress the people, and the more fanatical they became, the more they abused the word democracy. Their political regime, exercising unchecked power, is a negation of almost everything it pretends to stand for.

CHAPTER FOURTEEN

Tito's Military Contribution

I BELIEVE the Yugoslav Partisans were among the best underground fighters in this war. They were brave, hardy, skillful in maneuvering, agile in retreats, deadly in attacks. The reasons for their prowess are: first, all South Slavs are by nature good fighters; second, the South Slavs have an old, highly prized tradition of guerrilla warfare; and third, the Partisans were led by fanatical Communists.

In all Allied countries the Communists have been excellent guerrillas. They were among the foremost leaders of most underground movements. After Russia was attacked by Hitler on June 22, 1941, the Communists everywhere fought with fury, valor, and persistence.

Such a phenomenon is not new or strange. In all the ages, fanatics with a narrow, intolerant, flaming faith in a cosmic or millennial or universal ideal have been among the most eager to kill and most willing to be killed. The Nazis were a striking example. The Moslems, too, were long among the most deadly and death-defying soldiers on earth. Jewish fighters on certain great occasions have avidly faced death amid carnage and destruction. The Puritans under Cromwell were among the bravest and most irresistible warriors of all time, because they believed they were fighting for their God. The savagery of every religious war shows the terrific effect of a flaming faith.

Balkan Communism is such a faith. Tito's comrades were as apostles of Marx and Lenin. Some had foresworn all for the cause. They had already operated in a dozen lands. They had laughed at prisons, tortures, privations, even death. And having prepared their lives for the Day, they did not shrink when that Day came.

As was natural, not all of Tito's soldiers had that ardor, since many were drafted, others were time servers, still others disliked Communism. Actually, there were many cases of Partisan cowardice, desertion, graft, corruption. The Communist elect was fairly small. But it was large enough to inspire others and give the world an example of heroism. For such courage, in this age of killing, the Yugoslav Partisans deserve an honored place among the world's warriors.

However, when we have said this, we have still said very little about their military contribution to the Allied cause. As is not unnatural, they themselves make very extravagant claims, for which they deserve no special reproach. All warriors toot their own trumpets and have done so from the beginning of time. We cannot temper the tootings, but we must ask whether or not they correspond to the truth.

Before trying to ascertain the military contributions of the Yugoslav Partisans, we should consider the general question of the contribution of underground forces. In doing so, we would discover that "undergrounders" liberated no land in this war. Anglo-Saxons liberated France and Italy. The Russian armies, operating in south central Europe, forced the withdrawal of German armies from Greece. ELAS by no means liberated that country. The Russian Army was almost wholly responsible for the capitulation of Bulgaria and not the pro-Allied underground movement there. The Bulgarian Communist-led Fatherland Front contributed very little. In Slovakia, the underground, though brave, played a minor role and did still less in Czechia. Their military contribution in Belgium and Holland was small. In Norway, the heroic underground made a great moral contribution but did little of military importance. Only the final capitulation of Germany freed Norway. If we leave Europe and go to the Philippines, we see that the liberators of those islands were American soldiers, not local guerrillas.

This is no reflection on the resistance forces, but a historical fact. And it applies to Yugoslavia, as to other places. Tito and his Partisans, though fighting heroically, did not by any means free Yugoslavia. That was done largely by Russia, in conjunction with the Western Allies and Bulgaria. Indeed, much of Yugoslavia remained unliberated until the final collapse of Germany. No one drove the Germans out of that last area; they just vanished when the Wehrmacht surrendered to Eisenhower and Zhukoff. Tito's major military contribution was hampering enemy transportation, harassing enemy troops, and occupying Yugoslav areas that were evacuated by Germans, or held by inferior Axis troops or by inferior numbers of good troops.

Before attempting a somewhat more detailed appraisal of the Partisans' military activity we may well ask how the world was informed of the fighting in Yugoslavia during 1942, 1943, and much of 1944. First, through the Yugoslav radio called "Free Yugoslavia." This began to operate in 1942 and almost daily issued long military and political dispatches. The sending station was in Russia not Yugoslavia. Russian operators and paraphernalia had been sent to Yugoslavia to maintain communications between the two lands. The information, therefore, in the "Free Yugoslavia" dispatches was purely and wholly Partisan. It was what the Partisans and Russia wanted the world to believe. From beginning to end, it was Tito's propaganda. This does not mean that all "Free Yugoslavia" said was false. Indeed not everything America's OWI said was false. In fact, practically nothing in OWI's propaganda was actually false. But it was not the whole truth. It was part of a military campaign. Every single broadcast was conditioned. OWI was serving a fighting army. It carried on psychological warfare; it fought with words. So did Tito through "Free Yugoslavia." Often his words gave a very warped picture.

In addition to "Free Yugoslavia" broadcasts and to Tito's very active emissaries, who went to Western countries after Italy's collapse, Great Britain and America received reports from their own agents in Yugoslavia. Our armies had liaison officers with Tito's forces. Most were British but eventually many Americans also established direct contact with the Partisans. These men all wrote profuse reports, some of which they sent out by radio, others of which they brought out. They had headquarters in Cairo and Bari and other places. Hundreds of Allied officers, from generals down, daily tried to ascertain what Tito's Partisans were doing.

What they discovered or thought they had discovered was assembled in voluminous secret reports, and the few people who had access to the reports believed they knew what was going on. But this information was inadequate and one-sided, because no British or American liaison officer with Tito's forces had freedom of action! No American was allowed to wander about Yugoslavia studying the situation as a good journalist would. He could make no independent investigations. He could not freely ask priests or teachers or peasants or storekeepers what they thought of Partisans or what the Partisans were really doing or what support they had.

Neither could American liaison officers witness battles or skirmishes or even bridge demolitions, as a rule. They were stationed at corps or division headquarters and had to take the information handed out to them. They were constantly under the control of commissars assigned to them and were prohibited from making direct independent contacts. They could not leave their posts without specific permission. They could not visit a neighboring village without written authorization from Partisan officials. In many cases the local inhabitants were told not to mingle with American or British officers. Our agents were simply guests of Tito and obliged to do his bidding.

Naturally they tried to get information, because they were there for that purpose. But as a rule they reported only what they were told. If they reported a bridge blown up, it usually meant that the Partisans had told them a bridge was blown up. If they reported a Partisan battle against Germans, they got the report from a Partisan bulletin. And if they said Tito had ten thousand soldiers in a certain place, it meant that Tito said he had ten thousand soldiers in a certain place. If they said trains weren't running, it probably meant that Tito said trains weren't running. They usually reported what "Free Yugoslavia" was reporting. If these Allied officers had appeared sceptical and had aroused the suspicions of fanatical armed Partisans, they would have been in acute danger. They were under constant supervision.

Of course, there were certain things these men saw first hand. Their very presence in a certain locality showed that Tito dominated that locality. It was freed. And the fact that eventually scores of such men could report from various parts of Yugoslavia—except Serbia—showed that Partisans held areas in many parts of the country. Very few of these liaison officers ever fell into German hands and that in itself shows some Partisan strength. However, these men did not know exactly how strong or well armed the Partisan forces were, what local opposition they faced, or the political attitude of the inhabitants. Some of their reports on specific matters were excellent, but their overall appraisals will remain as examples of "propaganda serving as intelligence." Future British military academies will read many of these reports with chagrin and shame.

Another important factor entering into the gathering of information about the Partisans is the great political and human sympathy which some of the liaison officers and other Anglo-Saxons felt toward Partisanry. In very critical times for Great Britain and the Allies, the Partisans were "in there pitching." Thousands were homeless, hundreds were wounded, most were suffering privations. But they did not give up. Many were aggressive, filled with hope, and flaming with faith. They were sure of their gospel and seemed confident of the future. Many were certain they wouldn't lose.

And they were on our side. Their spirit moved many Americans and Britishers. Some of our men sang Partisan songs, danced Partisan dances, gave Partisan salutes, wore Partisan souvenirs. On British military cars—made in the U.S.A.—one occasionally saw Partisan slogans.

A Canadian liaison officer in Slovenia circulated printed appeals, bearing his photograph, and urging Slovenes, in the name of the United Nations, to join the Partisans. This Canadian presumed to try to make Slovene Catholics believe that Anglo-Americans wanted them to join Tito. An American officer wrote an article in an underground Partisan paper extolling the Partisans as equalling Americans at Valley Forge. Other American agents of Slav origin had Partisan relatives in Yugoslavia. Some are reputed definitely to have gone over to the Partisans.

Thus Partisanry became a cult. For a time Partisans in Italy were employed in the homes of some Americans who were engaged in the most secret of intelligence activity. Some Britishers vied with each other in playing up Partisans. In addition, some Americans and Britishers working with the Partisans shared their ideas. They rejoiced in the chance to aid the Revolution. It goes without saying that men singing Partisan songs, giving Partisan salutes, running about in cars bearing Partisan slogans, writing in Partisan papers, and looking for the coming of the Partisans' new world would not be objective gatherers of information. Such liaison officers misled their governments. Later, Winston Churchill admitted he had been misinformed. One of his chief deceivers was his son Randolph, who daily proclaims his mistake—now that it is too late.

Nevertheless, there are indisputable facts and here are some of them. The Partisans did considerable damage to railroads. It is true that they were unable to stop heavy military traffic on any major route, for more than a day or two at a time—on one or two occasions for a week—but they appreciably handicapped the Germans. The main German military line through northwest Yugoslavia, right across Partisan territory, succeeded in running practically all the time. It was double tracked most of the way from Maribor through Ljubljana to Trieste and beside it was a motor road. The Partisans boasted of dominating Slovenia and northern Croatia, but nine days out of every ten, during the whole war and especially when the Axis troops were holding our army cold in its tracks in Italy, those lines, both rail and motor, were carrying very heavy German military traffic. Enemy troops and munitions moved practically every hour. Finally a very vital bridge in Italy was blown up and traffic suspended for a week. But that demolition was carried out under British leadership and largely by Britishers. They had vainly waited months for Tito to do it.

Also the main lines from Zagreb to Belgrade and from Hungary to Belgrade ran most of the time, carrying heavy military loads. Likewise, the vital military line through Macedonia, of which the Partisans claimed to be masters, ran with but short interruptions. As a matter of fact, the Germans provisioned their troops both in Greece and Albania until the very end—through "Partisan territory."

So inadequate was the damage done by the Partisans to Yugoslav railroads that late in the summer of 1944, Allied air forces, operating from Italy, devoted a long period to the intensive and exclusive bombing of Yugoslav communications. Our airmen had to do what Tito every day for two years said he had done. So unreliable were Tito's reports on demolitions that in the summer of 1944, one vital branch of Allied intelligence quit using them. Yugoslavia is one of the most rugged lands in Europe. It has vast, thinly inhabited mountain areas, in which the railroad lines abound in bridges and tunnels and are completely exposed. Few lines of communications are more easily accessible to guerrillas. But in spite of this, the enemy continued to use most of the important railway lines to the very end.

In pointing out these facts and recalling the success and speed with which the Germans constantly sent troops and supplies anywhere in the Balkans across Tito's territory, I am not belittling the demolition work of the Partisans. They did blow up many trains and bridges. The line from Zagreb to Belgrade was fairly thickly strewn with derailed locomotives. Hitler and Pavelitch had to detach troops to watch those lines. Traffic was retarded, danger was increased, enemy morale was affected. Tito's men did useful work, of which the American Army is appreciative. But it seems to me strange that "an army of a third of a million," which Tito's propagandists said he had, couldn't permanently stop a single main line of enemy communications in the wild and mountainous Balkans.

Another one of Tito's useful military activities was to raid towns. For a while he was master of Bihach. Then he made Jaice his headquarters. For a short period he held Banya Luka. And at one time or another, in fact many times in some cases, he held a fair number of small towns in western Bosnia. This fact shows that Tito had daring guerrillas. They were able to rush into a town, overcome the local garrisons, and seize all military supplies, including arms. Almost always they were driven out again and from the larger places they were driven out without exception.

Usually the towns Tito held were rubble. And one may ask what was the sense of these raids. To what end were the cities ruined, the population killed and the Yugoslav nation crippled? Was there any object in razing a town and exterminating its inhabitants to "free" it? Yes, from the strictly military point of view. Because enemy garrisons were destroyed and enemy soldiers were kept in Yugoslavia that might have gone to the Russian front or to the Italian front. We Americans were hard pressed in Italy and the Russians were hard pressed on their front. If Tito traded ten Yugoslavs, including women and babies, for one Axis soldier, that was a military gain from our point of view. It was a terribly unequal transaction in human blood, but Americans accepted it, the British applauded it, Russians glorified it. We were all glad Yugoslav babies were saving our men. And by that blood Tito was moving toward power. He was laying up treasures in the political heaven. For that blood we sent him weapons and recognized his new regime. He could well sing the song, "There's power in the blood."

Also by their raids, Tito's Partisans hindered Germans in getting slave labor from Yugoslavia and in gathering provisions. This wasn't a very important point because Tito operated in very barren and thinly settled regions, that produced little food and provided little man power. Nevertheless, he did somewhat reduce Hitler's resources.

He also brought Pavelitch's puppet regime into disrepute. "Free Croatia," which Hitler had established and turned over to Quisling Pavelitch, was made a reproach and laughingstock before the world by Tito's depredations.

Besides these things, Tito made raids upon the islands, thus hampering Axis traffic in the Adriatic Sea. He was not able to occupy many of the islands until just before Hitler's collapse and the raids were terribly costly to the native inhabitants, but still they hindered the enemy a little. It was like burning down a house to steep a cup of tea, but we had the tea. And the house that burned was Yugoslavia's. For more than a year and a half we Americans have been feeding the poor, wretched refugees from those islands. The cost of those very meager military gains seems to me high.

The fact, also, that Tito's Partisans "liberated" certain regions in Yugoslavia had some military significance. His actual holding of distant isolated mountain areas didn't appreciably affect military operations on any major front, but it aided morale. Tito was a morale builder. The legend of his wresting half of Yugoslavia from Hitler and the fact of his setting up a provisional government under the very nose of Hitler's bloodiest stooge, Pavelitch, gave the democratic world a shot in the arm. For that reason Tito's liberation of a number of forests and mountains was helpful.

Militarily, Tito deserves well of the United Nations. But that doesn't prove, nor come anywhere near proving, the truth of basic Partisan claims; namely, that Tito practically freed Yugoslavia, that he had a formidable army, and that he engaged a large number of first-class German troops.

It is a fact that after the collapse of Italy in late 1943, Tito's Partisans moved into the vacuum left by Italy, rapidly enlarging their power and the extent of their freed territory. Tito was suddenly in possession of ports, islands, cities, railroads. If Tito had really had a strong force at his disposal he could have kept much of that, but he salvaged very little. The fall of Italy was a terrific blow for the Germans. They had lost Africa, were reeling back in Russia, were suffering heavy submarine losses on the seas and feared an American landing in France. Yet without much difficulty, with great rapidity, and with small losses, the Germans recovered all the vital Yugoslav points the Italians had vacated. They took over practically every Dalmatian island, occupied every Dalmatian port, and drove the Partisans from every city with any military or economic value. Tito's Partisans even with all their Italian arms were speedily pushed right back into the isolated mountain wastes.

As one surveys the whole area in which Tito and his Partisans fought, clear through the war up to the very end of 1944, he observes the following:

The Partisans were not able to take and hold any vital point anywhere which the Germans wished to retain. In spite of the Partisans' terrible need for supplies and weapons and the readiness of the Allies to provide them, the Partisans were not able to occupy a single Adriatic harbor—except isolated uninhabited beaches for night landings. Even where the Partisans received excellent harbors as a gift they couldn't hold them. They could not keep open a single road from the coast to the interior. The Allies had to bring all supplies by air, and take out the wounded by air.

One and only one important Adriatic island, named Vis, was securely "held" by Tito and that was held by Allied navies, Allied armies, and Allied planes. The British and Americans kept a liberated island to serve as the safe headquarters of the "liberator of Yugoslavia."

Not a single major city in the whole land was liberated by Tito and his Partisans. Belgrade, Zagreb, Ljubljana, Split, Mostar, Skoplje, Cetinje, and the rest were freed by the Red Army or the Bulgarian

Army or relinquished by retreating Germans or left in the hands of a weak, expendable Axis garrison, to cover the retreat.

Most of the troops the Germans used against Tito most of the time were not first-class, front-line soldiers. Many were not even Germans. In certain parts of Yugoslavia at certain times most of the Axis forces were Russians. They were deserters, called Cossacks by the Yugoslavs.

The areas "liberated" by Tito were almost exclusively wild, thinly populated, isolated, fairly unproductive mountain regions of almost no military importance for the enemy and of little economic significance. Quisling Pavelitch, during most of the war, was able to travel to almost any large city in "Tito's territory." Mihailovitch's men at any time could travel through "Tito's territory" from Bulgaria to the Adriatic or from Srem to Podgoritsa with speed and safety. Until the end of the summer of 1944, German troops passed directly and rapidly from Hungary through "Tito's territory" to Tirana, Albania.

The only part of Yugoslav Slovenia which Tito permanently held, before Germany collapsed, was a small mountain region south of Ljubljana, containing not a single important city and intercepting no vital line of communication. And there the Partisans sat without expanding for almost two years. North of Ljubljana they held no free areas whatsoever, although they operated in various places as guerrilla bands.

In the northern part of Croatia the only freed area was a small wild mountain region north of Celje and west of Maribor in the Carnic Alps. Also in Slavonia a small wild mountain district called Papuk containing no cities was in the hands of organized Partisans. Nowhere in Voivodina, meaning the whole of northeast Yugoslavia, was there a single freed area or much Partisan activity.

Not until the arrival of the Red Army were the Partisans able to "free" any appreciable part of Serbia. They held scattered mountain clusters, specifically Yastrebats and Kapaonik, and for a considerable period dominated a marginal region near the point where Serbia, Macedonia, and Bulgaria meet. Time and again Tito announced the capture of vital Serbian cities but later the Red Army according to official bulletins had to free every one of them. Tito had taken them only by radio or by raids, dashing in and darting out. When Tito raided a city he trumpeted the news throughout the world, but when he retired, as he usually did, he made no mention of it.

Until the collapse of Bulgaria, Tito's Partisans had completely failed to master Macedonia.

In other words, the only extensive areas which Tito managed to free with his own forces were parts of the heavily wooded or largely barren portions of southern Croatia, Dalmatia, Bosnia, Herzegovina, and Montenegro. He also held part of the wild, isolated Sandjak.

And why shouldn't Tito hold those areas? Did Hitler want to maintain troops in barren mountains? Did he want to waste soldiers in inaccessible forests or divert tanks to distant Bosnian gorges? The Yugoslav roads which Hitler wanted, he kept. The cities Hitler needed, he held. The ports he coveted, he retained. The transportation centers he required, he did not relinquish. He left Tito to rule over wastes. When Tito's radio daily told the world he had freed half of Yugoslavia, that was misleading. And when American journalists took up the claim and lauded Tito for freeing half of his land they were deceiving the American nation.

A notable example of how the world was misled regarding Tito's strength was a dispatch sent from Yugoslavia to American papers by an American correspondent temporarily representing the whole American press. He was taken into "free Yugoslavia" in an American military plane. Shortly after landing, he sent out a dispatch, which appeared in many American papers on May 8, 1944, with the date line "Somewhere in Yugoslavia," and began with the words, "A few weeks ago a high Allied official expressed doubts as to whether certain territories in Yugoslavia could be called 'liberated' in the strictest sense of the word." Then he proceeded to show how free it was.

He said he travelled twenty-five miles on a "Partisan railroad," had his baggage transported by groups of peasant men and women with oxcarts, saw Partisan patrols, conversed with peasants in their fields, participated in a Partisan Youth Congress (attended by eight hundred young men and women), rode in an auto through the night, heard Tito promise the Allies one hundred and fifty thousand—perhaps even three hundred thousand—Yugoslav soldiers to help crush Germany. "This," wrote the correspondent with a flourish, "is liberated enough for me!"

That is a rather idyllic picture of liberation. And Tito's radio had said that about half of Yugoslavia was in such a state of freedom. The impression which the reporter seemed to want to produce and which the casual reader would have gotten is that, in much of Yugoslavia, Tito's men managed trains, circulated in autos, carried on their regular work, held congresses, and prepared themselves to help take Berlin. Thus about half of Yugoslavia would be free enough for the American correspondent. But within a few days that whole camp, namely Tito's Central Headquarters and chief show place, the freest and best-guarded spot in Yugoslavia, was seized by the Germans. The reporter, with three other Anglo-American journalists and photographers, was captured and Tito himself, after plunging into flight, was saved by the Allies who brought him in an airplane to Bari, Italy. Later the American correspondent escaped from his captors and was liberated by American airmen.

Can you imagine a more misleading report? Actually Tito had extremely few autos and hardly a dozen trucks in use, in all Yugoslavia. He used part of a little one-horse, narrow-gauge, privately owned railroad, built and run by a lumbering company and meandering through largely uninhabited forests. It started at Jaice and ended at Knin, neither of which towns the Partisans held, and it served a few little villages devoid of military or economic importance. Near one of these villages, the correspondent had landed by night from an airplane which immediately took off again, touch and go. Tito had no permanent, secure airfield in all Yugoslavia, merely landing and take-off strips, available one night, perhaps seized by the Germans the next. So bereft of food were the Partisans, who claimed to have freed nearly half of Yugoslavia, that the few American visitors going there were asked to bring their own provisions, while airplanes constantly dropped provisions for Partisans.

It is true a youth conference was held during that May in Drvar, Tito's mountain lair, but it was long postponed because of danger from Germans and hastily dispersed because of German attacks.

You might try to imagine a "Company Train" puffing along behind a wood-fire engine, on a remnant of a narrow-gauge railway, serving half a dozen villages, situated in clearings amid small fields, gardens, and orchards in a vast Maine forest. And you might picture to yourself, also, a couple of old autos occasionally running along a thirty-mile road extending from one limit to the other of an area which a Robin Hood and his band had freed. Then you might imagine the oppressor so busily engaged in other vital points such as New York, Washington, and Chicago that he didn't much care what happened to Robin Hood in the isolated Maine woods. You might further envisage a romantic correspondent flying from Canada to a clearing in the Maine forests and reporting that Robin Hood had liberated about half of America and that it was free enough for him.

Then suppose that Robin Hood gallantly promised the reporter to send three hundred thousand of his men to help free the rest of the world and make all humanity happy. Subsequently, you might imagine that before the newsman's glowing dispatch had tingled itself through the ether, the oppressor had launched a surprise raid, pounced on the correspondent, and sent the Robin Hood rushing in full flight to the security of Canada in a hastily called Canadian plane. Well, in that case you might be inclined to think the reporter was feeding his readers taffy about Robin Hood freeing half of America. Many reporters have fed American readers taffy about Yugoslav Partisans.

TITO'S MILITARY CONTRIBUTION

The Allies saved Tito from the Germans, and later they carried him safely to the island of Vis, where they set up headquarters for him. They guarded him with their warships and airplanes and provided him with facilities to send out daily messages to the world, datelined "From the Headquarters of the Army of Liberation in Liberated Areas of Yugoslavia" and telling how Tito was beating Germans and preparing to help take Germany. Distinguished representatives from great lands visited Tito in his island, made safe by the Allied navies, and told the world they had been to see the Yugoslav Liberator in "Liberated Yugoslavia, kept free by a third of a million Partisans."

I am not saying that Tito was really as unimportant as he appeared to be there in his cave on Vis under British protection, but it is plain to informed people that the Partisans liberated only wooded and waste areas in Yugoslavia, that they gave freedom to very few people, that German armies constantly circulated through "Tito's territory," that Partisan claims were enormously exaggerated and that Partisan armies never at any time made headway against major groups of first-line German forces.

CHAPTER FIFTEEN

Collaboration and Accommodation

PRACTICALLY every aspect of recent Yugoslav developments is controversial but none so controversial as the question of "collaboration with the enemy." The Partisans, from the very beginning of their fight against the German invaders, have accused Mihailovitch of cooperating with the Nazis and Italians. Later the British took up this charge and Winston Churchill officially denounced Chetnik leaders—though not Mihailovitch himself—for aiding the enemy. The Russians have backed the charge with extreme vigor, and not a few American writers, broadcasters, editors, and politicians have swelled the chorus of denunciation.

Was this accusation well founded? That it was serious is, of course, beyond dispute. At a time when Russia and England were fighting for their very lives and when America was expending every energy to defeat Hitler's Nazis and Mussolini's Fascists, the War Minister of an Allied government was said to be helping Hitler and Mussolini. If it was true, Mihailovitch was working against us and for our enemy. And the charge was not lightly made. Mr. Churchill had his own agents with both Mihailovitch and Tito. Among them was his own son, Major Randolph Churchill, and two trusted advisers, Brigadier Fitzroy Maclean and Colonel William Deakin. At least one of the three was able and conscientious, namely Deakin. It was on the basis of original British reports as well as of Partisan and Russian accusations that Churchill made his public charge against some of Mihailovitch's Chetnik associates. It is true that Mr. Churchill has made many mistakes of judgment, but such a charge by him cannot be ignored.

Did not Mihailovitch collaborate with the enemy? The answer which I shall give to this question may satisfy nobody and may cause keen distress to most Serbs, but it is the true answer. I am sure that there was a species of collaboration with the invaders on the part of both Chetniks and Partisans. Both sides helped the enemy. And they did this because, as the war advanced, their primary interest was not in fighting Hitler, but in waging the civil war which Tito had provoked. After 1941, most fighting in Yugoslavia was waged by Yugoslavs against Yugoslavs for domination of Yugoslavia. Every group made use of the enemy for promoting this fight and thus helped the enemy.

From the point of view of England and America that was tragic and treasonable, but neither Tito nor Mihailovitch felt *primary* obligations to England and America. They were not fighting directly for England and America any more than England and America were fighting specifically for Yugoslavia. England was fighting for the Empire and America was fighting for its place in the world. President Roosevelt himself said it was a war of survival. He extolled this war of survival and urged America to make a supreme effort to survive. Likewise Mihailovitch and the Serbs of Serbia were fighting a fearful war for survival. The survival of Serbia was their supreme end, as the survival of Great Britain was the Britishers' supreme end. If it was a sacred duty in one case, it was surely an understandable consideration in the other. If Americans were right in applauding their President when he urged them to fight for survival, were the Serbs of Serbia villainous in wanting to follow Mihailovitch in fighting for their survival?

What did they consider most menacing to their survival? Without any equivocation, Tito's civil war! Was that not an absurd aberration based on blind prejudice and national vanity? Bulgarians, Hungarians, Germans, Italians, Croats, Albanians, and Moslems were killing Serbs, by the scores of thousands. So why should Mihailovitch get the idea that Tito's civil war was the main menace? Was that not an *idée fixe* due to Mihailovitch's personal ambitions, to "Fascist tendencies," and to his desire to save a ruling class? No, these motives did not play a leading role with Mihailovitch and the Serbs. The leading motive was exactly the same as that expressed in the poignant song, "There'll Always Be an England" or in "America the Beautiful" or in Generalissimo Stalin's exaltation of Mother Russia. If Mihailovitch was a Fascist, then Stalin, Churchill, and Roosevelt, who were fighting for their nations and who appealed to patriotism, were super-Fascists.

To most Serbs of Serbia, including Mihailovitch, Tito's civil war seemed execrable. They knew that Tito was using the World War to further a political revolution and impose a Communist government upon an unwilling nation. They had no illusions about that; they weren't fooled by bright, slick words glowing in a mild, fluorescent fog. They knew that Tito and his Comrades were determined to take advantage of Serbia's extreme tragedy in order to wipe out her traditional freedom and impose a foreign-sponsored dictatorship upon her. And that terrible realization took precedence over all other considerations.

They knew that when Tito called the humble Serbian peasants Fascists it was a lie, designed to weaken Serbian patriotism and dissolve Serbian unity. They knew that when Tito cried "Death to Fascism" it simply meant "Death to Serbian patriotism" and that when his followers cried "Freedom for the People" it meant precisely "Slavery for Serbia." They realized that the whole Partisan movement, which seemed very broad, was really the crusade of a small but powerful political clique for power. They were conscious that Tito, in his appeal for guns with which to fight Germans, really wanted guns to conquer Serbia. They foresaw, with complete clarity, that if Tito succeeded in this, he would destroy all self-reliant, independent Serbian leaders, weaken the church as a national factor, turn the schools into institutions for Communist propaganda, smother freedom, convert Parliament into a society of Communist cheerleaders, and use the press and radio for denouncing Serb traditions. In a word, they perceived that the Partisans were out to weaken Serbia as a nation. And they are as fond of their nation as Americans are of theirs, Russians of theirs, and Norwegians of theirs. So they decided to do everything to survive, just as Americans and Britishers and Russians were doing.

They had lived through centuries of Turkish domination, and from that experience they felt somehow or other they would be able to survive anything which Bulgarian, German, Hungarian, or Italian *armies* could do to them, since foreign occupation would be temporary, lasting a year or a decade or a century. But they were afraid that Serbia would be irremediably weakened if a Communist regime destroyed the foundation of Serbian patriotism and turned the new Serbian generation against all past sentiments. Consequently, they feared and hated Tito, more than they had Turks. When Tito talked of a people's uprising, he enraged the Serbs of Serbia, because they knew Tito was trying to crush the people. Every ideal he extolled seemed to them deception. And they could never forget that every step Tito had taken was of a political nature, designed to secure the domination of a totalitarian minority.

In 1941, he had raised the red flag and insisted on a separate Partisan army; in 1942, he had set up a tentative Partisan government; in 1943, he had set up what purported to be a permanent Partisan government; in 1944, he had won international support for the junking of the old Yugoslav state in its entirety. Tito had moved unflinchingly and unswervingly toward the goal of coercive political domination over all Yugoslavia including Serbia. On the first day of the struggle Tito had opened the civil war; to the last day he pursued it. It was he who took the initiative in destroying Yugoslav unity, in setting Yugoslavs against Yugoslavs and in pulverizing Yugoslav resistance to Germany. The Serbs of Serbia recognized that challenge and accepted it. They accepted the civil war and did everything possible to win it, regardless of consequences. That became their war aim number one.

And it inevitably led to actions that helped the enemy; it forced Mihailovitch into a method of fighting that amounted to collaboration. From the middle of 1943, Tito devoted his main energy to fighting Serbs and used his main forces in fighting Serbs. But in order to maintain a base of operation and to extend a freed area in which his regime could function as a state, he found it necessary, also, to fight Germans. Furthermore, to win the support of the Western powers and to obtain supplies from them, he had to fight Germans. Also he foresaw that the future place of every nation or group in postwar Moscow-dominated eastern Europe would be formally determined in accordance with the group's contribution to the war against the Nazis or "against Fascism." "Anti-Fascism" was to be the official card of admission, so Tito worked for such a certificate. It was like a birth certificate in an "Aryan" land, or in states with a "grandfather clause." This means Tito was fighting Germans some but Serbs much more and was calling them both Fascists. He put them all in one category. As a result of this action, both Germans and Serbs opposed Tito; and, in so doing, the Serbs, who were trying to defend Serbia, resorted to a form of collaboration.

To blink such a fact would be to distort history. That sort of cooperation marked many a battle. I am not saying that Mihailovitch consulted with any German commander, nor am I intimating that there were jointly planned campaigns or even jointly planned battles. Nor did Mihailovitch cease to resist Germans when they encroached on his freed area. But he knew where all German forces were stationed, and he knew in a Partisan-German clash exactly where and how each group would operate. Consequently, he struck his blows against Partisans where and when and as he thought they would be most effective. He certainly supplemented German action against the Partisans. For instance, the Germans didn't like to fight

Yugoslav guerrillas at night; they preferred the day shift. But Mihailovitch's Chetniks were good night fighters and often followed up where the Germans left off. That both Chetniks and German forces often fought against the same Partisan band in the same engagement is so widely and publicly known that to question it would be absurd. And that the Chetniks based many of their operations on this kind of fighting is beyond doubt. Was any other action conceivable as Tito in pressing his civil war attempted to seize Serbia and aroused the Serbs fanatically to resist! Civil wars in the midst of national wars always cause collaboration with a foreign enemy.

Now we may ask, did Mihailovitch collaborate with Serbia's Pétain, General Milan Neditch, Hitler's agent in Belgrade? Yes, his actions amounted to collaboration. I do not believe that Mihailovitch saw Neditch and drew up a common plan, but that Neditch's people and Mihailovitch's people constantly worked together is certain. Neditch's administration was honeycombed with Mihailovitch's men. Mihailovitch actually ran Serbia. At first Neditch vigorously and violently opposed this, but later I think was glad to be a sort of channel for facilitating Mihailovitch's hold on Serbia. Both Neditch's state forces and Mihailovitch's Chetniks fought Partisans, who were trying to occupy Serbia. Naturally they cooperated. They had one common aim, namely, to save Serbia from the Communists, and this aim was shared by most Serbs in Serbia. In a Serbian mountain battle against the Partisans, General Neditch's soldiers were in one sector and Mihailovitch's Chetniks in another and an agreement between the local commanders was very probable.

Also, most of Neditch's gendarmes were friendly with the Chetniks, as were a majority of the district or county governors, almost the whole administration, all the trained personnel, practically every teacher, and most of the judges. Very few Serbs in Yugoslavia approved of Neditch's vicious radio and press tirades against the Allies, and Mihailovitch sharply and constantly condemned him, as an enemy, but most Serbs in Serbia were united in trying to use Neditch's connections with the Germans for Serbia's advantage. Through Neditch's administration the Serbs got guns, ammunition, money, provisions, and placed them at Mihailovitch's disposal.

The overwhelming majority of the Serbs were intuitively or consciously led by a common aim, namely, to preserve Serbia from the Communist-led Partisans, and most of them worked together for its realization. If any Neditch man betrayed a Chetnik, Mihailovitch wreaked swift and terrible vengeance. And from Neditch propaganda most Serbians held aloof. But in practical matters, state officials and Chetniks worked hand in hand, and a Mihailovitchist always expected help from a Neditch policeman or soldier. This relationship was one of the means by which Mihailovitch was able to exercise control over practically the whole of Serbia, excepting only the larger cities. To ask if the people of Mihailovitch collaborated with the people of Neditch is almost like asking if the Serbians of Serbia collaborated with themselves for what they thought was national survival. They did.

Did they also collaborate with Italians? The Serbs of Serbia didn't, because there was no occasion or channel, but some "Across-the-river" Serbs in western Yugoslavia did; most of them secretly and with shame, a few openly and with arrogance. This is proven beyond all possible doubt. This collaboration arose and was continued in the following way. The two million Orthodox Serbs in the western Yugoslav provinces, sharing those lands with Croatians and Moslem Slavs, were more terribly persecuted than any other national group of that size in Europe except the Jews. They were killed by Germans, Italians, Moslems, and Ustasha Croatians. And later the nationally conscious members of the Serb communities were attacked by Tito's Partisans. The ring of persecution was complete.

Every avenue of escape was closed. The only choice left for many Serbs was extermination or an appeal for mercy to the least cruel or least fanatical or least efficient enemy. That was Italy. Literally, many Serbs in Montenegro, Herzegovina, and Dalmatia fled to Italian prison camps to save their lives. They preferred captivity at the hands of the Italians to death at the hands of brothers. As most persons who have been condemned to death feel a great relief when their sentence is commuted to life imprisonment, so Serbs who escaped from Yugoslav bullets to the comparative security of Italian prisons felt relieved. The Italian enemy came to seem almost a savior.

Compared with Moslem, Ustasha, and Partisan executioners, some Italians appeared as friends. The civil war, as is usually the case in civil war, had become more vicious and deadly than the interstate war between Italy and Serbia. To an anti-Communist, "Across-the-river" Serb, an Italian was more nearly a brother than was an armed Ustasha or Partisan.

Also, in the past, Italians and Serbs had not been especially hostile to each other. In the last war they were allies. The Queen of Italy was the daughter of the former Montenegrin King and a cousin of the late Serbian King Alexander. Furthermore, there had been a tendency among some Serb nationalists to consider Italy a sort of counterpoise for nationalistic Croats. In any case, Italy was considered a secondary enemy by many Serbs and in the moment of extreme peril they sought Italian protection.

Also, by a kind of military black market and perhaps blackmail, the Serbian nationalists obtained from the Italians arms, medicaments, munitions, and supplies in exchange for a sort of security agreement. Cops and robbers have been known to play a somewhat similar game. As emperors and fuehrers and duces and premiers made their deals on a grand, world-shaking plane, little, local Serbian undergrounders made their deals with Italians for arms, food, a pair of shoes, and a bed in a hospital.

That led to cooperation and some Serbs worked and fought beside the Italians against the Partisans. They helped introduce Italians deeper and deeper into Yugoslavia and tended to strengthen Italy's position in the Balkans. Some Chetnik leaders openly associated with Italian army officers and some Serbs used Italian weapons to kill

Partisans, who might have killed our enemy, the Germans. Beyond dispute, some members of the Serbian nation, our ally, were giving aid and comfort to our enemy, Italy.

Into such a deplorable situation had Serbia been maneuvered by events. Most nationalistic Serbs were distressed by this development, but felt they were caught inextricably in the coils of fate. The Serbs almost alone had turned Yugoslavia against Hitler, and they had borne the main brunt of Hitler's ferocious blows. They had done this to preserve Serbian independence, Serbian honor, and Serbia's place in a free world. But as a result they had lost everything, including world esteem. Croatia, which vigorously helped the German Nazis, seemed destined to be favored. Bulgaria, which was an active ally of Hitler, was slated for Allied preferences. The Serbs were eventually to lose their liberty and their unity, even after they had lost their lives in droves. Through five hundred years they had refused to accept the totalitarianism of Islam, and now they refused to accept the totalitarianism of Communism, even though that refusal meant giving aid to foreign enemies, thus making Serbs traitors in the eyes of their great allies!

Dark beyond measure was the night of those Serbs. The furious storms of war seemed to have swept them beyond the pale of their onward-fighting, upward-fighting friends. Russia began to win great victories. America was pouring out hope, marvelous weapons, and terrific armies. Heroic Britain was ending her period of defeats, and all the United Nations were about to move toward an epochal triumph. But as the very victory march was being prepared, near the head of which the Serbs had hoped to march, they were being denounced by the highest Allied tribunals as traitors. After being smashed by the Nazis, massacred in groups by the Ustashas, and executed in large numbers by the Partisans, the Serbs were being rejected by their great allies. Serb nationalists have wept as they told me of that. But even in their tears they were determined at all costs to continue to resist Communism.

Naturally, Tito's Partisans profited from these developments. Wisely taking advantage of a stupendous historical storm, they let the winds blow full into their sails and drive them steadily toward power. They were fighting beside the Allies against common enemies and were being acclaimed as the bearers of the flag of liberty. However, it is well to ask whether they also were not collaborating with the Nazis. I would say that they were not actively or specifically cooperating, but that after the fall of 1943, they accommodated themselves to the enemy in order to be free to pursue their civil war.

In a general sense, almost everything they did gave aid to Hitler. If they had not launched their civil war and broken Yugoslav resistance in two, the Balkan front against Hitler would have been much stronger. If they had not prevented a common resistance front from Bulgaria to the Adriatic, Yugoslavia would have been able to contribute much more to the Allied cause. If they had not used so large a proportion of Allied weapons and supplies for killing Serbs and had not directed so many American-British air attacks against their political opponents, rather than against the Germans, Hitler's armies would have suffered more. It goes without saying that if Communist Partisans had formed a special army and an independent political regime in the U.S.A., they would have hampered our war efforts, divided our loyalties, and given aid to the enemy. In that broad sense, the Yugoslav Communists actively and constantly collaborated with Hitler. Whoever provokes civil war in wartime "collaborates."

Similarly, by trying to invade and dominate Serbia the Partisans weakened permanent Serbian resistance to the Germans. Whatever faults or virtues the Serbs may have, one quality is certain; namely, their persistent opposition to all foreign encroachment, including that of the Germans. Among all the Balkan peoples, including the Hungarians, Rumanians, Bulgarians, Croatians, Turks, and even Greeks, the Serbs have most persistently opposed Germany's expansion into southeast Europe. That was one reason why Hitler encouraged Pavelitch's Ustashas to massacre Serbs. And Tito broadened that German-inspired crusade against Serbia. Thereby he directly strengthened Germany, thus aiding the enemy.

But that is not all. I wish to emphasize more specific aspects of Tito's relations with Axis armies in Yugoslavia. During certain periods and in certain areas he heroically fought the Germans, for which he deserves gratitude and praise. But after Hitler had stabilized the situation subsequent to Italy's collapse, in 1943, Tito and his Partisans observed an unwritten but no less real truce with the German occupiers. There was accommodation on most Partisan-Nazi fronts. Tito, by his action, said, If the Germans won't attack us, we won't attack them. If they'll leave us free to build up our Party, strengthen our administration and wage war against the Serbs, we'll leave them alone.

What is the proof of this accommodation? In the first place there was actual traffic between the two sides. On certain occasions captives and commodities were swapped across lines as in the gallant feudal battles, in the good old days of chivalry. Secondly, Partisan underground routes were often left unmolested by German patrols. A Partisan could pass from region to region in much safety as long as he left the enemy undisturbed. Partisan patrols made a point of not meeting Nazi patrols and vice versa.

More important than either of these comparatively small matters, the stable war front of the Partisans over against the Nazis shows how completely they accommodated themselves to the presence of German armies. If one should carefully read Partisan war bulletins and draw a German-Partisan battle line at the end of each month he would discover that that line was practically the same for the full year preceding November, 1944. In almost all cases the same towns are mentioned and we find the Partisans repeatedly taking the same places they had already taken. They stood in one place. Their aim was to build up a military-political force for seizing power in Yugoslavia, and they didn't want to weaken it by fighting with Germans. Both sides were busy elsewhere and were glad to observe that unspoken truce on most occasions.

Even more striking than the stability of the Partisan lines over against the Germans was the terrific energy and fanatical persistence with which the Partisans attacked Serbs in areas having little or no strategic importance for the Germans. The Partisans left the German vital supply lines largely undisturbed as the Germans fought Americans in Italy, while the Nazis left the Partisan rear quiet as the Partisans attacked Serbs in Serbia, Montenegro, and the Sandjak. And in fighting Serbs the Partisans used American weapons that should have been killing Germans. That was all Partisan aid and comfort to the enemy. A German was quite comforted when he heard a Partisan shooting Serbs with an American howitzer that was designed to be shooting Germans.

In addition to all these palpable facts contained in Partisan bulletins, persons who followed Partisan activities at first hand during 1944, report that in certain Partisan corps headquarters where American goods were most liberally sent, the Partisan commanders refused to use them in offensives against Germans, but saved them for the subjugation of Serbia.

I do not mean to intimate that the Partisans never fought Germans. They did and bravely. That was a vital part of their revolutionary struggle for power. But it was a preliminary part, a preparatory stage. When that phase of the revolutionary struggle was completed, as it was long before the war against Germany ended, the Communist-led Partisans left the main Yugoslav, anti-Nazi front almost as quiet as Mihailovitch did. Tito's civil war had brought about a situation where the main enemies of all Yugoslavs were other Yugoslavs and in which our Yugoslav allies used most of their energies and most of our supplies and most of the bombs of our air squadrons for the Balkans in killing Yugoslavs, thus leaving the Germans freer to kill Americans, British, and Russians. Old internecine Yugoslav hatreds partly caused this civil war, but the chief responsibility rests upon Tito. It was a sad picture and for generations will cause endless chagrin to the Serbs. But already most responsible leaders in most western lands have come to agree that Imperial Communism has become the world's greatest menace. The verdict of history will probably be that Mihailovitch saw earlier what other honest, wise men saw later, and that under his circumstances, most Americans or Britishers would have considered Tito's **Communism enemy number one.**

CHAPTER SIXTEEN

Britain Throws Its Support to Tito

DURING the month of May, 1943, the British Army sent a brave, intelligent, conscientious young Major, William Deakin, to serve as a liaison with the Partisans. Already Tito, with Russia's help, had set up a system of communications and was daily telling Yugoslavia and the outside world of his operations. Also, his Anti-Fascist Council had been functioning for many months as an incipient government, and the daring of Tito's activities, as well as their extent, had much impressed the British, who were vitally interested in Yugoslavia.

Tito's Partisans had a double significance for Great Britain. In the first place, they were fighters and the English welcomed the cooperation of every fighter who would kill a German. Secondly, they were led by Russian-trained Communists, and Britain was not pleased by Russian encroachment in Yugoslavia. Plainly, if Tito succeeded in his efforts to dominate Yugoslavia, and if he felt himself inseparably attached to Russia, he would deliver the shores of the Adriatic to the chief rival of the British Empire. As a matter of fact, Mr. Churchill had hoped to launch a major Anglo-American offensive in southeast Europe for the purpose of preventing such a Russian advance toward the Mediterranean, but Mr. Roosevelt had frustrated the plan. The Western Allies were preparing their main blows for other sectors, thereby forcing Churchill to leave the whole Balkan Peninsula wide open to Russia. During 1943, Russian armies were so busy themselves they were not able to take advantage of the opportunity, but Tito's Partisans appeared to be preparing the way for them.

Having that possibility in view, the British set out to win Tito for themselves. They hoped the Partisans would kill Germans and help liberate Yugoslavia for England, while Moscow felt sure the Partisans would kill Germans and help liberate Yugoslavia for Russia. Churchill entered ardently into this contest with Stalin for the soul of Tito, but it proved to be no contest whatsoever. Churchill never had a chance. He was deceiving himself. Tito's loyalties were as firm and as fixed as the stars. He considered England, with its Tory chief, his mortal enemy. It took the British Premier two years to become convinced of that. It is hard for British imperialists to understand Balkan character and, most of all, Communists.

When Major William Deakin dropped into Yugoslavia, he found Tito terribly hard pressed by the Germans who were at that moment engaged in one of their most elaborate and determined anti-Partisan drives. Tito was retreating under furious fire, in which both he and Deakin were eventually wounded and a number of leading Partisans were killed. However, the survivors extricated themselves very adroitly, reorganized their forces and continued their activity with undiminished resolution. Deakin, who is one of Britain's noblest and most idealistic empire defenders, was impressed both by the Partisans' valor and by their revolutionary ardor. He was thrilled to find men fighting the common enemy, as he saw them doing with his own eyes, and he was inspired to see fanatical men and women making what he thought would be a brave new world.

In both of these emotions, Deakin was very sincere. The extent and vigor of his longing for world improvement were illustrated by the results of the 1945 elections in Great Britain. I am not intimating that he voted the Labor ticket, but he shared many of the social aspirations of those who did. He was tired of old evils. He wanted a new Jerusalem. He was delighted by the boldness of the

Yugoslavs, whom he pictured to himself not as saving an old empire but as shooting into being a grand new social order. I found hundreds of responsible Britishers with that same adoration for the bloody Yugoslav builders of a coercive new regime. Naturally, Deakin sent his great chief in London glowing reports about the Partisans.

Naturally, also, he heard from Tito, not only thrilling reports about the Partisans, but very derogatory things about Mihailovitch and the Chetniks and the Serb nationalists. He saw, too, that as the Partisans retreated into Montenegro they were not only pressed by the German armies and Croatian Ustashas, but were harassed by Mihailovitch's men, against whom the Partisans had been waging civil war for about two years. Deakin personally saw the internecine strife in all its horror, and he perceived that it was weakening Yugoslav resistance. He was also told that the Serb nationalists were collaborating with the Italians. Direct from Tito's camp, therefore, as well as from other sources, the British government got the impression that among the Yugoslavs the Partisans alone were helping the Allied cause while Mihailovitch was hindering it.

In consequence, Churchill sharply ordered Mihailovitch to make his men cease working with the Italians and begin more active operations against the invaders. By the end of 1943, Churchill's relations with the Serbian nationalists had become so strained that he began openly and officially to call them traitors. He threw all his moral and spiritual support to the Partisans, and in January, 1944, he induced General Dushan Simovitch, a Serb from Serbia and the Premier of the revolutionary anti-Nazi Yugoslav government of March 27, 1941, to broadcast from London a message to the Serbian nation, urging it to join Tito. This was a categorical and sensational repudiation of Mihailovitch and of Serbia. The cycle of Serbian disaster was almost complete.

When Great Britain stood alone in 1941, little Serbia went to her aid. When little Serbia stood alone, in 1943, surrounded, partitioned, and invaded, Great Britain turned against her.

Churchill's government attempted to weaken the Serbian national spirit, to deprive Serbs of faith in their traditional patriotism, and to fill them with confusion. The greatest defender in modern times of traditional British loyalty, who was trying to preserve not only England but the whole Empire including Hong Kong, tried to break down the Serbs' love of Serbia and inveigle or force them to drown in Tito's torrent of totalitarianism.

The great British leader bitterly and publicly reproached Serbia in the British Parliament. Over the B.B.C. London radio, that could be heard in every Serbian village, Yugoslav orators of rare eloquence and flaming ardor scolded and cajoled Serbs and implored them to join Tito. The British station at Cairo took up the anti-Serbian refrain, Bari (Italy) chimed in, Jerusalem added its voice, and during every listening hour the most resourceful propagandists in the British world besieged Serbia with a barrage of words, calling the hard-working, self-respecting, home-owning peasants traitors, Fascists, and war criminals and ordering them to hasten and join Tito.

To that drum fire, stopping neither by day nor by night, was added the frequent and stentorian voice of Russia, sent from Moscow and Tiflis. Other Slavs swelled the chorus at impressive, all-Slav congresses and called upon Serbia to leave its ways of sin, reject Fascism, stop serving Hitler, and return to the Slavic fold. In Moscow were held all-Slav congresses; in London were held all-Slav congresses; in New York were held all-Slav congresses—which with one voice in the name of democracy, freedom, honor, and the century of the common man, urged Serbia to gather at the altar with her Slav brothers or be thrust into eternal darkness, where there would be weeping and gnashing of teeth.

Try for a moment to imagine a Serbian peasant—85 per cent of the Serbs are peasants—in a Shumadiyan village, at the end of an evening, at his radio. He has long been sad and discouraged. He has lost a son in the war against Hitler. Another son is a war prisoner in Germany. A son-in-law was killed fighting Partisans. He has two Serbian refugees in his home who managed to survive the Ustasha massacre in Croatia and fled to Serbia for safety. He has personally, and at the risk of his life, helped free an American aviator who landed near his village. He kept the aviator in his crowded house for two weeks, brought a doctor from a town fifteen miles distant to treat a sprained ankle, and finally took the aviator by night to Mihailovitch's camp from which he would be delivered to the American Army.

But this peasant in his cares and dangers hears over the radio that he's a traitor and a Fascist. He has always had great admiration—although little love—for England and now the British radio is calling him a knave. He has admired Roosevelt above almost all other men, not excluding his own King—but Roosevelt has forgotten Serbia and says not one word in her defense. This peasant has considered Russia his second fatherland and second motherland, but Russia now denounces him without restraint. He thought he was the banner-carrier of Slavdom on its most dangerous frontier, but now the Slavs of the world call him a deserter and enemy agent.

He never read a dozen books in his life, but he is well informed on world affairs and knows what Churchill has said about Communism and the Soviets. With a little more prescience he could have foreseen what Churchill would say even about Socialism in a coming election campaign. Indeed, he did foresee that, for when all of Churchill's impassioned propagandists, around the clock and around the compass, urged this simple Shumadiyan Serbian peasant to accept Communist Tito and his Communist Comrades, the peasant sadly said to his wife, "Churchill thinks Communism is good enough for us, but I bet he'd die before joining the ranks of a Tito in England." Millions of other Serbs said the same thing in bitterness and sorrow. They knew that Churchill's propagandists were lying to Serbians and trying to use Serbia for foreign interests.

At the moment when Serbia's morale was lowest and her spiritual defenses most nearly shattered, the greatest nations of the earth and Serbia's only friends upon the globe turned upon her one of the most terrible propaganda assaults to which any people has ever been subjected. The fury of that word tempest, shrieking through many transmitters and raging from tract-dropping bombers, seemed to blow Serbia, as Hagar, into a bleak and barren wilderness, where she was despised by Slavdom and denounced by the democracies. And all because she wouldn't accept the lordship of Communists, coming with guns and bombs and bayonets.

But the Serbs withstood the storm. Not only Mihailovitch, not only long-bearded Chetniks with guns on their shoulders, but the people. The common people. The papas and mamas, the sons and daughters. The men who fed pigs, the women who milked cows, the girls sickling wheat beside the river, widows lighting candles in churches for men who died to stop Hitler—they resisted this global intimidation. Future generations and centuries will look back on this propaganda drive against Serbia as a strange and marvelous spectacle. This little man at his Thermopylae, holding the pass of human freedom against friend and foe, this Serbian peasant who had learned of history from folk songs and of liberty from the trees and rocks and brooks and birds on his twenty-acre farm, stood alone before fierce Bulgarians, ruthless Germans, murderous Ustasha butchers, ferocious Partisans, mighty Britain, stupendous Russia—and defied them all. He refused to bow his head or bend his knee to Communist tyrants. And, sad at heart, he lit a little homemade candle in the church upon the hill, which his fathers had protected from Moslem hordes, and vaguely hoped that God and Serbia's past would alleviate his loneliness.

His act was not mere Serbian stubbornness nor the caprice of a wild man of the wooded hills. It came from the heart of Serbian history. It was elemental loyalty to all that a free man cherishes. It was the unwavering voice of fifteen generations. It was the imperious asseveration of battles and of wars, of graveyards and of church bells, of sowing times and harvests, of weddings and of births, of prayers at meals. It was the wisdom and the will gained by a free man in his own ancestral home, as part of a self-governing community. What spoke was five centuries of Serbian traditions and five centuries of Serbian faith.

These Serbs had won their homes and fields, their altars and their self-respect by war and work and loyalty. So they knew what freedom was. They were not supine tools of British might or Muscovite expansion. They were the masters of their hills and of their souls. Because they were, they had spurned Adolf Hitler. And because they were, they spurned all other foreign masters, even to Josip Broz-Tito and his mighty sponsors. They did not accept the blackmail. They refused to be terrorized. They allowed no spiritual night to sink into their souls.

But other things more substantial than the shades of darkness showered upon them and their children. These were bombs from Allied planes. More Serbian mothers and babies were killed by Allied than by German bombs. We Americans and the Britishers filled more mass graves with Serbians than did the enemy pilots. And we did it in a vicious civil war only slightly connected with our fight against the Nazis. Our planes, made by Americans to destroy Nazi soldiers and carrying bombs manufactured in American factories to smash the German war machine, were repeatedly used to kill Serbian women and children in civilian, residential areas. The American nation for a period allowed the Communist, Josip Broz-Tito, to direct a part of its magnificent and terrible air fleet, including pilots from American homes, against our Serbian allies. More than one gold star sadly gleams today from American windows because American boys were sent by a Croatian Communist revolutionist to bomb the wives and babies of his political opponents, who were striving to save their homes and fields and churches from Communist totalitarianism.

One of the examples was the double bombing of Belgrade on successive Easter days. Balkan Orthodox Christians, among whom the Serbs are numbered, celebrate three Easter days each spring. In 1944 their Easter came in April; and on the third Sunday of that month, the Belgradians in the best clothes they could buy or make, or the least shabby they had managed to preserve, set out for church. Normally Serbs talk of their church more than they serve it and are not distinguished by faithful attendance at Sunday morning services. But on holidays they make a point of gathering before their altars, in the presence of eikons of sad-faced saints, and of reverently hearing long masses sung by bearded priests. Since Easter is their greatest holiday, both earthly and celestial reasons draw most Serbs to church to share in its celebration.

In the spring of 1944, the attendance was unprecedentedly great because of grief and hopes, because of solicitude for war prisoners, intense worries about Serbia's future, and the belief that this might be Serbia's last war Easter. On "Resurrection Day" the Serbians greet each other with the exclamation, "Christ is risen!" and answer one another by saying, "He is risen, indeed." The name for the day is "Uskrs," meaning resurrection, and it seems radiant and bright after the preceding Friday's realistic celebration of the crucifixion and burial of Christ, usually lasting far into the night. As the Belgrade Serbs anticipated that approaching Sunday morning which would briefly swallow up their darkness and wipe away their tears, as they expectantly envisioned flowers and fragrance and sparkling priestly vestments and imagined their capital about to echo with joyous exclamations about an arisen Saviour, they allowed themselves also to believe that Serbia herself would soon arise and bring their sons, husbands, and brothers home again.

This was a most special celebration of the most special Serbian holiday, and as the morning church bells blended in a pleasing antiphony, sounding from one part of Belgrade to another, the streets of Serbia's capital filled with people. Among them were many men, with the aged predominating over youth, but a majority were women and children because three hundred thousand Serbian men were held as forced laborers or detained in prison camps. Belgrade that Easter morning was predominantly a day of mothers and their children.

Suddenly, as the movement on the streets was at its height, the sound of rapidly approaching planes was heard. Belgrade still showed hideous, yawning wrecks from the terrible German air attack of Palm Sunday, 1941, so that the drone of Sunday airplane motors brought terrifying memories. However, that first feeling of horror quickly vanished, for the great birds above were friendly planes. They were Allied planes. Indeed, they were American bombers that Roosevelt, the great champion of liberty, had sent from across the seas to crush the tyrants. It was like an American Easter greeting to an isolated nation, a harbinger of approaching resurrection. The Serbs felt proud to be allies of the pilots of that mighty armada sweeping through the skies to kill their enemies. They waved as they stood gazing at the Easter birds above them and from their hearts they cried, "Christ is risen!"

And the airplanes gave lightning answers with their most deadly bombs. They dumped their loads on the civilian quarters of Belgrade and flew back to their base in Italy. They poured death and ruin on their Serbian allies. Whole residential blocks were instantly reduced to rubble with hundreds of people beneath the wreckage. Blood trickled out from under twisted girders. Heartbreaking cries replaced the Easter songs. The Friday of crucifixion and interment had come again, and wailing filled the skies, as mothers in spite of their wounds strove to disinter their children.

There was no military object in the vicinity. No German garrison or post was near. No vital line of communication approached the area. No factory or workshop turned out war material there. It was one of the most exclusively non-military, residential districts in the country and the Easter raid turned out to be a massacre of America's defenceless allies.

But in the abysmal sorrow that fell upon the Serbs, there was more bewilderment than bitterness and almost no malevolence. The Belgradians saw it was a useless slaughter, bringing carnage to the innocent and leaving the enemy untouched, but they could not believe Americans were deliberately trying to kill Serbian civilians. They laid the holocaust to some awful blunder.

All that long, sad day the Serbs dug the bodies of relatives from the ruins of their houses. And all during the sad night that followed they still dug for loved ones in the mountains of rubbish that once were bright, intimate homes. Tears of almost unbearable sorrow flowed down their cheeks at the thought that Americans had added this blow to the others which had befallen them. As the church bells of the second Easter morning tolled a sorrowful dirge over the city and a multitude of men dug mass graves for the mutilated bodies that lay in crude, handmade coffins in improvised morgues, again the sound of planes was heard over the city and again American bombers appeared in the sky. This time the people fled in terror. But whither could they flee? The rushing about was just a vain and futile panic. Again the bomb crates unloaded, again death showered down on residential Belgrade. Houses leaped up in clouds of dust and splinters. Women and children were blotted out. To what had seemed almost endless rows of little coffins for little Serbian boys and girls were added other dozens and scores. The mass graves were made to yawn deeper and wider; the long lines of the bereaved were lengthened. The coffins were lowered, one upon the other as cord wood in a warehouse, and mounds of earth were piled upon them. Grass has grown upon those mounds, flowers fringe them round and each All-Souls Day Serbs gather to light candles and shed tears before the piles of women and children killed by Serbia's American ally. Someday, when true freedom comes, American tourists will wander through Belgrade cemeteries and will ask about those strange, grass-covered, flower-rimmed hillocks, and for many generations Serbs will sorrowfully say, "Those are the graves of Serbian women and children that American boys massacred at Easter time in 1944."

And these Serbian tourist guides may also recall, I hope without bitterness, that after those bombings Tito's radio broadcasters sternly ordered Serbs to stay out of Belgrade because it might be bombed again. He warned the Belgradians that if they wanted to save themselves they must seek refuge in the country.

Could anything more clearly explain the reason for that Easter air massacre in residential Belgrade? Was that not a wanton act in Tito's civil war, performed by American boys mistakenly in the service of a foreign Communist, using our army to impose totalitarian slavery upon an ally? Was it not a terror raid, added to the constant propaganda bombings, all designed to break down Serbian resistance? Were not we doing to Serbs who defied totalitarian Tito exactly what Nazi pilots had done three years earlier to those same Serbs for defying totalitarian Hitler?

And Belgrade was not the only target for such air attacks. Time after time Tito propagandists of British and of Slav origin, speaking over the B.B.C. London radio, announced that Allied fliers from Italian bases were peppering Yugoslavia "under Marshal Tito's directions." We Allies hit the places he told us to hit and killed the people he told us to kill. There was no equivocation about it. Britain's official radio told the world that our Allied air armadas were in the service of a Communist revolutionist carrying on civil war.

Behold now two other places that we Allies smashed for Tito. One is the city of Podgoritsa, the second largest settlement in barren Montenegro, situated "at the end of the world" on the wild fringe of Yugoslavia where it meets still wilder Albania. It was on no railroad line except a meager ten-mile road running to the shores of an inland lake. Montenegro is practically without railroads and has no vestige of a main line. Podgoritsa was not an arsenal or a port or a military center, though it contained a German garrison. It was a provincial residential city, serving an isolated province far from all the main scenes of global strife. Its only importance was that it lay on a route from Yugoslavia into Albania, though it was by no means the key to a pass or gorge. It lay amid a fairly level plain, one of the few in Montenegro.

For Tito, however, it had much significance, because it steadfastly repulsed the Partisans. It was an anti-Communist center and hindered Tito in the pursuance of his civil war. Many of Tito's political and military leaders were Montenegrins, as, for example, his Chief of Staff. One of his major corps of Partisans was stationed in Montenegro, and it was commanded by one of his most ambitious chiefs, who was determined to become master of Belgrade and all Serbia. To feed and clothe and arm this Partisan force, the Allies had sent hundreds of air sorties over the Black Mountains, dropping provisions and guns. But in spite of this, the Partisans could not even open a lane of transport to the coast near by, in order to get more supplies, nor could they occupy the principal Montenegrin towns. They held only the wilder areas of a wild land. Podgoritsa stood out resolutely against them, a stronghold of anti-totalitarianism, a main center of the moderate, responsible, frugal, religious Montenegrin people, such as had given eternal glory to the little mountain land. They were what Marxists so scornfully call the bourgeoisie. They were such people as had kept Montenegro free from Turkey and made it the pride of Slavdom, such as had performed its epic deeds and written its epic songs. They were now making a brave stand against their own totalitarian brothers such as their fathers had long made against the totalitarian sultans. Strange to say, some renegade Montenegrins whose fathers had helped the sultans were now helping the Partisans. A few of the chief Communists were from Podgoritsa.

Nevertheless, the Podgoritsans held out. Tito's armies, which were going to help take Berlin, couldn't even take little Podgoritsa at their own back door. So Tito called on his Western Allies to help. A mighty air blow was arranged, a powerful bomb-carrying armada hopped from Italy over the black Montenegrin peaks and razed Podgoritsa. A little Nazi garrison was smashed, a few German guardsmen were killed, and many hundreds of Yugoslavs were murdered. An Allied city was swept off the map, Allied women and children lay dead beneath the debris, Allied arms and legs and heads were strewn about, an anti-totalitarian stronghold was erased and Partisans in Italy, eating at tables that Americans provided and wearing clothes Americans furnished, joyfully drank red wine and happily congratulated one another on a great victory over the enemy—a Yugoslav enemy in a civil war. What the sultans could never do and the Axis could not do, the Western Allies were helping Tito to accomplish, namely, to impose totalitarian enslavement on Montenegro.

On those superb bare heights there were other sturdy towns that had not bowed to Communist-led Partisans. One such was Nikshich, nestling in Montenegro's west central ranges. It had no industries, housed no arsenal, turned out no war materials, had no military warehouses, was not a center of Nazi military operations, was scores of miles from the nearest railway line, and was on no main road. It contained a small German post and was inhabited by eight thousand Yugoslavs, of whom nine-tenths were Montenegrin Serbs. The humble homes, lining drab, badly paved streets, contained poor people that had struggled hard through all the generations to get enough to eat, to wear, and with which honorably to present themselves before their altars, their elders, and their consciences. However, poor as the Nikshich people were, they loved freedom, had a strong sense of responsibility, and opposed totalitarian Communism. Therefore they resisted the Partisans. Partisan "divisions" operated near by, scouring the country for its last meager provisions, but as Partisan chiefs told eager American journalists of freeing half Yugoslavia, they couldn't free modest little Nikshich, in sight of their military headquarters. That is, Tito couldn't "free" Yugoslav Nikshich from its Yugoslav inhabitants.

So he called on his allies and an annihilating air expedition was arranged. Instructions were given by Tito's liaison men, pilots of American and British airplanes were briefed, bombs made in American and British war factories were loaded onto the fleet, and off flew boys from the western democracies to wipe little Nikshich from the face of the earth. The hop took less time than is required for an ordinary American commuter to get to his office, and with the whir of motors, the pressing of buttons, and the pulling of triggers, Nikshich and its inhabitants were smashed. A tiny company of third-rate Axis guardsmen were killed or taken or put to flight, mass graves in Yugoslav graveyards were filled with our Yugoslav allies, surviving children cried for dead mothers, surviving mothers wailed for dead children, Partisans closed in for the kill, or what was left of it, and the surviving Nikshichians sought new shelters as Allied radios told of destroying the enemy in Nikshich. The "enemy" were mostly Yugoslav women and children, who were opposed to Communist totalitarianism.

Crude little Nikshich in the mountains, modest Podgoritsa on a plain beside the Albanian border, and Belgrade, Serbia's white city on the Danube, all mourning for their dead and weeping amid their ruins, symbolize the significance of Allied support of Tito. When Yugoslavia's Communist revolutionists received the support of mighty democratic powers, the off-chance of a thousand years was realized. The perfect revolutionary situation was created. When Tito wanted guns to kill his political rivals, he merely shouted for guns to kill Germans. When he wanted to destroy Serbs, he just called them "the enemy" and the Allies ardently helped in the destruction. When he wanted to further Communism, he called it anti-Fascism and we rushed to his aid. When he wanted to popularize ruthless totalitarianism, he called it democracy and Americans placed an armada at his disposal. The more of our Serbian allies he killed, the longer was the list of "enemy" casualties he could announce over his radio and the more help he got to kill more Serbs. Tito could rest secure in his well-protected cave on well-protected Vis and inform his Western Allies how to expend their lives and substance in installing his totalitarian regime. He had Britain's Premier sending ministers to Vis, and when Britain's government invited Tito to visit a British Commander-in-Chief in Caserta and sent a boat to fetch him, Tito blandly spurned the General's offer and sent the boat back empty, as his Partisan Comrades laughed at "old man Winnie."

CHAPTER SEVENTEEN

We Plunge Deeper Into Yugoslavia's Civil War

DURING the spring of 1944, Mr. Churchill called the Yugoslav King, along with the exiled Yugoslav government, from Cairo back to London. The King hesitated to comply with the summons but was attracted to London by his sweet and gracious fiancée, who wanted to get married quickly. Peter wanted to get married, too. So he flew back to London, arriving on March 18. Six weeks later he fired his Prime Minister, Bozhidar Puritch, an uncompromising, anti-Tito Serb, whose chief quality was reactionary stubbornness. To perform that act Churchill had ordered young Peter to London.

The British Premier had reached the conclusion that Tito was going to be master of Yugoslavia and he wanted to salvage something from the old order, at least the throne. He planned definitely to discard Mihailovitch, along with all the Serbian ministers connected with him, after which he hoped to effect some kind of understanding between Tito and Peter. In other words, he wanted the youthful monarch to change his royal purple to a Communist red. It seemed rather evident even to casual observers that Tito wouldn't accept any king as master, least of all a Serbian Karageorge, the emblem of Serbian nationalism. However, Churchill believed he could make a deal.

In the negotiations that followed, the Croatian laborer Brozovitch played rings around the astute, gifted, and experienced Marlborough.

The head of a rather fictitious AVNOJ, leading a non-existent state, badly beat the Premier of a world empire. As Tito's Partisans ate British food and wore British uniforms, Tito himself imperturbably thumbed his nose at Great Britain's greatest hero.

His Majesty's First Minister repeatedly endured from a revolutionary refugee insults such as Britain's First Minister had not been accustomed to accept from any sovereign on earth. That was England's rich reward for helping Tito to power.

After the old Yugoslav cabinet was dismissed and Mihailovitch was thrust out in disgrace, Churchill persuaded King Peter to try to create an interim Yugoslav government that would establish good relations with Tito and prepare the way for a balanced Yugoslav regime, embracing all elements, from raging Communists to defiant Royalists. Churchill realized well enough that the Yugoslav oil and water, which he had been trying for three years to blend, had stubbornly refused to mix, but he thought this phenomenon was due to the special samples of Yugoslav oil and water he had on hand. So he asked for new specimens.

It is certain that the British government hoped to outmaneuver Tito and his Communists. Some Britishers, as many wishful-thinking Americans, tried to persuade themselves that the Yugoslav Communists were nice tame folks, really Abraham Lincolns at heart. They hoped to find similar varieties of nice tame Serb nationalists and gentle Croatian Agrarians with which they would concoct a nice coalition that would leave Tito in a minority. Churchill was going on the principle, "If you can't beat 'em, join 'em." He hoped to smother Tito's Partisans in an avalanche of supporters who would favor England.

Churchill's daily and nightly occupations certainly made him aware of what Adolf Hitler had done to a similar coalition in 1933, but Yugoslavia was a small state and Churchill had a King in his pack, so he hoped to outplay the obscure Balkan Piades and Brozovitches, recently out of jail. He understood the Balkanese little, the Communists still less. Tito is now complete and absolute master of his country as well as the big shot of all southeast Europe, while Churchill is sitting on an opposition bench even in his own England.

For the delicate task of decoying flocks of anti-Tito Yugoslavs about Tito, without his realizing what was going on, Mr. Churchill had King Peter choose a Croatian lawyer of much distinction, some ability, humble origin, and good character, Dr. Ivan Subashitch. He had been "Ban," or Governor, of Croatia and at that moment was in America. From Tito's point of view, it proved to be a perfect choice; from England's, a disaster; from Serbia's, a catastrophe. For a time, Subashitch was not only the new Yugoslav Prime Minister, but the whole official government. He could get no adequate Serbs from Serbia to serve him as Quislings and no Croatian democrats either. He ran over to Tito's Vis during the middle of June, 1944, and after long consultations fixed up a little rump cabinet, containing himself and another Croat, Dr. Juraj Shutej, along with an "Across-the-river" Serb, Dr. Sava Kosanovitch, and a Slovene diplomat, Professor Isidor Tsankar. Later Tito sent two quite anomalous members to the cabinet but refused to accept the slightest responsibility for their actions. One was a Slovene with an authoritarian record; the other a Sandjak Serb politician of minor importance, good intentions, and a weak character. These men were figureheads. They were the mites Tito had "chipped in" to Churchill's good will collection and Tito was ready to repudiate their every act. He had Mr. Churchill, going and coming. It was heads England loses, tails Tito wins.

The Subashitch "cabinet" was a diplomatic fiction, more futile even than it was false. Tito accepted it, for it served him as a ticket for British food, clothing, and munitions—mostly made in America.

After long negotiations between Tito and his comrades, on one side, and Subashitch and his frail partners, on the other, all taking place on the island of Vis, under British military protection and under the benevolent observation of a British Minister Plenipotentiary, a number of vital agreements were reached. They were announced as a step toward Yugoslav and Allied harmony, but in their implementation turned out to be no more than a plot against Serbia.

Some of the most important points reached were that Subashitch should funnel all possible Allied aid to Tito, that Tito's revolutionary AVNOJ should serve as the factual government of Yugoslavia, that Tito's army was to be recognized as the one fighting force in Yugoslavia, and that all Serbians were to be urged to join Tito. Also, the Yugoslav nation in Tito-controlled elections, which would be held in Tito's good time, was to decide whether or not it wanted King Peter back. Mr. Churchill had granted Tito every political concession he had asked for, and to make the measure full, pressed down and running over, Churchill had induced the young Yugoslav King to play the role of a Serbian "Lord Haw Haw." Peter consented and commanded his Serbian nation to enroll under Tito's banner, thereby repudiating Mihailovitch.

That was a spectacle for the centuries to behold! There were the hard-pressed Serbs under a barrage of anti-Serbian Allied propaganda, under a rain of anti-Serbian Allied bombs, under the guns of anti-Serbian Axis armies, under day and night attacks by Communist-led guerrillas, yet in the hour of most terrible anxiety, their king, champion, and protector, operating from a free land where he could make free decisions, ordered them to give up the fight and join the Communists. They felt he had so disgraced his throne in his efforts to save it that it wasn't worth saving. The kindest among the Serbs said, "Peter's treason was due to irresistible pressure." The more vehement among them cursed their king with the most obscene words in Serbia's vocabulary.

Churchill and his little royal charge had shot the works and after Peter had kissed Tito's feet they expected Tito to kiss King Peter's hand or at least shake it. For that ceremony the British had brought Peter to Malta and were planning to rush him to Allied Army

Headquarters at Caserta, Italy, whither Tito was also to repair. Then in the presence of high American and British generals, the King of Yugoslavia, the scion of the first Black George, who defied the Turkish Empire, would solemnly pledge allegiance to his subject Josip Brozovitch. The wine was ready, the banquet table was set, photographers were on the alert, the celebrities waited—but Marshal Tito didn't come. He said he had been told by the democratic Yugoslav people that they didn't want him to tarnish Yugoslav democracy by shaking hands with an effete king. Mr. Churchill uttered ferocious words, while Tito and his comrades on Vis celebrated their defiance with vulgar Yugoslav imprecations, and little King Haw Haw realized not only that he had hawhawed for nothing but that he had been unworthy of the least Shumadiyan peasant watching his herd of pigs in the woods.

However, the chief significance of the meetings at Vis between the Partisans and the Subashitch delegates under British tutelage was not that the Allies and their stooges had sold Yugoslavia to Tito for nothing, but that they together had plotted the subjugation of Serbia. To realize the full meaning of their conspiracy one must recall the men who met on Vis and see what they represented. The chief participants were Subashitch, a Croat; Tsankar, a Slovene; Kosanovitch, a furiously anti-Belgrade "Across-the-river" Serb; Tito, a Croat; Ribar, a Croat; Kardelj, a Slovene; Smodlaka, a Croat; and a number of Montenegrin Communists. Not one single representative of non-Communist Serbia was present. It was not a negotiation between two sides, because only one side was there. It was not an attempt at reconciliation and understanding, because only one party to the quarrel was called. It was Tito talking with his pals. They were not resolving a quarrel or planning Yugoslav harmony; they were plotting.

Their aim was to smash Serbia. As preparation for the meeting, Tito's agents had announced that Machek, head of the Croat Peasant Party, had come over to Tito with his whole party, meaning most of Croatia. To make this assertion the more convincing, the Partisans presented Magovats and Gazi, two authentic former members of the Croat Peasant Party, who actually were working with Tito. The Partisans also asserted that August Koshutitch, Machek's most faithful lieutenant, was on the way to Vis to join Tito. It was made to appear therefore that Croatia was behind the Partisans. Very fluent Slovene Communists and especially Tito's foremost associate, Edward Kardelj, assured Subashitch that all Slovenia was with the Partisans. The Slovenes were just raring to go. Montenegrin Communists, who were thicker than flies on Vis, assured the men from London that an anti-Partisan in Montenegro was a rarity, and "Tempo," the delegate from Macedonia, even more emphatically said that Macedonia was with Tito. All that was left was Serbia. All they had to do was to crush Serbia.

And they all agreed that now was the chance of a lifetime to do it. Serbia was alone and isolated. Russia was against her, England was against her, the King had fizzled, Mihailovitch was called a traitor, the huge United Nations propaganda apparatus was largely at Tito's disposal, and Allied agents, especially British, were working night and day to recruit Serbs for Tito. If Subashitch had been inclined to disbelieve that, he could read whole sheafs of reports from the British agents themselves.

In addition, Serbia was very weak. Nearly a quarter of a million Serbian men were in Germany as prisoners of war and forced laborers, mostly prisoners of war. They were there because of fighting Hitler. Also scores of thousands of men were pressed into forced work in Serbia, so they were out of the ranks of Serbian fighters. Then, too, the Serbian nation seemed groggy. It appeared bewildered and confused by the propaganda and conduct of the Allies. Then was the time to strike and strike hard. If Serbia succumbed the Partisans would be entrenched in power and the conspirators would be big shots all the rest of their lives.

The Croat Ribar, the President of AVNOJ, said, "Now's the time."

The Croat Tito said, "Now's the time." The Slovene Kardelj said, "Now's the time." The Communist Montenegrins chorused, "Now's the time." Tito's representative from Serbia, the veteran fanatical Communist, Mosha Piade, whom no Serbian Serb considered a Serb, said, "Now's the time." And King Peter's London government, led by the Croat Shubashitch, enthusiastically agreed that then was the time to smash Serbia once and for all. This all took place under British sponsorship. A British minister was on the island of Vis, acting as a sort of governess to the London Yugoslavs.

The Croatian-Communist Conference reached a unanimous agreement and set to work with the help of the great Allies to deliver the final blow to Serbia. Telling the world of their grand offensive "against the enemy," the Partisans directed practically all their blows at Serbia. Tito concentrated many of his forces in the Sandjak, which served as a base of operations. He sent a special staff, accompanied by Russian officers, into the area which he held in lower Serbia, and an American correspondent flew in to give him encouragement. Other Allied officers were there trying to break down Serbian unity. They acted as missionaries and tried to persuade Serbian peasants that the Anglo-Americans wanted them to join Tito.

When they appeared in a Serbian village wearing British battle dress and speaking for Americans and British, one can imagine the effect. America was then loved in every Serbian cottage and the British were still respected by Serbian peasants. Anglo-Saxons were thought to be good, just, honest people, above the intrigues of the Balkans. Popular Serbian proverbs told of American and British integrity. Anglo-Saxons were considered the models of fairness. They were "the people who didn't lie." The Serbs had even introduced the word "fair" into their language. Fair and Anglo-American were synonymous.

At that time a uniformed American or Britisher could appear anywhere in Serbia, outside of a few cities, and receive immediate protection, food, and medical care. He could actually ask help from a

Neditch policeman, without fear of betrayal. He could steal into Serbian saloons or inns five hundred yards from a German or Bulgarian post and would immediately become the center of admiration. He would be protected as an angel from heaven. And all that, in spite of the killing of Serbs by Anglo-American bombers and the daily radio and leaflet propaganda against Serbia. A fallen American aviator, who had bombed Belgrade, might lie with a wrenched knee in a Serbian peasant's only bed and even if that peasant heard Serbian Communists in London denouncing Serbia as the home of treason, over the British radio, still the sorrowful, bewildered pig-raiser would nurse that American back to health and eventually take him to a place of safety.

When British and American agents in the service of Tito urged such Serbs to join the Partisans and told them that Communists were democrats just like Franklin Roosevelt, would it be any wonder if some of the Serbs tended to waver? So strong was their confidence in America and England that when Tito sent his own native Communist agents into Macedonia he took pains to clothe them in British battle dress and to pass them off as Serbian-speaking Britishers. The Macedonians spurned native Partisans but would listen to the British.

In addition to this propaganda aid, much more substantial help was flown in. Air strips were laid out as near Tito's fighting lines as possible, and on every suitable night, American-made airplanes carried American-made weapons and munitions to Tito and his comrades to use against our ally Serbia. Battles raged in a dozen mountain clusters and every day Tito told the world how many enemies he was killing. Three-fourths of those "enemies" were just poor Serbian peasants, each with a pig and a sheep, a little whitewashed cottage, and perhaps a dozen acres of hilly land, which he was trying to defend from Communist invaders. And those peasants, fighting for their children and homes and their precious traditions of freedom, were denounced by some Americans as Fascists.

The plot against Serbia, which the Croatian Subashitch and the

Croatian Tito made on the island of Vis under British tutelage, failed. Tito and the Partisans, in spite of all Allied aid, never took Serbia. Russia had to do that, helped by Bulgaria. The Red Army eventually marched in, drove out the Germans, and then handed the Serbian nation over to Tito, as an Austrian emperor might give Slovakia to a favorite cousin. Naturally the Serbian people, following the advice of Mihailovitch, did not oppose the Russians. On the contrary, they welcomed the Red soldiers and tried to aid them.

As a result of all this, Tito became master and could erect gallows as he wished, but he had not succeeded in breaking Serbia's resistance to Communism nor in smothering its desire for freedom. Serbia defied Tito to the last. Only an outside army enabled the Communist chief to set up his dictatorship. Tito placed his totalitarian yoke on a bound ox.

For the part of the young King and Dr. Subashitch in this anti-Serbian plot, the Sovereign and his ambitious Premier received only the scorn of Russia and the loathing of the Partisans, who didn't need subservient monarchs and didn't want superfluous bourgeois relics. As soon as Tito marched into Belgrade behind the mighty Red Army, he reduced the chief Croat conspirator from London to the role of an unwelcome office boy, whose smiling face served naïve Anglo-Americans as a guarantee of Yugoslav democracy and of Yalta's inviolability. Tito declared the King unwanted and had a rubber-stamp Parliament ratify the decision. He forced Subashitch unconditionally to join the Partisan Front and before long arrested him. That was the exit of Premier Subashitch, the bait dangled over Yugoslavia by Premier Churchill.

By that time, Mr. Churchill's London stooges had learned that Tito's picture of the situation in Croatia was wholly false. To be sure, Mr. Magovats of the Croat Peasant Party had once helped the Partisans, because he had been assured that the Partisans' main aim was fighting against Germans and was promised that an intact Peasant Party bloc might work in a common Liberation Front beside a

Communist bloc. But when he saw that the Communists were determined to lord it over the Peasant Party and absorb it, and when he also perceived that the supreme Communist aim was not to fight Germans but to impose a dictatorship upon Yugoslavia, he objected. His refusal to serve as a Communist agent provoked immediate reprisals and Tito replaced him with a more supple, subservient Croatian peasant named Franjo Gazi.

The vice-president of the Croatian Peasant Party, Dr. August Koshutitch, whose allegience the Partisans were claiming, actually did leave Zagreb and went to see Tito, but on learning that the Communists demanded complete subordination, he refused to assent. As a result, the Communist chief, in spite of his safe conduct promise, put the Peasant leader in jail. Tito also told his propagandists to whoop it up, and Koshutitch, who had spent half a lifetime in danger, in jail, or in exile, because of his uncompromising fight against autocracy and for peasants, was branded in Tito's radio and press as a "dirty Fascist." He was kept in prison until 1947.

The president of the Croatian Peasant Party, Dr. Vladko Machek, not only had refused to go along with Tito, but had been so successful in keeping his followers true to democratic ideals that Tito's propagandists began to denounce Machek night and day as an arch-Fascist and traitor. Although Machek was being held in prison by the Nazis, Tito heaped special vituperation upon him, calling him an enemy of the people. Finally when Germany collapsed and Tito was able to march unopposed into Zagreb, Machek moved out toward the approaching Americans. As American soldiers took him under their protection, they saved from Communist fury one of the bravest and most devoted champions of common men and women in southeast Europe.

Before closing this chapter on the plot against Serbia, it is well to describe the successful efforts of Mihailovitch and his Serbian supporters to save American aviators who had fallen while bombing Yugoslav objectives or Axis bases in Hungary, Slovakia, and Rumania.

By mid-summer, 1944, well over a hundred such pilots had been safely collected at Mihailovitch's headquarters. They had been fed in Serbian homes, tended by Serbian doctors, given loving care by simple Serbian women whose sons were dead or in German prison camps. In the mountains, Mihailovitch built adequate runways for the landing and taking off of large, loaded American bombers. Communications were established between Mihailovitch and the American air bases in Italy. The new Serbian airfield was effectively guarded by Mihailovitch guerrillas, who enabled American planes, divided into two fleets, to land and take off. They came on two different nights and succeeded in evacuating every American pilot without mishap.

All this was done at a time when Allied broadcasters were denouncing Serbia as Fascistic, indeed on the very nights when Partisans, using American weapons, wearing uniforms made in America, and accompanied by Allied military missions, were trying to kill Mihailovitch and smash the Serbian nation. When the first fleet carrying rescued American pilots arrived in Italy, they told of Serbia's desperate need of medicaments and asked that a little aid be sent. American bombs and guns were daily killing and wounding Serbs in Serbia, and as these Serbs, our allies, asked for a few kits of first aid, they were sternly told that a little would be sent for the still unevacuated Americans. The British kindly let us aid Americans even in Serbia. An anti-Communist Serb of irreproachable character, much distinction, and considerable political influence was smuggled into one of the planes and taken by the grateful American aviators to Italy to tell the world Serbia's story. He was instantly nabbed by the British, clapped into confinement, and treated with as much severity as a guy called Goering, when Herr Goering later fell into Allied hands.

Two things the British wanted at all costs to avoid: one was to let the story of American-British active participation in Tito's civil war get to the outside world, and the other was to permit any act that might offend Tito. Suppose that Tito, the prospective ruler of a Yugoslavia which he couldn't free and the commander of an army which couldn't hold a single vital point, should hear that the people of the United States of America and of the British Empire had been given a chance to listen to the story of a sincere and noble Serb, who had spent a long life fighting for common people! God forbid! Mr. Churchill's emissaries humbly hastened to assure Tito that the arrival of the Serb was due to American disloyalty and that the old fellow would be sent right back. Through American intervention he was allowed to stay, but in confinement.

Some members of the Allied forces in Bari, Italy, even went so far in their determination to aid Tito as seriously to discuss methods of "disposing of Mihailovitch." But they could agree on no feasible plan and ceased considering the matter. At least we were spared that dishonor. We refrained from doing to our Serbian ally what neither Germans, Italians, Ustashas, nor Bulgarians were able to achieve. We disposed of many Serbian women and children and tried to dispose of Serbia itself, but at least we abstained from a personal act of treachery toward Serbia's Mihailovitch.

CHAPTER EIGHTEEN

Tito Is Installed

THE mighty Red Army, which with its valor and brilliant strategy contributed so vitally to the overthrow of Hitler, took Belgrade on October 20, 1944. A few days later Marshal Tolbukhin and Marshal Tito paraded through the streets of Yugoslavia's liberated capital, in a victory celebration, at the head of picked Soviet and Partisan troops.

The old "white fortress" swam in red. Soviet and Yugoslav flags, each of the latter with a Partisan star added, shared honors on every high edifice. Huge pictures of Stalin and Tito adorned available walls. "Long live Soviet Russia," "Long live Partisan Yugoslavia," were blazoned from banners spanning the streets. The grim height, which had so often faced Teuton and Turk there at the confluence of the broad Sava and the sweeping Danube, became the stage for a unique celebration.

After some of the most awful years in Serbian history, the last brutal Nazi had been expelled from the city in which the Serbs three and a half years earlier had defied Adolf Hitler and his cruel totalitarianism. Serbia was free again. And the chief liberator, along with America, Britain, and the valiant Yugoslavs themselves, was Russia, the Mother of the Slavs, the traditional champion of Serbia, the chief guardian of the Holy Eastern Orthodox Church, of which all Serbs were members. After another long Serbian night, there rode into the dawn the Russian St. George that had slain the Nazi dragon. Never had the converging waters of those rivers seen a more radical historical change. One of history's most dramatic spots was witnessing one of history's most dramatic days. It was a victory parade such as fathers describe to their sons through a dozen generations. If the Serbs through five centuries sang of the day when invincible Turkish warriors smashed King Lazar's armies and swept over a prostrate Serbia toward that same Belgrade, will they not sing for five millenniums of this triumphant day, when Serbia and Yugoslavia and the Balkans were all made free?

One would think so. But actually, as the church bells rang and the red banners snapped and the brass bands boomed, most of the Belgradians remained in their homes. According to an eyewitness, who has been an ardent and tireless propagandist for Tito, four out of every five Belgradians shunned the celebration. The streets were largely empty. Drums echoed down deserted boulevards. The people who had been freed wept sadly before their eikons. The tramp of the liberators' feet sounded to them strangely like the boots of the former invaders. The noise of jubilation had a funereal undertone.

Was not that a strange attitude for a liberated nation to take toward the liberators? It was, indeed, strange, but not surprising, because the Serbs in Serbia's capital and in every Serbian village knew that those marching soldiers had not brought freedom. To them the celebration meant only that Russia was installing Tito as master of Yugoslavia. And they did not associate Tito with freedom. They did not believe that Tito was leading a glorious people's revolution, designed to free common Serbs from "Serbian despots," but rather that the common people of Serbia were being delivered to totalitarian Communists by a foreign power.

Both political and military events had impressed that conviction on the Serbs. For example, it was foreign soldiers and not Partisans who had cleared out the Germans. The Red Army entered Bucharest on August 31, 1944, reached the Serbian border on September 7, entered Bulgaria on the same date, and held a victory parade in Sofia a few days later. This brought the Bulgarian Army into the war on the Allied side, as a result of which Serbia had friendly armies on both her northern and eastern borders. Two Bulgarian armies began immediately to fight against Germans in Serbia and Macedonia. The moment had come for Tito's supreme achievement, in order to show the Serbs, the Yugoslavs, the world, and all future generations that the Serbs had flocked to the "Liberation Army" and enabled it to liberate Serbia. It was the climax for which the Partisans had spent months in preparation, gathering Allied weapons and hoarding those which they got from other sources. And Tito desperately tried to come in on the home stretch with a grand finish, but he failed.

The Russians crossed the Danube from Turnu Severin into Serbia on October 3, 1944, they freed Negotin on October 5, Zajechar on October 17. The victorious Red Army entered Belgrade three days later. At that time Tito was not even holding Valjevo, which he had temporarily taken in a raid that he had triumphantly trumpeted throughout the world. The above dates are from official Russian war communiqués. It took the Red Army and the Bulgarians two months to free the places Tito had repeatedly said he had freed. With the help of the Bulgarians, Skoplje was freed on November 15, and Macedonia was cleared of Germans by the end of November. The Bulgarians helped free the Sandjak and in December were released to fight against the Germans in Hungary.

Greece was largely free from Germans by the end of October, and Nazi troops had also evacuated Albania by that time, under constant Partisan pressure. The Red Army took the last German posts in Budapest on February 13, 1945, and entered Austria about the same time, but Tito still found himself stalled in western Yugoslavia by the meager remnants of inferior German divisions. He who had told American correspondents that he was going to send three hundred thousand soldiers to help fight Germany couldn't even liberate the western areas of his own land after the Russians and Bulgarians had put him in possession of the eastern part.

His Partisans entered Bibach on March 30, 1945; Sarajevo on

April 6; Ljubljana, the chief city of Slovenia, on May 5; and Zagreb, the chief city of Tito's own Croatia, on May 8. Germany had capitulated on May 8. In other words, Serbia was freed by the direct intervention of the Russian and Bulgarian armies; Croatia and Slovenia were freed by the Allied armies through the annihilation of the Wehrmacht. The Partisans marched triumphantly into a Belgrade, Zagreb, and Ljubljana that had been freed for them. The Allies handed liberated Yugoslavia over to Tito. In view of that, it is not strange that four Serbs out of five remained sadly at home when the Communist-led Partisans held their Belgrade victory parade. They felt as though some emperor was giving a living nation, as a gift, to some importunate courtier. They stayed at home, not because they didn't want liberty, but exactly because they did want it and knew they hadn't got it.

What was Tito's foremost activity after he became master of Serbia and then, step by step, of all Yugoslavia? He did exactly what Adolf Hitler had done under similar circumstances; namely, he tried to exalt his name above every other name in the country. He tried to make himself appear as a god to the people. The country was still horribly devastated and only partially freed. Most Yugoslavs were ragged, badly housed, inadequately fed, and without regular incomes. Yet the chief concern of the Partisans was to aggrandize their chief and establish their domination.

When Hitler tried to make a god of himself by terror and propaganda, the world condemned his action as tyrannical. It was considered a sign of totalitarian absolutism. The Nazis' use of the state, the army, the schools, the press, the radio, and all other institutions to exalt one man, seemed to most people the subversion of popular government. The organizing by the Nazis of little girls and boys, of youth, of women, of farmers, of workers, and of every group in such a way as to increase adoration for Hitler, is generally considered an attempt to strengthen absolutism. It is held by most democratic observers to have closely resembled the practices of Oriental despots.

By universal agreement, kings who make themselves objects of worship are called absolutists. Yet the activity to which the Partisans gave their chief attention, after they received absolute power, was to create for Tito the spiritual status of an Eastern monarch.

A poem appearing in Tito's publication *The Youth Movement* in June, 1945, is typical of the sentiments which this propaganda aroused. This poem is so ecstatic that translation is difficult, but in the author's outpouring of adoration are found such phrases as the following:

> "You ask about Tito,
>   who he is,
>
> "Tito—that is us,
>   all, . . .
>
> "And he is full of us,
>   and great. . . .
>
> "Tito was born in anger,
>   and longing for achievement, a titan.
>
> "He was born holy from
>   the first Communist cell,
>
> "**And he was born again,**
>   in the first revolutionary shrapnel.
>
> "He was born once more
>   in the brigades of Kocha and Peko
>   in every
>   new
>   brigade
>
> "And he lives in every fighter,
>   under his heart he lives and breathes.

"He attacks with him. . . .

"And he is full of us

And great

And we live in him.'

That is what Radovan Zogovitch wrote of Tito. The Marshal was an object of adulation for the poet; he played the role of a divine inspirer and comforter. This hymn of adoration, resembling the songs Christians sing to Christ and the prayers they secretly utter in hours of consecration, could be matched in many Partisan publications. The guerrillas were very short of paper, but they had enough to create an extensive literature of adoration. This converting of Tito into a popular idol began in Partisan publications for little tots and continued through the most serious political reviews.

The Partisans were taught to think of dear, gentle Tito at sunrise, of tireless Tito in the noonday's heat, of all-wise Tito as the sun sank in the west, of omniscient Tito as the stars filled the skies, of irresistible Tito smiting his enemies as lightning crashed from crag to crag.

At meetings the staccato two-syllable name was repeatedly shouted with ecstasy, sounding like the hoof beats of a thousand galloping horses or a hundred locomotives clicking over the rails. As one heard that rapturous, grim, sharp chorus of "Ti-to-ti-to-ti-to," he was reminded of similar echoes of "Hit-ler-hit-ler-hit-ler."

Tito was said to be with Partisans in hunger and fear. He was beside them in battles, in prison, in long, consuming marches. He assuaged their sorrow, softened their pain, mitigated their loneliness. To live for him was honor; to fight for him, distinction; to die for him was glory, they said. He gave his smiles to the little ones, clasped the hands of the brave warriors, put his strong arm about the faltering. In his eyes were the red stars of Russia, in his bright countenance the glow of a new world. He was the harbinger of eternal righteousness, the guarantor of final triumph. He was Croat and Slovene and Serb, all in one.

It goes without saying that there is much strength and beauty in such adoration. Tito really has a strong, pleasing personality. Fighters need religious emotion and many Partisans found it in Tito-worship. It will be interesting for someone sometime to make a choice collection of adoration poems in Hitler-worship and to match them with similar poems in Tito-worship. If we go a step farther and compare them both with the adoration poems in the worship of Oriental despots, we shall again find great similarity.

Egypt, Babylonia, Persia, Japan, Germany, and Partisania, all meet in mystical, absolutist adoration, which stifles self-respect and kills democracy. Many a time have I seen women gather before a picture of Hitler and say, "Our dear leader." I have seen children place flowers in reverence before his candle-lighted shrines. And I have seen Partisans show the same emotion toward Tito.

You may recall that before Alexander the Great began his attack upon the Orient, he made a mysterious visit to North Africa, where he had himself installed as a son of the sun god. He thought the Orientals might fall for him as a deity, as well as a conqueror. That was Alexander's propaganda line. That stunt for impressing the simple was one of the very first acts in his greatest adventure. Likewise, Tito's Partisans tried to install Tito as a kind of god. His pictures covered the walls of buildings, were stretched across the squares, adorned every camp, office, and school. And as eikons of God the Son are exalted beside those of God the Father in Balkan monasteries, so pictures of Tito and Stalin were constantly placed side by side—as were their statues.

Tito was Marshal of Yugoslavia, Hero of Yugoslavia, Premier of Yugoslavia, War Minister, Commander of all the Armed Forces, head of the Liberation Movement. Whenever he got a new title or was invested with a new office, journalists vied with one another in praising him, poets laureate outdid one another in lauding him, newspapers contended with one another in displaying his pictures. The speeches made at each new investment were collected in books, and on reading them one wonders whether the courtiers in Tokyo, Peking, Teheran, and Nineveh had anything on modern Yugoslav Partisan sycophants. If one saw a mass of youth standing with uplifted hands in Nuremberg, crying "Hitler," another crowd standing in Milan with uplifted hands, crying "Duce," and another standing in Belgrade with uplifted hands, crying "Tito," one could hardly tell the difference.

Tito is trying to jump the gun on an old Yugoslav custom, and become a legend while still living. The Yugoslavs are among the world's most energetic and assiduous folklore producers. They have built up marvelous cycles of folk stories and songs about their heroes. Some of their gifted sculptors, drawing inspiration from this folklore, have produced heroic statues, recognized as among the world's best. Singing of heroes is a Yugoslav characteristic—but until now their songs have been of dead heroes, of half mythical heroes. Now Tito and the Partisans are trying to coerce Yugoslav myth-makers and force them to make a Saint Sava or King Lazar of him while he is still alive.

To do this, Tito has placed himself at the peak of a vast propaganda pyramid made up of the press, news agencies, radio, meetings, the army, the AVNOJ, sports clubs, youth societies, and women's organizations. Countless meetings are held all over Yugoslavia for extolling Tito.

Here are the meetings as reported in a single day, May 16, 1945, by R.B. (Radio Belgrade). There was: a meeting of workers in Sarajevo, a conference in Skoplje, an anti-Fascist mass meeting in Zajechar, a conference of youth (Pioneers) at Chachak, a meeting of anti-Fascist women in Cetinje, an anti-Fascist meeting in Trieste, and a conference in Gatsko.

On May 24 and 25, there was: a congress of Pioneers at Ouzhitse, an election of a Committee of Liberation in Ljubljana, the election of a new Committee of Liberation in Tuzla, the election of another Committee in Nevesinje, a meeting of intellectuals in Sarajevo, the election of a Liberation Committee in Dubrovnik, a workers' conference in Zagreb, and the election of a new Liberation Committee in Cetinje.

Here are some of the regional congresses held during a ten-day period: a Regional Congress of Pioneers in Belgrade, a Regional Meeting of twenty thousand Anti-Fascist Women in Zagreb, the First Congress of Anti-Fascist Women in Bosnia-Herzegovina, an Anti-Fascist Congress in Ljubljana, a Regional Conference with one thousand participants in Rieka, an Anti-Fascist Women's Conference in Belgrade, the First Regional Congress of Croatian Youth in Zagreb, the Second Regional Congress of Slovene Youth in Ljubljana.

Each one of these major conferences is national or even international in scope. When the Anti-Fascist Women hold a conference in Belgrade, women come from Slovenia, Montenegro, Croatia, Macedonia, Bosnia. And when the Bosnian pioneers hold a congress in Sarajevo, youth pours in from Belgrade, Skoplje, Zagreb, Ljubljana, Rieka. And guests are often invited from Russia, the U.S., France, Czechoslovakia, Greece.

This propaganda activity has aspects of the epic and grandiose. In a sad, devastated land with poor communities and full of hungry people we see thousands of women, youths, and men, following uniformed leaders from one end of the land to the other. There aren't enough trains and trucks to carry badly needed UNRRA supplies from ports to interior cities, but we see Anti-Fascist Women converging on Ljubljana from every part of the kingdom to sing songs, shout slogans, curse the enemy, inflame hatred against all non-Partisans and shout Tito—Tito—Tito, as they listen to eloquent orators and gaze upon Tito's pictures. The congresses pass burning resolutions against the Fascists of the world, pledge eternal fidelity to Tito, and rush back to Belgrade where they hold another congress with all railroad and hotel expenses paid by the state. If there is any energy left after their rousing hot gospel meetings led by the world's most accomplished exhorters, the delegates conduct similar meetings in their home towns where they separate the saved from the sinners and divide all Yugoslavia into Partisans and "Fascists" who hate and fear one another.

During a period of about six months not fewer than twenty-six hundred conferences and twenty-seven hundred mass meetings were held in the Serbian district of Ouzhitse, attended by 337,225 people. That amounts to about twenty-five meetings a day in a fairly small, somewhat mountainous peasant area with no more than one hundred and fifty thousand inhabitants. This means that every man, woman, and child went to at least two meetings in that period.

In addition to that, fifty-six hundred grandmas and grandpas were attending adult education courses, with as many as 108 to a class, and in one brief season all got certificates, which is a pedagogical world record of mass production of enlightenment. And that at a moment of complete educational upheaval. Usually I do not vouch for the accuracy of Balkan figures, but it is true that the Partisans carried on a furious propaganda activity. The twenty-five daily meetings in Ouzhitse were matched in every other county.

And they did not remain without results. Tito was acclaimed far and wide. Worshipful Partisans constantly called him "the greatest man in Yugoslav history," "the greatest son of Mother Yugoslavia," just as Hitler was repeatedly extolled as "the greatest man in all German annals." For example, it was reported, "Yesterday arrived in Zagreb the greatest son of our people." "May 25 will be celebrated most solemnly because it is the birthday of our greatest son, Marshal Tito." He is repeatedly called "the greatest," "the wisest," "the most gifted." As the Tito-controlled daily, *Politika*, reported on June 18, 1945, "The women at an Anti-Fascist Congress held in

Belgrade suddenly interrupted a chant 'Ti-to-he-ro, Ti-to-he-ro' by passionately crying 'We are Tito's; Tito is ours.' "

Tito does not shun such celebrations. On the contrary, he rushes from one end of the country to the other to present himself at them. For example, it is reported that on a certain day he spoke at Belgrade, two days later at Zagreb, five days after that again at Zagreb, four days later at Ljubljana, then at Celze, Osijek, Belgrade, Mladenovats, etc.

And he does not appear empty handed. In less than a month he distributed at least 1707 decorations to his Yugoslav followers as well as many to Bulgarians. He seems even to outdo the Fascists and horrible "bourgeois capitalists" in kidding hungry people with little pieces of tinsel. And his pockets are filled not only with decorations, but also with wonderful telegraphic testimonials. Every day at a Tito celebration in Yugoslavia telegrams pour in from all over the earth, all plugged by the press and radio. Within a week he had telegrams from Gatsko, Trieste, the Kremlin, Sofia, Bihach, Ljubljana, Zagreb, Marseilles, Buenos Aires, Ohio, etc. The sad, unshod, ragged Yugoslavs beheld the wonderful spectacle of the world rising up to acclaim their greatest son.

On his birthday, Yugoslav youth from every part of the kingdom engaged in a vast relay race converging on Belgrade, whither they rushed over hill and mountain to bring their hero Tito the homage of a nation. From Trieste and Gorizia, from Klagenfurt and Maribor, from Subotitsa and Podgoritsa, from blue Ochrid and drab Negotin sped the boys with vows of eternal allegiance to Tito. And that same evening there was held a solemn meeting in honor of Yugoslavia's Marshal at which were present the ambassadors and ministers of the United States, Great Britain, the U.S.S.R., Turkey, Greece, Bulgaria, France, and the three Royal Regents, generals and cabinet ministers, Partisan chiefs, youthful heroes, devoted anti-Fascist women. What European king since the demise of the Bourbons and Romanoffs had been so lauded!

Such is the build-up of one man in Yugoslavia. Such is the carefully fostered legend. As a Roman of ancient times, called Diocletian, deified himself and made the whole Roman Empire not only serve him as emperor but worship him as a god, so Partisans now build Yugoslavia on the myth of one man, Tito. As Diocletian massacred the early Christians for refusing to degrade themselves by worshipping him, can anyone doubt that the Partisans are degrading liberty and massacring democracy in trying to make Yugoslavs worship one of their fellow citizens? Shall free Americans call that democracy and liberation of the people?

CHAPTER NINETEEN

Fascists in Tito's Ranks

A LARGE number of Fascists have associated themselves with Tito and been given important positions in his regime. By the word "Fascists" in this case I mean actual, open supporters of Mussolini, Hitler, or Pavelitch. In addition to such persons, who flopped out of actual Axis ranks directly into Tito's ranks, there are many other questionable Partisans who are merely reactionary or menial or sycophantic or corrupt. They typify what is said to be the old world which Tito is destroying. They are the antithesis of all who are said to be working for the common man. Nevertheless, such fleshpot addicts have streamed to Tito by the thousands.

This aspect of recent European political revolutions deserves careful study. Without doubt it will someday be shown in detail, with names and numbers, that German Communists streamed into Nazi ranks and played vital roles in Hitler's movement. From the very inception of the ideology of modern mass movements, from the great shows in Nuremberg and Moscow to bloody fights at the barricades, Nazis and Communists have been similar in emotions, aims, and practices. They originated from a number of the same sources, were trained in the same revolutionary schools, read some of the same books. And as Communists flocked to the German "Liberator," Hitler, after 1933, so Nazis have flocked to the Yugoslav "Liberator," Tito.

I shall not attempt to give a long list of them with their biographies, for that would be tedious, but shall point out a few striking cases. One such Fascist who has especially come to my notice and with whom I am personally acquainted is the Slovene, Franz Pierts. For months he was the foremost airman in Tito's Army of Liberation. He won Tito's special confidence and during 1944 was sent by Tito to train Partisan airmen in North Africa, under British supervision and with American supplies. We Americans and British intimately worked with Tito's Colonel Pierts.

He always presented himself as a stern, fierce-visaged, fanatical Partisan, utterly devoted to Marshal Tito and the common man; but before he entered Tito's services in 1943, he was head of the air service of Dictator Pavelitch, the arch-Nazi of Zagreb. Pierts recruited men for Pavelitch's air force and led them in daring fights against "the vicious Russian Bolsheviks." He was a major Axis hero, the pride of Mussolini's "Independent Croatia," a favorite of the Wehrmacht, a slayer of Reds. He was especially eager to hobnob with German officers, and by having his pictures featured in Nazi military publications, he brought lustre to his own name as well as renown to Fascist Croatia. Copies of such publications are still available and the military intelligence of America, England, Russia, and other United Nations have in their files pictures of Colonel Pierts, wearing Nazi uniforms and an imperious Nazi smile. He was the perfect type of a ferocious Ustasha Nazi, blindly intolerant, a hater of Yugoslavia, a killer of Serbs. But, when Germany's defeat became apparent, he flopped to Tito, seeking a good job.

However, before he flopped either to Tito or to Pavelitch he had been an officer in the Royal Yugoslav Army. He had taken a solemn oath to serve the Yugoslav king and defend the Yugoslav state. For that he had been trained and for that he was paid. Nevertheless, at the moment when Yugoslavia was attacked by Germany and found itself in direst need of Pierts's services, he deserted the Yugoslav Army and flamboyantly went over to the Germans, joining the German stooge, Pavelitch, after which he worked with all his might against Yugoslavia.

A further point! Before he entered the Royal Yugoslav Army he was in Franz Joseph's Austrian Army. Indeed, he got his very name from his Emperor Franz. Thus, in the course of his military career Pierts has given his oath to four different states and twice deserted them in the midst of war. Such is the character of Tito's foremost hero of the air.

A no less notorious case is that of Marko Mesitch, the commander of Tito's Guards, corresponding to the old Royal Guards. Mesitch finished the Yugoslav military school for officers and entered the Yugoslav Army, after giving a solemn oath to king and country. When Germany attacked Yugoslavia in April, 1941, Mesitch immediately deserted and joined the enemy which was obliterating the state he had taken an oath to defend. He signed up with Dictator Pavelitch, raised his hand in a Fascist salute to his new "Poglavnik" (Fuehrer), whom he hailed as Croatia's greatest son, and ardently joined Croatia's fiercest pro-Axis fighters. He did not content himself with fighting in Croatia, but led a force of Croatian Nazis against the "very source of all evil," Bolshevist Russia.

He became the Axis hero of the hour, an idol of every bloody, democracy-scorning, Yugoslav-shattering Ustasha. His pictures appeared in Nazi papers, he was lauded over Axis radios, on his manly breast were pinned Nazi medals. He basked in glory as the state he had sworn to defend writhed in bloody, smoking ruins. But Mesitch didn't just sit around basking. He plunged forward and ever forward against Russia. He led his brave Croatian volunteers across river, swamp, and endless steppe, smiting Russian Reds. Above him snapped bright Nazi banners, over him zoomed furious Nazi stukas, blasting "a glorious way" for Mesitch through Russian women and children. In his ranks resounded the martial hymn "Deutschland Ueber Alles," giving new strength to the Ustasha warrior.

Into the Ukraine plunged Mesitch, past Kiev, beyond Kharkov, through Voroshilovgrad, clear to the forts of Stalingrad. Nazi cannon boomed, Nazi drums beat, pictures of Fuehrer Hitler and Poglavnik Pavelitch gleamed above them and Mesitch heartened his fellow Ustashas by pointing out the Urals and the Caspian, by promising them they would soon be trampling on the dead bodies of Bolshevik Russia and decadent Slavdom.

Then he got captured; after that he flopped. He took another military oath. After a little briefing and a little reorientation, he organized an anti-Nazi Croat brigade and began fighting against the Germans and the Ustashas, getting his picture in another kind of paper, and lining up for a new sort of medal. Eventually the hero got to Yugoslavia, threw his arms around Tito's neck and became a leading Partisan, Liberator, Democrat, Champion of the common man. After swearing three oaths in the year and deserting twice in the middle of war, Mr. Mesitch sat down to excellent American food, strutted about in beautiful uniforms, and raised his arm in clenched-fist salutes to his new leader, whom he called the greatest son of Yugoslavia, as many American "liberals" cheered.

One of Tito's even more resplendent Fascist heroes is Sulejman Filipovitch, who became one of Tito's cabinet ministers. He is in his fifties, a restless, forceful, ambitious Moslem Yugoslav from Bosnia. The Croatians call him a Croat; the Serbs, a Serb. At the age of 18 he participated in the Sarajevo assassinations that provoked the First World War. At that time he was apparently a flaming Serbian nationalist. After the First World War he went to Zagreb for further studies and soon joined the Yugoslav Army as an officer, giving the oath to king and country. By 1941, when the Germans attacked Yugoslavia, he was a colonel and during the first days of fighting commanded a regiment in Serbia. But on being captured his Serbian nationalism suddenly vanished. He milled around a while with the thousands of other prisoners, as the Nazis were separating the good Yugoslavs from the bad. The bad, all of whom were Serbs, were sent to prisoner-of-war camps in Germany, while the good were released to help Poglavnik Pavelitch, the fierce Croatian dictator, butcher Serbs and fight Russians. Colonel Filipovitch had no difficulty in convincing the Nazis that he was a good Yugoslav and was released to join the Croat Ustashas.

He took an oath of allegiance to an archenemy of Yugoslavia and set out to destroy the dynasty he had served for twenty years. He was made commander of an Ustasha regiment that soon won fame under his leadership as a killer of Serbs. Moslem Filipovitch and his soldiers ravaged back and forth through "Independent Croatia," as sultanic armies had done centuries before. The Serb members of Filipovitch's former Yugoslav regiment were lying in German camps. And there was Filipovitch leading ferocious Ustasha killers through the towns and villages of Kordun, Lika, Bosnia, Herzegovina, massacring the very families of his former soldiers! He and his Ustashas bayoneted priests in their churches, attacked mothers in their homes, battered out babies' brains in the market places, machine gunned old men and boys in groups and left corpses in stacks or windrows or piled in ditches. He fought against Chetniks, he fought against Partisans, but mostly he fought against women, children, and defenceless old men, and when terror-stricken survivors saw wide swaths of fire, ashes, debauchery, and death streak across a valley or over a plain, they knew that Pavelitch's Sulejman Filipovitch had passed their way—had passed as Sultan Sulejman the Magnificent had passed centuries earlier.

After about a year of this, Filipovitch flopped again—this time right in the midst of battle. He deserted the great Vozhd Pavelitch and joined another Croatian, Tito, to whom he soon swore eternal allegiance—after it had been arranged that Filipovitch was to be a Partisan big shot. In three short years he had given three oaths and twice deserted. He had passed from revolutionary Serb nationalist, through a routine officer's career, to a flaming Croatian nationalist, and was now a champion of the common man, reaping the plaudits of American admirers.

I shall not continue with this list of notorious, active Fascists who left the services of the bloody Pavelitch to accept and hold high positions with Tito. If men so well known to Yugoslavia and to the world could become Tito's most intimate helpers, one can readily see how thousands of rank and file Croatian Ustashas were accepted into the Army of Liberation.

Long before the collapse of Germany and the surrender of Zagreb, Ustashas had entered Tito's ranks by companies. That was their way of "working their passage home." They put a star on their caps and were transformed from Fascists to champions of the people. They passed from the bench of war criminals up to the judges' bench where they could condemn war criminals. They were as the thief who rushed through the street with the crowd, shouting, "Catch the thief."

Now we may pass from Tito's out-and-out Fascists to the merely reactionary or base or traditionally dictatorial among his followers and associates. First, let us mention Tito's Ambassador in London, Dr. Ljuba Leontitch. Concerning him the New York *New Leader* wrote on July 7, 1945, "Leontitch arrived about a month ago accompanied by a considerable staff. He is a Croat and a lawyer . . . the founder of the Yugoslav Fascist organization—Fascist not in any vague or generic sense, but in a precise and specific sense—known as 'Orjuna.' Leontitch assumed the title of 'Veliki Chelnik' (Grand Fuehrer). The organization, founded after Mussolini's march on Rome, was a copy of the Italian Fascist original—it even adopted the black shirt as its uniform. It was used to break up meetings and strikes, and had a special body of storm troopers, who perpetrated deeds of violence. They would disperse Communist and Socialist meetings, often with bloodshed. They did much to embitter relations between the Serbs and Croats. Leontitch went over to Tito after the collapse of Italy. He has now been fitly rewarded for his past services."

This activity with Orjuna does not necessarily mean that His Excellency Ljuba Leontitch was in Fascist ranks during this war. It merely means that he had been very active in a brutal, direct-action, Fascist-like organization, that he was in the service of extreme Yugoslav centralism, and that he is the type of man who serves dictators. The name one gives him is immaterial, but beyond all question, his activity and methods are the antithesis of Lincolnian democracy. His attitude embodies Tito's loudly proclaimed principle, "In Yugoslavia there's no democracy for the enemies of democracy," meaning political opponents of the dictatorial government.

A prominent member of Tito's intimate entourage, once sent as a Partisan delegate to Moscow and constantly lauded as an exalted example of "new Yugoslavia's" intelligentsia, is the Croatian sculptor, Antun Augustinchitch. The Partisans are very proud of him. They say with awe that he is the greatest Croat sculptor after Mestrovitch, and even more impressively that "he is a progressive, though was not active in politics till recently."

Actually, during the whole of his career, forty-eight-year-old Augustinchitch has been a typical court sycophant, serving every regime in order to get honors, renown, adulation, and cash. Some artists have done that since the time of the Pharaohs. They resemble false prophets who live easily by courting kings and flattering the mighty. Yugoslavia is a rather poor country, inhabited largely by peasants who don't flock into sculptors' studios to buy statues. Thus sculptors live from orders given by the state or regional governments or communities commemorating dead heroes. Therefore, to get ahead, namely, to get orders and subsidies and gifts, an artist must have political friends.

And Mr. Augustinchitch was careful to make them. He cultivated the royal court with much assiduity and persistence—also with success—and later he poured out his heart in praise of the Croatian tyrant Pavelitch. That was not unnatural; when the sculptor saw that the Yugoslav court had collapsed he sought to win the favor of its successor, the Fuehrer-Duce-Vozhd court in Zagreb. It was a rather artistic step. Dictators like to have their statues stuck all over the place. They don't wait till they're dead to have their bronze likenesses placed in squares, market places, parks, and before the grand cathedrals. They want sculptors to make statues quickly. And through Pavelitch, Augustinchitch might have found favor even with the All-High Adolf. So the Croat sculptor ardently served the bloody creator of "Independent Croatia."

But when it became apparent that Pavelitch could not maintain his position, and Tito's star began to ascend over all the Balkans casting a glow that came clear from Moscow itself, Augustinchitch sought another court. And his search went not unrewarded. He became the sculptor laureate of the common man, the immortalizer of Liberation, the proud possessor of a place in an airplane flying to Moscow.

The number of Yugoslav intellectuals with records identical with that of Augustinchitch is legion. They ardently followed the trail, brush in hand, chisel in hand, pen in hand, or lyre in hand, always with hat in hand, from the court of the Karageorges to that of Pavelitch and then over Partisan paths to Tito. Most famous and notorious of them all is seventy-two-year-old Vladimir Nazor, "the greatest Croatian poet." He became president of the Anti-Fascist Council of Croatia, which made him practically President of "Free Croatia." He is a picturesque figure with many of the typical qualities of a self-adulating prima donna.

He received and enjoyed most of the subsidies, funds, and favors that a gifted and subservient poet could expect from Yugoslavia's rather generous old "Fascistic regime," then served Pavelitch as a poet laureate, singing his praises in a way that would bring blushes even to the poets of Persian monarchs or Arabian caliphs, and after giving the gory Croatian Poglavnik an immortal place among tsars and Caesars, Nazor found his way to Tito.

Tito also has his court priests, the most distinguished of which is a Croatian, Monsignor Svetozar Rittig of the Roman Catholic Church. For a long time this "devout prelate" was one of Tito's chief show pieces. He not only wrote widely, prayed reverently and exhorted earnestly, but was brought out at all the important Partisan conferences and impressively presented to the liaison men or special representatives from the West in order to convince Americans and Britishers that Partisanry was good old New England democracy with distinguished priests giving it an odor of sanctity. The road which Monsignor Rittig followed to reach Tito's camp bore a strange resemblance to that of all courtiers, whether profane or sacerdotal.

I remember him first as hastening into the service of King Alexander after His Majesty's imposing of the dictatorship of 1928. The Yugoslav Constitution had been suspended, Parliament dismissed, democracy temporarily suppressed and a burly, ruthless Serb soldier made dictator over Yugoslavia. After ten long years of turmoil, insecurity, and parliamentary quarrels the King had decided to force unity upon his people—as many kings have attempted to do in similar circumstances. The Croats believed that the dictatorship was directed against them and bitterly opposed it, even to the use of bombs. They felt all the more rebellious because their great leader, Stephan Raditch, had been shot in Belgrade. At that tense moment Monsignor Rittig won great prominence by springing to the aid of the royal dictator. He drummed up Croatian delegates and conducted them in special state-provided trains to Belgrade to display their loyalty to the new autocratic regime. The few Croatian peasants who followed their Reverend Pied Piper to Belgrade got free rides and free lunches and a good time was had by all, but the Monsignor won the scorn of most of his countrymen for so demonstratively serving a dictatorial general who had replaced Parliament.

That venture into high politics was soon forgotten and Mr. Rittig spent the following years in rather uneventful obscurity until the war with Germany, the collapse of Yugoslavia, and the rise of Dictator Pavelitch gave him another opportunity to shine, which he did with almost blinding scintillation. After the Poglavnik, or Fuehrer, had installed himself in power, with Hitler's and Mussolini's blessings, and set out to exterminate the Orthodox church, along with the Orthodox priests and many of the worshippers, in the new Croatia, Monsignor Rittig appeared in the most famous church in Zagreb and warmly praised the new dictator, commending him to the people as a Croatian St. George. The godly man who had helped King Alexander's dictatorial Serbian general suppress Croatia, now helped a Croatian conspirator crush Yugoslavia, kill Serbs, and defame the Karageorges. But Monsignor Rittig's God did not seem to heed "his faithful servant's" exhortations and Dictator Pavelitch's affairs showed signs of bankruptcy. Consequently, the priest found his way to another Croat conspirator. He burnished up his old sermons, warmed up his old prayers, and placed Tito in the high places to which he had once elevated Pavelitch. Communist Tito glowed and his Communist Comrades smirked as the priest recruited Yugoslav Catholics for the Communist crusade. An American after talking with this eloquent clergyman wrote back home that democratic Tito resembled George Washington praying at Valley Forge. It is significant that although thousands of Yugoslav intellectuals followed Nazor and Augustinchitch, very few priests followed Rittig.

There are many active war criminals in the ranks of Tito's Partisans—I mean men who killed women and children and massacred civilians for political reasons. By war crimes, I mean acts similar to the killing of Polish officers at Katyn and the atrocities perpetrated in Nazi concentration camps. American journalists, congressmen, and photographers have acquainted the American public with war crimes. Such atrocities were not restricted to Germany nor to the Nazis. At least two groups of people committed them in Yugoslavia. One was made up of Croatian Ustashas, whose crimes consist of the plundering, burning, raping, torturing, and mutilating of living persons, the causing of slow death, and mass assassinations. These horrors have rarely been surpassed in a part of the world long used to horror. Such Ustasha war criminals are now sheltered in Partisan ranks and are active in the Partisan regime. Not only will they never be tried, but they are clamoring for the extermination of persons who fought for the Allies against these Nazi agents.

Another group of war criminals filling Partisan ranks are Communist executioners who systematically exterminated the more solid leaders in Serbian or even Croatian communities. This was usually done through individual assassinations, according to carefully worked out plans. Each town and county and province was thoroughly studied, as it might be by an American committee making a Community Chest drive. The teachers, mayors, judges, reserve officers, leading peasants, and influential merchants were listed and marked for death, as "enemies of the people"—and there was no passover. Nor was there any "city of refuge." A man or woman could not even flee to a church for safety as in the savage times of the dark ages. The Communist Liberators allowed no such avenue of escape to the men they had condemned.

As night came, the executioners stole from house to house, killing their victims, often with American weapons. Sometimes they shot them in bed; at other times they simply stuck bayonets through them; occasionally they carried them off and left them dead beside the road. Not infrequently the bodies were never found. Against such treacherous actions there was no defense and no redress. If Mr. Yovanovitch fled, that very act placed him beyond the law for the Communist cell in his locality. If he remained at home, he was a potshot, to be picked off as a duck on a nest.

Among the Communist assassins and Fascist war criminals are also found a few Chetnik leaders who flopped to Tito's side when his victory appeared certain. The most notorious of these was Major Djuritch, whom General Mihailovitch was about to discipline for allegedly serving the German occupiers. One day he was denounced by Tito as a knave; the next day received by Tito with open arms as a champion of the people.

I would not intimate that all Partisans are of this sort. But a large part of them are marginal, bitter, impatient, intolerant men and women, including many Fascists, many venal courtiers, a few of the basest Chetniks, and no small number of Communist criminals.

CHAPTER TWENTY

Balkan Pan-Slavism: Tito's Relations with Bulgaria

ONE of the most persistent and fundamental of Tito's aims is to unify all the Balkan Slavs in Communistic Partisanry. They number at least twenty million and include some seven million Bulgarians, living in a pleasant, mountain-filled, fairly fruitful land about the size of Ohio, lying east of Yugoslavia.

The Bulgarian peasant nation is among the most industrious, frugal and progressive in Eastern Europe and in spite of a scant Asiatic blood strain is as Slavic as any group in the Balkans. The Bulgarians are very closely related to the Serbs in culture, language, and religion, but they and the Serbs have long been hostile toward one another. Since 1885, these two peoples have fought four wars, three of them since 1912. Plainly, if that old strife could be converted into friendship, the authors of that change would deserve the praise of the world. And at present the Bulgarian and Yugoslav governments maintain friendly official relations. Fraternization is the order of the day—and night. These two Slav neighbors have beaten their swords into plowshares and lovingly plow each other's fields. The Bulgarians recently cared for thirty thousand Serbian children in Bulgarian homes. Friendly delegations constantly make visits from one land to the other. Medals and greetings are frequently exchanged. And the radios of the two countries vie with one another in expressions of friendship, as do the newspapers.

On first impression, this is the most inspiring change that has taken place in Balkan politics for many years. However, first impressions are often deceptive and Bulgaro-Yugoslav relations deserve careful study. At the beginning we must see what kind of a Bulgaria is maintaining such intimate relations with Tito's Yugoslavia. We must also try to ascertain Bulgarian motives and Tito's motives and ask whether this warm official affection is based on mutual hostility toward a third or fourth party and whether it is shared by the people.

The question as to what kind of a Bulgarian regime has established friendship with Tito is easy to answer. Bulgaria's present government is a replica of Tito's. They are both revolutionary governments, both Communist-led, both warmly attached to Soviet Russia, both brutally totalitarian, and both dependent on revolutionary armies.

The most striking single illustration of the nature of the Bulgarian regime is the fact that it has been directed from the beginning by one of the ablest and most famous Communists in the world, the Bulgarian George Dimitroff, former secretary of the Comintern and long a member of Russia's Communist Presidium. He enjoyed international fame two decades before Tito came to the attention of the world.

Shortly after the First World War he became the most forceful leader of the Bulgarian Communist Party—though not its nominal chief—and in the fall of 1923 launched a revolution against Bulgaria's dictatorial regime. The revolution was crushed and Dimitroff fled through Serbia and Germany to Russia, where he soon won an enviable position among the first organizers of world revolution. He attained an international stature not far below that of the chief Russian Bolsheviks. He survived all the purges, enjoyed Stalin's confidence as much as he had Lenin's, and won undying fame by defying Goering at the Reichstag fire trial in Leipzig in December, 1933. Such is the man behind Bulgaria's new regime.

This does not mean that during the first year of Bulgaria's Communist regime Dimitroff held governmental posts such as Tito held in Yugoslavia. To use a Bulgarian expression, he "functioned more as the Holy Ghost," since he was physically absent from the scene. He served as a living legend among the Bulgarian Communists, as a combined John Brown, Lincoln, Lenin, and St. George. He was called "the greatest son of Bulgaria," "the most gifted Balkan Slav," "the champion of the poor," "the liberator of the exploited." While still in Moscow, he was the first candidate on the government ticket for the Parliamentary elections that were to take place in August, 1945. He returned during November of that year. The Dimitroff saga, the long Dimitroff anti-bourgeois struggle, Dimitroff ideals, and actual Dimitroff leadership have determined the character of the present Bulgarian regime. With the dynasty removed, his power is practically absolute.

Bulgaria's Communist government came into power by a revolution in the early morning of September 9, 1944. Rumania had capitulated, the Red Army had occupied Bucharest, entered Bulgaria, and was on the way to Sofia. The former transitional Bulgarian government, led by an Agrarian, Kosta Muravieff, who was the brother-in-law of the martyred Peasant chief, Alexander Stamboliisky, had already ceased fighting against the Allies, had adopted an anti-Nazi policy, and was trying to make peace. When the attempt was spurned by the Red Army, which was advancing through Bulgaria unopposed over carpets of red flowers amid red banners, all authority broke down and every Bulgarian became his own master. At that moment a group of conspirators, organized in the Fatherland Front and led by Communists, reached out their hands and took the reins of power, which they still hold.

They had long been carrying on a rather ineffective underground activity, causing little damage to the German occupiers and bringing little aid to the Allies. However, they had uncompromising anti-Nazi aims, had shown unreserved devotion to the Big Three, and had set up a secret apparatus ready to seize power. The Communists used it, just as Tito used his Liberation Front.

The Bulgarian conspiratorial Partisan movement, or Fatherland Front, consisted of the Agrarian League or Peasant Party, the Communists, the Socialists, and Zveno, the last of which was a military league or cabal with very few political adherents. Zveno was strong because of its military power and the Socialists because of their moral power. They both had prestige but not many votes. This means that the chief might of the Fatherland Front was due to the Peasants and the Communists. The Peasants were by far the more numerous throughout the country, and the Communists, the better organized and better led. The Communists were city people, long accustomed to underground activity, well trained in subversive acts, ruthlessly dictatorial, vigorously disciplined, and inspired by Soviet ideals.

The Bulgarian Communists are among the bravest, most devoted, most efficient, and cruelest revolutionists I have known. From the age of sixteen to sixty they defy every opponent, accept every danger and press unswervingly toward their goal. They had been outlawed and for two full decades had been subjected to repressions that were sometimes savage; yet they remained strong and active, in caves, catacombs, and sewers. They had a hagiography that was glorious and a saga of heroism that danced as stars before every rebel's eyes. They made stirring declamations, sang ringing songs, and chanted thunderous slogans that picked them up and placed them beside all the heroes of all the nations that had ever fought the good fight for common people. Most of the Communists were intellectuals, some were workers, a few peasants. Their program was a political Second Coming. They were worshippers before Lenin's altar—audacious, savage, ecstatic political Pentecostalists, preparing for the Day. It came during the night of September 8 and the faithful went to meet their messiah, Marshal Feodor Tolbukhin, leading his triumphant Red Army toward Sofia. Chief among the bridesmaids was Mrs. Tsola Dragoicheva. She soon became the mistress of Bulgaria.

It was plain that the Socialists and Agrarians would be no match for these able and experienced Communists, backed by Russia and the Red Army. The non-Communists were soon brought to order. The purging of the Socialists was fairly easy. The Communists simply brushed them aside. Communists physically took possession of their organizations, laying hands on Socialist clubs, the well-developed cooperative organization, "Napred," and the party paper. The Communists had the brute force and used it.

A few Socialists, fearing perhaps a resurgence of political reaction but most of all desiring jobs and posts, went with the Communists, serving them as tools. They form a show window which the Communists like to display to the world as a proof of Fatherland Front democracy. Actually, the Communist-serving Bulgarian Socialists are among the most despised renegades in their country, serving tyrants in violation of all Socialist principles, mostly for the sake of personal rewards.

The bulk of the Socialist Party remained staunchly loyal to Socialist ideals. The foremost leader, Krustyu Pastouhoff, was given a seven-year prison term for criticizing the Communists, and many of his loyal supporters were sent by the Communists to join him.

The purge of the Peasant Party was more difficult and more painful. The Communist-Peasant struggle resulted in an internal upheaval, the resignation of four cabinet ministers and grave international repercussions. The size of this party, its historic traditions, the almost unanimous anti-Communist sentiment of Bulgaria's peasants, who form 75 per cent of the population, the boldness of the Agrarian chiefs and their perfect anti-Nazi, anti-Fascist record, enabled the Peasants to carry on a long, anti-Communist resistance. Indeed, they are still fighting the Communist regime.

The ablest, most influential, most radical, and most aggressively anti-Nazi Peasant leader was Dr. G. M. Dimitroff, who has been fighting reaction for two decades. He began working for the western democracies and against Hitler long before Bulgaria entered the war, at a time when Bulgarian Communists along with Mother Russia were whooping it up for Nazi Germany and calling the Anglo-Saxon powers imperialistic, capitalistic oppressors. Because of Dr. G. M. Dimitroff's anti-Nazi activity, his aggressive opposition to King Boris, and his efforts to organize a union of all democratic elements in an anti-Nazi front, he was condemned to death and managed to flee the country just a step ahead of the Gestapo. Some uninformed or unscrupulous American writers have said that G. M. Dimitroff, commonly called "Gemeto" to distinguish him from the famous Communist, George Dimitroff (who is no relative), was a right-wing Agrarian. That is completely misleading—Gemeto and his colleagues are of the old "Pladne group," constituting the extreme left wing, which has always advocated a United Front with all radical elements and made the utmost endeavors to work with the Communists. The most typical leftist Agrarians in Europe were the Gemeto-Kosta-Todoroff group of Bulgarians. Among its other Peasant leaders were Nichola Petkoff, George Yourdanoff, Asen Pavloff, all "tried by fire," that is by prisons, by the police, and by concentration camps. Petkoff is now in prison.

These men and other equally brave colleagues worked with the Bulgarian Communists in the Fatherland Front for six months before they became irrevocably convinced that they were collaborating with tyrants. They demanded freedom of political action in the Front, and when this was denied tried to follow an independent, democratic course. They were bitterly attacked by the Communist Party, which was helped by the Communist militia, the Communist police, the Communist Gestapo, the Communist-led army, and the bitter persecution still continues. Gemeto was arrested, escaped, and fled to the house of the American Political Representative to save his life. Their group was physically expelled by Communist bruisers from a phony Agrarian Congress, packed by Communist-led Peasant tools. Subsequently, the rump Peasant Party, emanating from the phony Congress, accepted the Communist dictatorship and consented to work as Communist agents. This means that the Fatherland Front, as now constituted, consists of out-and-out Communists, Communist-Agrarian puppets, Communist-Socialist puppets, and a few Zveno military conspirators, serving the Communists as puppets. The first Parliament elected by the regime, in November, 1945, had the same composition as the "Front"; it was a hand-picked Communist-led body of rabid "yes-sayers." The Parliament chosen a year later at elections marked by terror, falsehood, and violence had a group of genuine opposition members.

The Fatherland Front, which has largely controlled Bulgaria since September 9, 1944, is managed by a Central or National Committee, of which the Communist, Mrs. Tsola Dragoicheva, is Secretary or Chief. As long as George Dimitroff was in Russia she was guided by remote control. For more than a year, she was the most powerful Bulgarian Communist on the spot. Now she shines only in the light of her effulgent master.

Mrs. Dragoicheva, in an official report of about one hundred pages, tells us what the Fatherland Front did during the first half year of its existence. According to her, it formed 7292 committees throughout the country, which "controlled" the government, "mediated" between the nation and the government, and in many cases "functioned as the government." The committees were created by local revolutionary groups, which means they were self-appointed. Mrs. Dragoicheva herself says, very emphatically, they would not have been able to establish themselves had it not been for the help of the Red Army. According to the regime's own spokesman, it owes its existence to Marshal Tolbukhin's soldiers in Bulgaria.

According to her official report, about 59 per cent of the members of the 7292 all-powerful committees were Communists, about 36 per cent Agrarians, over 3 per cent Socialists, and about 2 per cent Zvenoists. In other words, at the beginning there were about three Communists to two non-Communists and five Communists to three Agrarians or Peasant Party members. The leadership of the Central Committee was flamingly Communist with Tsola Dragoicheva herself giving orders. Officially, also, as Mrs. Dragoicheva says, Partisan veterans were favored above all other Bulgarians in getting key positions wherever they wanted them. Up to 90 per cent of these veterans, according to her, were Communists. Such was the original composition of the Fatherland Front, but after the purge of Peasants, Socialists, and the 2 per cent of Zvenoists, it contained no committee member anywhere in the land who was not either an official Communist or a Communist agent. In the fall of 1945, a part of an insignificant Radical Party joined the Communists. As the Bulgarians say, the group went to Communist headquarters in a single cab. It later faded out.

One of the first tasks of the Fatherland Front was to attempt a complete spiritual reorientation of Bulgarian life. It proclaimed that September 9, 1944, when it seized power, marked a new era. Aping Mussolini, Mrs. Dragoicheva called that September morning the beginning of a new dispensation. It is as January First in Year One of new Bulgaria. Mrs. Dragoicheva has the same sentiments as a more famous absolutist, who spoke rapturously of a new millennial Reich. And like her totalitarian forerunner, Adolf, she is leaving nothing to chance. The Bulgarians are ordered vigorously and assiduously to recognize and promote the new cultural epoch. All "religious-superstitious aberrations" are to be replaced by "scientific truth." The perpetuation of old religious superstitions is forbidden as an offense against the new state.

This means, in plain terms, that Marxian ideology is to dominate. The Marxian apocalypse and the Leninist Second Coming are to delude the nation. Pupils have been explicitly forbidden on holidays to sing such a beloved hymn as "Holy Father," much resembling "A Mighty Fortress Is Our God." Prayer for divine help is considered a cowardly escape for primitive minds, belief in a divine purpose is a childish myth, faith in spiritual healing a sign of mental weakness, and expectation of spiritual continuity is "pie in the sky." They are relics of Fascism. Individual responsibility is swallowed up in mass action. Everything is done to submerge the individual man and woman. For instance, declamations and solos are forbidden at school exercises. Mass declamations and mass singing are required, by express ministerial orders. Everything is done to promote regimentation and to smother individual initiative.

The idol of the new spiritual order has been the swaggering, pistol-toting, man-killing, institution-destroying Partisan. Kindergarten teachers were ordered to tell tiny children of these heroes. All schoolteachers were commanded to make pupil and student programs center about Partisan celebrities. Partisan pupils came to school with pistols on them, and occasionally caused trouble. Into that beautiful ideal, according to official reports, Bulgaria's spiritual life was to be transfigured.

How does the transfiguration affect Justice? Bulgaria has a brand new Justice—as new as Tiglath-pileser—of which its creators are very proud. They had sound movies taken of its mass executions, and sent them all over Russia, the Prime Minister said. This Justice found impressive expression in the sixty-eight People's Courts, scattered throughout Bulgaria.

The courts were set up by self-appointed Fatherland Front committees. They did not emanate from nor were they controlled by the Ministry of Justice, the Cabinet, or the Supreme Court. Groups of men and women formed committees and these committees established courts to kill people whom they didn't like. Anyone could be a judge who was twenty-one years old and a Bulgarian citizen. Especially sought for judges were the Partisan-veterans and others who have suffered in fighting against the established state institutions during the last twenty-two years. As the Premier and the Communist Secretary, Tsola Dragoicheva, jubilantly announced, "the condemned were now the condemners."

The purpose of the courts, as officially described, was "razplata," meaning paying back or getting even. It was lynch law. The courts were a device through which the Communists wiped out their political opponents. If the American Communists, William Z. Foster, Joseph North, Sam Sillen, Mike Gold, and Benjamin Davis, with the cooperation of a few other self-chosen left-wing totalitarians, should set up a court to hang, after a day's trial, Hoover, Landon, Vandenberg, Dewey, the *Times*'s Sulzberger, and the *Tribune*'s McCormick, with photographers filming the dangling victims, we would have a picture of Bulgaria's People's Justice in the new order.

The Bulgarian courts based their political decisions on the most repressive laws in Bulgaria's modern history. Not only did the Communists preserve the drastic wartime laws promulgated by pro-Nazi governments to suppress civil liberties, but they decreed a basic new law "For the defense of the Regime," making "Fascist" criticism of the Fatherland Front government a capital offense. Later they increased the scope even of that law to catch every editor or speaker whom they wanted to silence. This makes opposition activity extremely difficult. Prison, a beating, or a concentration camp await almost every vigorous oppositionist, and even death stalks him at terrifyingly close range. One of the flagrant examples of Communist terror was the speech of dictator George Dimitroff on the eve of the October 27, 1946, elections in which he warned every opposition voter to remember the fate of Drazha Mihailovitch.

Most of the press is the mouthpiece of the government; only three opposition papers have been permitted, and all of them have been suspended at frequent and occasionally long intervals. Now one is definitely prohibited, one indefinitely suspended, and one stopped by Communist labor union chiefs. Bulgaria has no opposition press. The radio is exclusively in the hands of the government.

History also is being transfigured. And books are brought into line. Hitler showed the way there. They are not burnt, because

Bulgaria too badly needs paper. They are merely purged. All libraries are purified, even private ones. And new books are to be purified even before they're written. The Propaganda Minister, according to an official report, is kindly looking after that. He tells writers what works to translate and also what new books to compose. Of course, folderol about moonbeams or mother love or spiritual grandeur is eliminated. Scientific stuff about the class war, the Soviet millennium, heroic rebels, and American "Fascism" is extolled. Even lullabies are to bristle with the class war.

Also, according to official data, a gigantic cultural spy system has been set up. The government has appointed councils to spy on the provinces and note what people sing and play and how deep their dirges are. The nation is commanded to give only happy entertainments. Teachers are commanded to spy on pupils; the Communist Parents' Association to spy on teachers.

Films are distributed exclusively by the Propaganda Ministry. New propaganda theaters have been opened. Right-thinking poets, artists, and actors are given sinecures.

The staffs of schoolteachers and professors have been thoroughly purged and only those with right thoughts retained. A professor who somehow slipped through the net and made a non-Marxian statement to a student was vehemently attacked in Parliament and his immediate dismissal was demanded. What the Communist Parliament demands is carried out.

The student body has been sieved and is being re-sieved to strain out all people without right thoughts. No student can enter the university without a certificate of right thinking from a Fatherland Front (Communist) Committee. Youth and children are forced into "Progressive" (Communist) Societies.

The army has been brought into Communist hands and serves as an agency of the Communist Party. It is directed by Bulgarians who served in the Soviet Red Army. These officers are aided by more than four hundred Communist commissars who have officerial authority and indoctrinate both men and officers. Great pictures of Stalin and George Dimitroff beam from Bulgarian army barracks, over which in many cases red stars glow and red flags wave.

The most influential body in the provinces is the militia. It is largely self-directed and is often above the government and laws. It dictates to many government officials, makes its own rules, and often tells courts what sentences to pronounce. There is no state institution or government department, not even the army, that can control the militia in some parts of the country. In many of the provinces it is master, taking what it pleases, dispossessing whom it pleases, physically eliminating Bulgarian citizens according to its will. It and the People's Courts have killed no fewer than twelve thousand Bulgarians, mostly ordinary, independent, solid community leaders, along with a few war criminals and Fascists. The militiamen are heavily armed, most of the leaders had long been subversive, working as rebels against previous governments, and some are ordinary bandits. Brigands can with impunity rob Bulgarians in the name of the new order and "for the good of the common people." Such operators become heroes. Does anyone believe that many judges, state officials, or teachers would dare to refuse the demand of such heavily-armed, brutal, capricious militiamen?

According to a new Bulgarian law, the police or militia can arrest any Bulgarian and force him to work for the state six months—or more—on the pretext that he is not engaged in a useful occupation or is idle. There is no redress. It is a police measure, requiring no warrant.

And propaganda pressure is almost as formidable as physical terror. The Fatherland Front holds meetings all over the land. For example, the Secretary, Mrs. Dragoicheva, proudly reports that during one quarter in one county the Fatherland Front held 2759 indoor meetings, 353 outdoor mass meetings, and gave 1342 entertainments. Altogether more than twenty-three thousand meetings were held in about five months. That is one hundred and fifty a day with extras on Sunday.

In towns or cities in which Bulgarians were to be brought before People's Courts, the Fatherland Front's propaganda became almost hysterical. Special vengeance meetings were held with armed men drumming up audiences. A special state-maintained daily paper, *People's Justice*, was widely distributed. Day and night the radio beamed furious imprecations against the accused and fervid appeals for "justice." Teachers cried for "justice," students demanded "justice," Partisan-veterans shrieked for vengeance, and as a climax, there marched through the town or city of the forthcoming trial, ominous "processions of black widows," or "of women with black kerchiefs," moaning, wailing, and shouting for vengeance. They were the mothers, sisters, wives, or relatives of persons who during the last two decades had suffered in the fight to overthrow Bulgarian governments. Since the Communist-bourgeois fight in Bulgaria has been very bitter, there were many "black widows" and "black orphans."

The spectacle of hundreds of bitter, bereaved women, uttering Biblical curses, calling down cruel imprecations, and crying for the swift avenging of dear ones is moving. It resembles a classic Greek drama or the Jewish exiles at Babylon, beseeching Jehovah to beat the brains of enemy babies against the rocks. Such dirges did not predispose judges toward objectivity. And as the judges convened, crowds demonstrated with furious cries before the courthouse; they even shouted curses in the courtroom. Such were the forces bringing in the new cultural era. Most of the principal shouters for "vengeance" were Communists and relatives of Communists who had long been actively subversive.

One may say without exaggeration that almost every aspect of Bulgaria's new order resembles Hitler's Third Reich in brutality, ruthlessness, the suppression of freedom, the perversion of truth, and the repression of public opinion! One exception is better treatment of Jews; another is a small degree of liberty for some Socialists and Peasants.

Now we may ask why Tito has formed such intimate official relations with such a Bulgaria. In the first place, he may have wanted harmony and peace among the Balkan Slavs. This is a noble motive and a basic Communist doctrine. Communists have some excellent points in their programs.

However, of more importance is the fact that such Bulgaro-Yugoslav fraternization is directed by Russia. Tito and George Dimitroff are following the directions of a single master. They are organizing the twenty million Balkan Slavs to serve as Soviet Russia's spearhead in the Balkans. This is the most formidable indigenous power that has existed there for centuries. Serving the Soviet Union and using Macedonia as an entering wedge, it brings Russia closer to Salonika than she has been since San Stefano Bulgaria was created sixty-eight years ago.

Does this Bulgaro-Yugoslav *rapprochement* promote Balkan tranquillity? The answer is conditioned on two considerations. One is that the Balkan Slavs are united by dictators serving a foreign power. Can despots truly unite nations? And will freedom-loving Balkan mountaineers unite in subjugation? Usually nations unite to win liberty. In 1912 Bulgaria, Serbia, and Montenegro united to free the Balkan Slavs from Turkey. Whether Bulgaria, Serbia, Croatia, Slovenia, and Montenegro will now unite to serve domestic and foreign absolutists seems problematical. It may be that Tito and Dimitroff will make Balkan Slav unity odious for many decades.

In addition, Bulgaro-Yugoslav unity may be used to disrupt rather than solidify Balkan harmony. Its main purpose may be Slav expansion.

So far, indeed, it has been used for that purpose.

A friend of the Balkan Slavs rejoices at the thought that all the Bulgarian and Yugoslav peasants from the Black to the Aegean Seas might now tend their fields in peace and devote their energies to gardens and vineyards, orchards and schools, but closer study shows that self-imposed autocrats are already oppressing these Slav peasants and setting them against their neighbors, as has not been the case since Turkish domination ended.

As a result of this close cooperation, Bulgaria, a defeated member of the Axis, continues to show extreme aggression toward Greece, our victorious ally. She recently admitted the harboring of armed guerrillas fighting in Greece against the Athens government and categorically refused on one occasion to let the United Nations enter Bulgarian territory to study the question of Bulgarian aid to Communist conspirators seeking to set up a rebel state in northern Greece.

Also, the Bulgarian government, strong in Tito's encouragement and Soviet support, demanded during May, 1947, the immediate recall of an American colonel, alleged to have spoken about the Sofia regime in an unfriendly way and required the American Military Mission to hand over to the Bulgarian militia a Bulgarian employee accused of belittling the Bulgarian Communist leaders and their system.

CHAPTER TWENTY-ONE

The Role of Macedonia

ONE of Marshal Tito's major innovations was the setting up of "Free Macedonia" as one of the independent states in Federative Yugoslavia. The five other constituent units are Serbia, Montenegro, Croatia, Slovenia, and Bosnia-Herzegovina. Two of the six units, namely, Slovenia and Macedonia, are involved in very serious international difficulties. The "Macedonian Problem" is one of the most explosive and dangerous in all Europe, implicating not only the small Balkan states, but the Old World's two major empires. Macedonia is the vortex of a whirlpool of bitter conflicts. If Tito could find a way to resolve them he would deserve the gratitude of mankind. But did he achieve this by creating "Free Macedonia"? Perhaps he accentuated the conflicts. Let us see.

The term Macedonia was in common use even before the time of Alexander the Great, also called Alexander the Macedonian. The region embraced by the term may have changed some during the last two thousand years. In any case, it now includes territories incorporated into or claimed by four states, Yugoslavia, Bulgaria, Greece, and Albania. It is inhabited by representatives of those four nations, with some Turks and a few Aroumanians added. The total area is about the size of West Virginia and the population about two million five hundred thousand.

Macedonia passed under Turkish domination more than five hundred years ago and remained a part of the Turkish Empire until 1912, when a military coalition of the small Balkan powers drove the Turks out. During that long period of foreign rule, the various nationalities inhabiting Macedonia became almost inextricably mixed. Greek, Latin, Slav, Turanian, and Albanian lived side by side in the dozen larger towns, while Greek villages lay near Slav villages and Albanian hamlets were found just across the gully or around the mountain from Turkish hamlets. Naturally the claims of the various nationalities egregiously overlapped and ambitious states aggressively backed one or another of the conflicting claims. No similar area has been the center of more irreconcilable, irredentist longings.

The principal modern claimant, or perhaps one should say the most aggressive claimant, was Bulgaria and the Bulgaro-Macedonians. Up until 1912, a majority of the inhabitants of Macedonia were Slavs. The second largest group was Greek. Naturally the Slavs were in conflict with the Greeks. But they were also engaged in a furious internecine Slav fight, because the Bulgars claimed the Slav Macedonians as Bulgarians, while the Serbs claimed them as Serbs. Consequently, there was a fierce, five-cornered struggle among Turks, Albanians, Greeks, Serbs, and Bulgarians, with Bulgarians often pitted against the field, and with Turkey playing one Christian group off against another. And above these bloody combats were the Great Powers, frequently intervening to restore harmony and each trying to protect its own interest. The Teutons and Russians both wanted to dominate Salonika, Macedonia's chief port, while Great Britain and France were determined to prevent them from doing it.

The rival local claimants maintained conspiratorial organizations for the purpose of realizing their aims by force. These organizations and the Balkan states supporting them provoked revolutions, wars and many acts of terror. For fully fifty years Macedonia has been a scene of violence, a classic stage for political murders, plunder, treachery, and the burning of villages. Helpless, homeless peasant refugees have constantly fled across Macedonia, with mothers carrying babies on their backs and with burning homes lighting midnight skies. In 1903 there was a major revolution and during the following decades frequent raids, assassinations, massacres, and bomb outrages. There were wars about Macedonia in 1912, 1913, 1915, 1924, 1941–1945. Wherever Macedonia appears on the pages of history, the word is written in letters of blood.

And the recent cause of much of the blood was Bulgaria. It was the chief aggressor because it believed Macedonia was inhabited by Bulgarians, whom it must free. "Freeing Macedonia" was the main aim of Bulgaria's foreign policy and was considered the holy duty of almost every Bulgarian patriot. Macedonia was imprinted deeply in Bulgarian hearts, it echoed in Bulgarian songs, and gleamed bright or grim from Bulgarian poetry. At one time or another, almost every modern Bulgarian boy has dreamed of being a Macedonian revolutionist or chetnik. "Freeing Macedonia" has also been almost as vital an element in Bulgaria's internal politics as in its external politics. Many a Bulgarian government has been overthrown because of the Macedonian question.

The strongest, bloodiest, ablest, and most famous—or notorious—Macedonian revolutionary society was a Bulgarian creation called the Internal Macedonian Revolutionary Organization or IMRO, which came to be a symbol of terrorism. Its greatest revolutionary act was the uprising of 1903, beginning on August 2, or "Ilin Den." This was a bold attack on the Turks and was accompanied by many brave deeds. However, in the course of a few weeks it was suppressed with characteristic Turkish cruelty, which left burned villages and nameless graves and sent thousands of Macedonian refugees rushing toward Bulgaria. Nevertheless, in spite of all the suffering, frustration, and defeat, Ilin Day came to be an almost holy date among Bulgaro-Macedonians. They consider the leaders of the uprising, especially Gotse Delcheff, the greatest of the great. He is the Macedonian Patrick Henry, while Ilin Day is the Macedonian Fourth of July—which failed.

And the most significant aspect of these vital but sad events, indelibly imprinted in the hearts and spirits of Bulgaria, is that IMRO, Ilin Day, and Gotse Delcheff were Bulgarian. They are part of Bulgaria's drive toward Salonika and beyond. They are a symbol—the most explosive symbol—of Bulgarian expansion and Bulgarian irredentism. They have been synonymous with Bulgarian antipathy toward Serbs and Greeks.

As a result of the wars and revolutions that took place after 1903, Macedonia was repeatedly divided and when Hitler attacked Greece through Bulgaria in 1941, 50 per cent of the area was in Greece, 40 per cent in Serbia or Yugoslavia, and 10 per cent in Bulgaria. Naturally, these were contiguous areas. By that time, because of purges, massacres, and exchanges of populations, most of the inhabitants of Macedonia in Greece were Greeks; all of the inhabitants of Macedonia in Bulgaria were Bulgarians; and most of those in Yugoslav Macedonia were Slavs or Albanians, with some Turks. Until the middle of the 1930's, most Bulgarians claimed the Slavs in Yugoslav Macedonia as Bulgars and IMRO continued to work for their liberation—not from Turkey now, but from Yugoslavia, or more specifically from Serbia. However, IMRO's terrorist activities gradually dwindled and by 1941, the terrible Macedonian problem had been tentatively settled by cutting the Gordian knot. Bayonets had established the borders. The Serbs were coercively making Serbs of the inhabitants of their Macedonia, and the Greeks had settled Greeks in their Macedonia.

I am not pretending that from the ethnological point of view this was the right solution. I have followed Macedonian developments intently and on the spot for a third of a century and believe that in 1912 most of Bulgaria's ethnological claims were just. Most Macedonians were Slavs, most Slav Macedonians were more nearly Bulgars than Serbs. However, vast changes took place during the three decades after 1912 and the forcible solution of the Macedonian problem by Serb and Greek swords, along with the diplomatic decisions of the Great Powers, had been accepted, even by the Bulgarian government.

Many Bulgarians had grown tired of fighting all their Balkan neighbors because of Macedonia and were inclined to let bygones be bygones, in spite of the great sadness in their hearts. They still sang and talked of Macedonia and they cried and prayed about it. They felt as the Jewish exiles in Babylon and they reverently watched grand Ilin Day processions which were annually held throughout Bulgaria, but by 1941 most Bulgarians did not want to provoke a war for Macedonia any more than Mexico would provoke a war for southern California. The Macedonian question was more nearly closed than it had been for half a century.

But Hitler opened it up again. When he attacked Yugoslavia and Greece in the spring of 1941, he used the Bulgarian state as a base of operations and the Bulgarian nation as an ally. In payment for this help he gave Bulgaria all of Yugoslav Macedonia and much Greek territory. The Bulgarians immediately occupied the areas, formally annexed them, set up civilian administrations, re-established Bulgarian civilians there, and built roads to connect the "liberated provinces," permanently, with the Bulgarian "motherland." When the Germans were expelled from the Balkans late in 1944 and Bulgaria capitulated, Greece and Yugoslavia received back their lost territories. Consequently Macedonia's boundaries were re-established as they had been at the beginning of 1941. Thus, at the beginning of 1945, Macedonia, which had changed hands many times and been the scene of countless battles, was back about where it was in 1918 and the situation appeared once more to have been stabilized.

But that appearance was deceptive because an extremely dynamic new element had entered the situation. It was the creation of "Free Macedonia," a federal unit in Tito's Federative Yugoslavia. This new creation is a political bomb—time bomb, not atomic one. Free Macedonia covers 10,230 square miles of territory, which makes it a little larger than Massachusetts. It has about one million inhabitants, most of whom are Slavs, but beside them is a large Albanian minority. Free Macedonia has a government of its own and claims for itself the attributes of a sovereign state. Its capital, the city of Skoplje, or as the Bulgarians call it, Skopie, is rather pleasantly situated on the Vardar River, about one hundred miles from Sofia and two hundred from Belgrade.

In it is a new radio station which is said to be one of the most powerful in the Balkans. And its function is not merely to serve the peasants in the narrow valleys and on the rather barren mountains of Free Macedonia in Yugoslavia but to serve the whole of Macedonia, including both Greek and Bulgarian areas. Indeed, it is to keep all Balkan Slavs daily and nightly aware of Macedonia, its problems and its aims. A daily paper called *New Macedonia* appears, a university functions with Macedonian professors, schools flourish with new Macedonian textbooks, a Macedonian army fills the barracks, the Macedonian language is in official use, and a rigid control is exercised over all economic activities. Skoplje or Skopie and the Macedonia of which it is said to be the queen, are undergoing a revival unique in the history of that area. A dream has come true. For decades Macedonians have shouted, "Macedonia for the Macedonians," and now at last the vision is a reality. Macedonians run Macedonia—that is, the part in Yugoslavia.

This is an exhilarating sight! One is thrilled to see dreams come true and is inspired to see a people freed. But even in one's exhilaration, he must not fail to study the situation carefully. Who are the Macedonians that now run Macedonia and whither are they directing it? Among them are old revolutionists. They have revived the spirit of IMRO and are trying to complete the old Ilin Day uprising. They are turning Macedonia toward Salonika. They want an integral Free Macedonia. And in this they are backed by the Yugoslav Communists.

Free Macedonia is doubly revolutionary. Its leaders are rabidly nationalistic and fanatically Communistic. This is a mighty combination. Macedonia offers an unusual opportunity for the study of social dynamics. Its government is a combination of IMRO, Communism, Bulgarian nationalism, Yugoslav expansiveness, and all-Slav solidarity. Every one of those elements is notoriously explosive. Combined, they constitute a political block-buster ever ready to go off.

Note for a moment the IMRO ingredient in this explosive mixture. The President of Free Macedonia, Dimiter Vlahoff, is the most famous old Macedonian revolutionist alive, and a number of his colleagues have also been active Macedonian conspirators, shooting guns and throwing bombs. They consecrated their lives long ago to the liberation of Macedonia in solemn, mysterious night meetings, before a Bible. They signed their oaths with their blood and went into the hills to kill or be killed. They have repeatedly demanded an "integral Macedonia." They have promised the liberation of all Macedonians. They have stressed the necessity of "freeing Macedonian Salonika, of restoring to Macedonia her God-given seaport." And they have often told eager young Macedonian admirers how they once threw bombs and blew up buildings in Salonika. They and their friends have sent Macedonian revolutionary songs tingling down every glade and reverberating through every mountain cluster.

These men are now attempting to complete that old "sacred task." They have made the chief official day of new Macedonia that glorious old "Ilin Den," which they are now determined to avenge —as the American defeat at Bunker Hill was eventually avenged.

The Macedonian State Printing Office in Skoplje is named "Gotse Delcheff," in honor of the famous revolutionist. An army brigade is named "Sandanski" after another noted member of IMRO.

And Macedonia's Communist banners burn as hot and red as its old revolutionary flags. Vlahoff came to his post of President direct from Moscow. He and the "great George Dimitroff," both Bulgarians, worked side by side in Russia for years and they are working side by side now. Practically every member of the Skoplje government is a crusading Communist, as are most members of local city or district governments in Macedonia.

Nowhere in the Balkan Peninsula is Communism more openly, ardently, and proudly proclaimed. Tito has constantly tried to convince the Western world that his regime is liberal-democratic. Tsola Dragoicheva in Bulgaria tries to convince the Bulgarians that she tolerates non-Communists. But the government of Free Macedonia stoops to no such "pussyfooting." They are as outspoken as their Moscow Comrades. They are Communists and glory in it. They have set up a Communist regime and tell the world to take it or leave it. They want Communist officials, Communist teachers, Communist officers, and Communist editors. They pour out Communist words over the radio and send them streaming from their presses. They follow Russia's line and make no apology for it. They consider themselves a Russian outpost, serving Russia's interests, and feel strong in that role. They tell the world that they're with Russia and Russia with them.

They exult in the reforming fury that moved Lenin and Trotsky. Of course, they're going to turn things upside down. That's why they're there. That's what a revolutionist is for. They have put their hands on practically all the little factories, many of the farms, every promising enterprise, and use them for the glory and aggrandizement of their regime. They confiscate what there is to be confiscated and control whomsoever is left to be controlled. They feel that time is short and there is much to be done to get the Communist conflagration spreading from Skoplje.

Also the Bulgarian fire in Macedonia burns very brightly. The official Macedonian language is essentially Bulgarian, not Serbo-Croatian. The Macedonian radio speaks largely in Bulgarian, the Macedonian papers print largely in Bulgarian, the new schoolbooks are written in the Bulgaro-Macedonian tongue.

The Macedonian army contains many Bulgaro-Macedonians who

long lived in Bulgaria and some Bulgaro-Macedonian officers trained in Bulgaria. As a matter of fact, the Bulgarian government officially gave Free Macedonia a fully equipped Macedonian brigade, sent from Sofia. When in Bulgaria in 1945, I saw Bulgaro-Macedonian refugees from Greece returning to Yugoslavia from Bulgaria, whither they had fled in 1944. They told me they were going to Free Macedonia to help in the fight against Greece.

New Macedonia's attitude toward Greece is that of Sofia in its most nationalistic moods, or of IMRO in its moments of greatest revolutionary fervor. Free Macedonia considers Greece an imperialistic Fascist oppressor, crushing the Slav Macedonians in Greece. The Macedonian government cries to the world of Greek terror, just as Sofia long shrieked of Turkish terror. The Skoplje papers report atrocity stories directed against the Greeks, just as Sofia papers for years seethed with stories of atrocities perpetrated by the "unspeakable Turks."

From Skoplje run underground lines of conspiracy into Greece, just as they used to run from Sofia into Turkey. And into Free Macedonia flee Macedonian refugees from Greece, just as Macedonian refugees used to flee into Bulgaria from Greece. Free Macedonia is a Bulgarian revolutionary station for operations against Greece. And not without importance is the fact that the President of Free Macedonia is from Greek Macedonia. This Communist revolutionist is from the very same town as Bulgaria's last Fascist Minister of the Interior. The Fascist Stanisheff was hanged as a war criminal, but the Communist Vlahoff is carrying out Stanisheff's Bulgarian irredentist policy, with Yugoslavia and Russia behind it.

There also functions in Free Macedonia a semi-autonomous Holy Eastern Orthodox church, which is endeavoring to free Macedonia's ecclesiastical activity from the control of Belgrade. That would make cooperation with Sofia easier and would increase Macedonia's prestige and feeling of independence. Such a Macedonian church would strongly appeal to Macedonia Slavs in Greece. It would be an ideal vehicle for Bulgaro-Macedonian irredentism.

Pan-Slavism, also, intensifies Free Macedonia's expansionist ardor. The Macedonian nation is the world's most enraptured Cinderella. It has emerged from a fearfully long sojourn in Turkish and Balkan kitchens and is now given a place of honor beside marshals and rulers. It has been brought into the all-Slav family amid booming cannon, blaring radios, and thunderous applause. Macedonia and Russia sit side by side. Macedonia, Bulgaria, Poland, and Czechia march hand in hand. Macedonia, the Ukraine, and Slovakia dance together, with newly emancipated Macedonia honored as the belle of the ball.

This all-Slav solidarity is a thrilling experience. It makes a Slav feel even stronger than an American or Britisher. Hard-pressed, long-tortured Macedonia no longer fears any big, bad wolf. The domain of its great comrade and champion extends from Port Arthur and Archangel direct to Skoplje. The Russia, "before which America trembles and England bows low, leads Macedonia by the hand!"

When there's a Pan-Slav Congress in Sofia, Macedonia is there. When the Slavs are all called to Moscow, Macedonia is there. Why, the Slavs from Moscow, Warsaw, Prague, Sofia, Zagreb, and Bratislava gather in Skoplje as Macedonia's guests! In all-Slav choruses you hear Macedonia's voice, in all-Slav orchestras you detect Macedonia's violin—even bass drum. Macedonia has no fear from poor little orphan Greece. Free Macedonia feels its soldiers are the vanguards of a stupendous Slav host, directing the sharp point of a gigantic Slav spear.

Naturally, Tito and the Yugoslav government are not indifferent to all this. They realize the dynamic force of Macedonia, its value as an imperial channel and as an instrument for South Slav aggrandizement. Tito joins with Bulgaria in nurturing and strengthening

Macedonia's independence and irredentism. In Yugoslav periodicals and papers, Free Macedonia is presented as part of integral Macedonia including Greek territory. And when, because of provocative Bulgaro-Macedonian activity in Greece, the Greeks get rough with Slav Macedonian agents, Tito issues vehement anti-Greek threats over all his senders.

In view of that, the question as to whether Tito's Free Macedonia will bring harmony to the Balkans is self-answering. It is already causing constant friction. It may eventually exacerbate Serbo-Bulgarian animosity. It hangs as a Damocles sword over Greece. It is a Soviet dagger directed at an artery of the British Empire. It could be a Croatian instrument in the Croat-Serbian fight. It is a charge of dynamite with many fuses in a very delicately balanced world.

In an ordered Balkans or a Balkans moving toward stability, a Free Macedonia might be an ideal solution of an old and bitter problem. But in the extremely unstable Balkans of the present time, it is an element of disruption.

CHAPTER TWENTY-TWO

Has the Federalizing of Yugoslavia Brought Harmony?

ONE of the outstanding features of the "new Yugoslavia," which Tito and his Partisans boast of having created, is the organizing of the state in six self-governing units, that are also subject to a central or national government. This granting of independence to Slovenia, Croatia, Macedonia, Montenegro, Serbia, and Bosnia-Herzegovina is lauded as Tito's greatest reform. The drawing of Bulgaria into close relations with the new Federation is said to make the reform even more important.

If Tito's federalization of Yugoslavia really meant the establishing of good relations among Serbs, Croatians, Slovenes, Bulgarians, and Macedonians, I would consider it one of the greatest achievements in Balkan history and would join in singing Tito's praises. I know of no Balkan need more urgent than finding a way to make the small nations there free, secure, and neighborly. I have seen myriads of good, honest men and women, scattered over Balkan hills and plains from the Black Sea to the Adriatic, working their fields, tending their sheep, milking their cows, whitewashing their little wicker houses, praying in their village churches, sending their children to school, all trying to create a better life, yet eternally frustrated by wars. These Balkan Slavs closely resemble one another in almost every respect and have common interests; yet they hate one another furiously and often butcher each other savagely. As a result, they constantly live in a state of insecurity and partial subjugation. They need mutual confidence and friendly cooperation above all things.

The ideal way of satisfying this need is clear, namely, through the establishment of a United States of South Slavs. And that is what Tito is said to be preparing. Although the Balkan countries are much more populous than the original thirteen American colonies, they are in a stage of economic development not unlike that of ours in 1776 and have the same longings for freedom, peace, and neighborliness as our own forefathers had. Consequently it would not seem unreasonable to expect them to form some kind of a federal union, as our fathers did. Is it not probable that Marshal Josip Broz-Tito is now playing the role of a Balkan George Washington? May he not turn out to be the father of a harmonious new federation, the United States of the Balkans, a U.S.B.?

Before answering that question it will be well to admit that no federal union is ever made without bloodshed. To create and establish our American Union we fought two terrible wars. The Swiss also fought internal and external wars. The unification of Italy, Germany, France, and even of Great Britain, was accompanied by much bloodshed. Bismarck was not the only unifier who used "blood and iron." Practically every unifier has done it. In view of this inescapable cost of liberation and unification, it would not be strange if much force were required to unite the South Slavs in a satisfactory state. Consequently, one should not condemn Tito merely for using force. Garibaldi, Grant, Cromwell, and Napoleon also used force in establishing national unity.

Two mighty factors usually operate to effect national unification; one is an imperative emotional or religious appeal and the other is the aid or supervision or active intervention of a super-state. Such factors might facilitate the unification of Balkan Slavs. An illustration of how these forces work is provided by the old Austro-Hungarian Empire. The Hapsburgs, using the emotional appeal of the Roman Catholic church, united Czechs, Slovaks, Germans, Croatians, Slovenes, Hungarians, and Italians in a fairly permanent and moderately satisfactory way. There was much oppression in Austria-Hungary but also considerable prosperity, a pretty good administration, and some freedom. Compared to some of the regimes that have followed the Hapsburgs' collapse, those old days seem almost like a golden age. The forces that held the very diverse fifty million people of Austria-Hungary together were the prestige and power of a mighty dynasty and the lure of an impressive religion, presented with masterly skill. For centuries, Roman Catholicism gave millions of Central Europeans a loyalty above class, group or nationality attachments, while the old, renowned monarchy with its armies, courts, and economic power overawed or suppressed local rebels.

Such forces, operating in the Balkans, might aid unification. An outside empire, with vast prestige and power might force the small nations there to repress their local hatreds and work together in a grander plan, for a more glorious aim. Also, some spiritual ideal might be conceived that would swallow up Roman Catholicism, Eastern Orthodoxy, Islam, Serb chauvinism, Bulgarian chauvinism, and Croat chauvinism. That new ideal, of course, would have to be carried by a flaming, tempestuous emotion, that would sweep up the other divisive emotions.

Where could one find two such miracle-working agencies for transforming the Balkans? Certainly no single existing ecclesiastical religion could provide the necessary emotional hurricane; therefore a secular religion would have to be invoked. Well, a hot secular religion already exists, in the form of Communism. Its lure and impact for Balkan Slavs is increased by a Pan-Slav setting or aura. Communism came to the Balkans from Slav Russia. It has served as a vehicle for spiritual *rapprochement* among many Slavs. It is closely associated with the unprecedented Slav triumph over the Teutons and is inextricably bound up with Russia's overpowering position in the world. Pan-Slavism serves as a grand secular cathedral, in which the Balkan Communists may hear the Marxian mass. The Communist saints are there, adorning the rosy Slavic walls; the Slavic liturgy rolls sonorously over the Maritsa, the Vardar, the Sava, and the Drina rivers; Slavic marshals, warriors, emperors, and revolutionists occupy the honored places by the altar, and imperialistic Slavic Communism forms a Jacob's ladder to a new heaven. Is it not conceivable that this terrific, august and awful secular religion might sweep up the youngest generations of Catholics, Orthodox, and Moslems in the Slavic Balkans?

In addition, the strongest land empire on earth is actually and physically in the Balkans, guiding this mighty emotional force. Russian soldiers, officers, diplomats are stationed in Bulgaria, Macedonia, Serbia, Croatia, Montenegro. Russian trucks and American-made, Russian-occupied jeeps roll along the Balkan roads. The vital decisions in each province are made by or in conjunction with Russians. The recent liberation of each Slav Balkan nation was directly effected by Russia, with Allied help. The future place of Bulgaria and Yugoslavia in the world depends on Russia. For Bulgaria, Macedonia, Montenegro, or Serbia to go against Russia now is unthinkable. For them even to reject an individual Russian command is almost inconceivable.

Consequently, Russia can coordinate every action from Ljubljana to Varna. Balkan Slavs, from Dobrudja to Montenegro, are actively working together, singing similar songs, repeating identical slogans, giving similar broadcasts, carrying out identical policies, writing similar sentiments in their papers, using similar administrative methods, and following one great plan. If they continue to tie their future to the future of ascending, advancing Russia, moving toward a pinnacle of glory, will they not be assured of reaching a position of international importance which until now they have never even approached? And if they understand that, is it not certain that they will stick to Russia's plan for Balkan unification and cooperation?

I shall not attempt to answer that question just yet, but must say that Tito seems to be in an unprecedentedly favorable situation for establishing a Federative Yugoslavia and for bringing in Bulgaria, either as a member or as a close affiliate. And it should be added that Tito got away to a good start. For a considerable period after the collapse of Yugoslavia he and his Partisans were almost the only bearers of the Yugoslav idea. The Croatian Quisling, Ante Pavelitch, opposed Yugoslavia with all his might and main. He pictured Yugoslavia as worse than the devil himself. The Croatian Peasant leader, Dr. Machek, was neutral toward Yugoslavia during the first year of the war. He said no word in its defense. The Serbian leader, General Mihailovitch, worked mainly for Serbia, at first, and many of his followers were bitterly opposed to the restoration of Yugoslavia. This left Tito almost alone, for a while, as the champion of Yugoslavia, and he made the most of the opportunity. Not only in words but also in acts. In all of Tito's organizations, Serbs, Croats, Slovenes, Montenegrins, Bosnians, and even Moslems worked harmoniously together by day and night. Tito stressed this Yugoslav activity as one of the chief points in his program. He played it up in his papers, pamphlets, speeches, and on the radio. So he now appears before his countrymen with an indisputable record of having worked indefatigably for a Federative Yugoslavia.

And more important than the foregoing favorable circumstances is the desire of most Yugoslavs that the state be organized on a basis that would give every group self-government. The historical Yugoslav units have as passionate a longing for "states' rights" as most Americans have had and as many still have.

Nevertheless, as we carefully examine the situation in its entirety, we see that Tito's Federative Yugoslavia has fatal defects. Here are some of them.

In the first place, Tito's plan is phony. It is insincere and deceptive. It is a campaign promise made, in the heat of a furious political fight, for the purpose of luring followers. During this political struggle, the Croatian Partisans repeatedly wrote and spoke of a *sov-*

ereign Croatia, with a Croatian army defending an *independent* Croatian state. The words sovereign and independent have been strongly stressed. Likewise, there is a sovereign Montenegro and a sovereign Macedonia. The latter is supposed to have an independent Macedonian army. Now, is it conceivable that in a territory no larger than the state of Oregon, there will be six independent, sovereign states, working together without authoritative central control? Can Yugoslavia, lying in the most bitterly disputed area in Europe, have six armies and six state departments? Can it administer its forests in six different ways, have six economic systems, and six systems of education?

No, that whole plan was a political slogan based on falsehood. Actually, in every vital respect, Yugoslavia has the most ruthlessly exacting centralized government in the history of that state. Real freedom and autonomy for any part of Partisan Yugoslavia is proving to be a myth. Neither King Alexander nor Prince Paul, neither Dictator Zhivkovitch nor Fascist Stoyadinovitch exercised such rigid central control as does Tito. To make a brutal comparison, federal independence for the various Yugoslav units is as illusory and phony as the Atlantic Charter has proved for Germany or Poland. The plan is not working because Yugoslav unity and harmony cannot be based on a falsehood.

Secondly, Tito-worship cannot replace Roman Catholicism and Eastern Orthodoxy. I, who write this, am a rather aggressive Protestant, so am defending neither Catholicism nor Orthodoxy. I know that both have grievous defects and that they have been abused by unscrupulous rulers. But compared with either, the worship of Tito is wretched, shabby, and degrading. In spite of all the Pan-Slav tinsel, the rousing Communist creeds, and the hot Marxian Pentecostalism, Communistic Tito-worship will not permanently grip most Yugoslavs. In fact, it does not grip many now. Its idolatry is crude and repellent. As we crush "Hito-worship" in Japan can we install Tito-worship in Yugoslavia? The old Yugoslav religions have got the new cult beaten in every respect. They are more aesthetic, have a greater heart appeal, affect women more deeply, exalt the family to a higher place, offer an incomparably grander ultimate reality than a mere Federative Yugoslavia or a Transplendent Russia or an All-Glorious Josip Broz. In addition, they are inextricably intertwined with national traditions and holidays, with birth, marriage, and death. A Tito gravestone gives little comfort.

Tito has set out to establish a Federative Yugoslavia on the humiliation and repression of two world churches. He has hoped to exalt a flaming emotional ideal that would sweep Catholics and Orthodox Christians out of their churches up into a higher faith, that would supply a Yugoslav imperative and wipe out sectarian differences. It is a grand dream, such as every national leader has had, but Tito is failing. Old religions, especially in peasant lands, are not easily superseded. It took Christianity centuries to supplant paganism in that very Mediterranean world. Also, the pristine fury of ideological Communism is waning. What we see now is sordid imperialism or an even more sordid local political conspiracy, called Communism. The Communist cult is already using a moribund liturgy.

There are indications that the power and prestige of Roman Catholicism as well as of Eastern Orthodoxy are mounting. Europe's sad, wretched men and women are terribly tired of destruction and devastation and hunger and death. They feel an aversion toward cruelty, dirt, and vulgar sloganeers. The Church seems a comforter, a mother, a teacher. It seems clean and pure and above petty lies. The persecutions to which Tito is subjecting it only enhance its value. The Holy Virgin·or the "Mother of God" seems indeed heavenly, when they contemplate a coarse, gun-toting, loud-mouthed Partisan girl. A priest, in spite of all his defects, may seem angelic in comparison with a brutal Partisan commissar, compelling every person in his block to go to Tito-meetings. Rulers have been fighting the Church in Yugoslavia for more than a thousand years and they always get licked. Milan Stoyadinovitch tried it less than ten years ago and the whole Serbian nation rose from mines, furrows, workshops, and officers' barracks to stop him—and it stopped him.

Let any objective reader imagine the ultimate effect in Serbia of Tito's decision to entrust vital church matters to a Jewish Communist, Moshe Piade! It is he who is taking land away from the Serbian Orthodox monasteries. I, a Protestant, certainly have nothing to say in defense of monks or monasticism, but the few monasteries existing in Serbia are humble institutions. The buildings are rather primitive, the land surrounding them limited, and the income from the monks' farming is barely enough to provide a few monks a living. Furthermore, these modest monasteries have been as holiday camps for the nation. Anyone and his family may go there and sojourn for the night. Usually the tourists are given a bean stew or whatever dish of the day may be available. They sleep on bright homespun rugs on earthen floors, after worshipping in little churches. The nation certainly has not felt that the Church was exploiting it by retaining a few thousand acres of monastery lands.

Especially since those lands are historical monuments. The monasteries have rested there in the valleys, on the hillsides or among the woods for many centuries. They were there before the Turkish invasion. They remained there even as Moslem armies swept across the country, carrying crescent-decked banners. They guarded the cross in secure vaults, defended the Serbian faith and on innumerable occasions served as hearths for lighting revolutionary fires. Even more frequently they were hiding places for heroes fighting Serbian oppression. These little monasteries are as inextricably bound with Serbia's fight for liberty as are Plymouth Rock or Bunker Hill with America's fight. And now, as the Serbs will say, "a Communist Jewish infidel" is trying to destroy them. His aim is to weaken the Serbian spirit and undermine the Serbian church. Can Mr. Piade do what sultans, emperors and Adolf Hitler failed to do?

Every American in considering this matter should bear in mind that the Serbian church is an outstanding example of a people's church. It is far from wealthy. Its church edifices are modest. Its priests are not a favored class apart. It is meagerly endowed. The Congregational church in New England is far richer than the Serbian Orthodox church in proportion to membership. The Baptist church of Texas has far more property than the Serbian Orthodox church, and New York Methodist pastors are gilded plutocrats in comparison with Serbian pastors. When Tito orders a "Communist Jewish infidel" to confiscate Serbian church property, the Serbs feel as Kansas Baptists would feel if the Communist William Z. Foster ordered a New York Jewish atheist to confiscate their church property.

I shall say nothing of the spiritual qualities of the Serbian church, but will again point out that this church played a very vital role in bringing Yugoslavia into the war on the side of the democracies, that it stood more militantly adamant against the Nazis than the Federal Council of Churches of Christ in America—even in the most terrible days—and that the clergy of Serbia resisted Tito almost to a man. With the Orthodox church reviving in the world, Moshe Piade's crusade against it in Serbia will only bring discredit to Tito and along with that to his idea of Federal Union.

As for the Catholic church, to which not far from half the Yugoslavs belong, does anyone believe that Tito and his Communists can repress it in Yugoslavia? I am not intimating that it has furthered or now furthers national Yugoslav unity. I would rejoice if all Yugoslavs could be snatched out of their fanatical religious sectarianism and lifted up to some beautiful, new, all-embracing spiritual religion. But my personal longings are very different from hard reality. The stubborn fact is that the Catholic church, which was brought to western Yugoslavia centuries ago, has so worked itself into the lives of the people there, is such a powerful world organization and is on such a global wave of power that Tito's weak Partisans cannot defeat it. Until some far greater prophet than Tito or Stalin comes to carry us *all* onto the Mount of Transfiguration, Yugoslav harmony will have to be established through the churches, or at least with the churches, not by suppressing or supplanting them.

To understand the extent of Tito's failure in his attempt to give Yugoslavia a new emotional synthesis, we should try to imagine the Communist Party, led by William Z. Foster and aided by a few totalitarian, big-city intellectuals, trying to bring Americans to a higher spiritual unity by crusading against all our churches and sects, restricting our private church schools, curtailing our religious press, and obliging us all, from the age of four years up, to get all our spiritual food from state and party propaganda about Marxian revolutionists, "Fascist oppressors," and "monopolistic capitalism." In such a case, revolt would flare up all over the land, and America would unite not around Mr. Foster but against him. Spiritually, Tito is not uniting the Yugoslavs, in spite of his tireless propaganda. He has not created a higher synthesis, only another divisive force.

Besides this, the basis of Tito's power and authority is entirely too small to support a stable, harmonious, Federated Yugoslavia. A small minority is trying to impose a new federative arrangement on a majority. That can be done, if the majority is static or lethargic or cowardly, but not if it is dynamic and daring—as the Yugoslavs are.

We Americans have had sensational illustrations of a minority trying to impose its will on a majority. One such was national prohibition. It failed, even though a large part of the Americans were for prohibition. An even more striking case was the failure of the Northern carpetbaggers to dominate the South after the War between the States. The Northerners then tried to do to the South what Tito's Partisans are trying to do in Slovenia, Croatia, Serbia, and Bosnia, namely, coercively to enforce "love and brotherhood." The South had been utterly defeated. It had surrendered unconditionally. We had set up new regimes in each state, at will, and forcibly established a new order of federal love. But within a few years the South, even in its weakness, swept those imposed regimes away, and that

HAS FEDERALIZATION BROUGHT HARMONY? 241

kind of reconciliation became as a stench throughout the land. It only increased the passionate attachment of the South to its own ways and intensified its hatred for the North.

If the North after a total victory could not impose distasteful regimes on South Carolina and Mississippi, how can Tito's Partisans impose stable Communist regimes on the equally unwilling people of Slovenia, Serbia, Croatia, or even Montenegro?

Tito has now showed his colors. He has established his state apparatus. The personnel has been definitely appointed, the leaders have been installed in their places. The Yugoslavs clearly see who their masters are to be and they perceive that they are fanatical Communists. The camouflage has been removed, the mask discarded. Communists run Yugoslavia's central government and every one of the six provincial governments. Tito holds the same place in Yugoslavia as Mussolini did in Italy; the Yugoslav regime is as much under the control of Communists as the Italian government was under the control of Fascists. And these Communists constitute a very small minority.

A mere handful of extremists run Slovenia. They are not much more representative of the Slovene nation than the first carpetbag government was of South Carolina. They are rejected by the devout Slovene Catholics, by most Slovene liberals, most peasants, the conservatives, and even by most workers. They are no more acceptable to most Slovenes than Earl Browder to most Kansans. They will make Tito's Federal Union as obnoxious in Slovenia as the new regime was in 1870 to most Alabamans.

In Serbia, the opposition to Tito's central government and the local provincial government is almost complete. The Serbs of Serbia successfully resisted Tito until the very day when the Red Army entered the country. He has not won the Serbian peasants nor the Church nor the old parties. His methods and teachings are in conflict with Serbian traditions and national sentiments. Tito is considered almost as much an invader and foreign occupier as were the

Nazis. He is arousing as vehement an aversion to the term "Federative Yugoslavia" as Virginians long had for "damn Yankees."

In Macedonia, the revolutionary Communist minority will have more success in imposing itself because the masses of the Macedonians have long been cowed by terrorists and accustomed to ruthless foreign rulers. Also, Free Macedonia lures many of them.

In Croatia, the "Federative idea" is decidedly popular as a theory. The Croatians have long worked for federation as the bare minimum; most preferred even more, namely, complete independence. To satisfy that aspiration, Tito has promised that Croatia will be a sovereign state in the new Yugoslavia. The promise in itself is acceptable, but Tito's method of applying it is intolerable to most Croatians because the application means the negation of a false promise.

One must keep in mind that Croatians defied Hungarian masters, they opposed Serb tyranny almost unanimously, and most members of the Croatian Peasant Party rejected Dictator Pavelitch, though he promised to make "Free Sovereign Croatia" the light of the Balkans. All those are recent historical facts. In addition, the Croatians are devout Catholics and have an active body of priests. Croatia looks westward; it considers itself part of the Christian world. Clericals and the Peasant Party are combining against Tito's autocracy. After Croatia's long record of opposition to foreign masters, one can hardly believe it will accept Tito's Communist domination. And the Croatians, one must not forget, are very virile rebels.

So are the Montenegrins. They have the most sensational record of all the Balkan peoples in defying tyranny. No master has been able, for a protracted period, to impose himself on Montenegro. In as much as Montenegrin Communists play a grand role in Tito's regime and Montenegro appears to be lording it over Yugoslavia, the people may temporarily revel in the glory. Also, many Montenegrins are flattered by the honor their adored Russia is showing to leading Montenegrin Communists. Consequently, the new Yugoslavia for a time may seem a wonderful vehicle for enabling Montenegrins to be big shots. However, when the Montenegrin masses see that their Communist masters have deprived them of their patriarchal freedom and given most of them nothing in exchange, the traditional Montenegrin hatred of autocracy may again express itself.

In any case, Montenegro is a comparatively small factor. The outstanding fact is that within the three main groups of Yugoslavia, namely, the Slovenes, Croatians, and Serbs, Tito is followed by comparatively small minorities whose brutal coercive methods and teachings arouse abhorrence for any system they impose, including the six-state federalization. Tito's Yugoslavia is a pyramid resting on its peak, and therefore is unstable.

Furthermore, new Bulgaria adds another disruptive element. Bulgaria is united ethnographically, is comparatively well off economically, is in an aggressive, patriotic-revolutionary mood, and is favored by Russia. Its population of seven million hardy people is larger than that of any Yugoslav unit. If Macedonia comes under Sofia's domination, Bulgaria will be almost twice as strong as any of the "states" in federal Yugoslavia. It might take the leading role and play one Yugoslav unit off against another. In any case, a dynamic Bulgaria "on the make" and feeling reckless because of real or imagined Russian support, brings more danger than stability. It is to be remembered that Bulgaria has provoked, or participated in, Balkan wars in 1885, 1912, 1913, 1915, and 1941. Whether attacking or being attacked, it is not a stabilizing factor, especially at a moment of uncertainty.

To understand the nature of Tito's Federative People's Republic, one should try to place himself there, amid the people, and observe how it affects them. Never before in history have they lived together in one state, except from December, 1918, to April, 1941. They have been divided by bitter enmities for centuries and the recent war intensified their mutual hatreds. Their places of worship, given names, garments, holidays, ways of making the sign of the cross feed their animosities.

And now comes Tito with Liberty and Union. He arrives in a victory chariot, drawn by the splendid steeds of Slavdom and Russia. Both Balkan Slav-ruling dynasties have been removed, clearing the way for union. A new day is proclaimed. Serb, Croat, Slovene, Macedonian, Bulgar, all dance together, singing hymns of freedom.

But what comes of it? Repression, from one end of Yugoslavia to the other. There is one army with unified command, one powerful secret police watching every house and keeping a record of every family, one Party imposing political and cultural unity from Slovenia to Macedonia, one uniform torrent of broadcasts, one press, one system of state-controlled economy, one torrent of propaganda flowing down every valley and over every plain, one system of People's Courts, one Presidium, one dictatorial Politburo.

All that is as rigid as a prison with six cells. One will is imposed everywhere; one source gives the commands. "Tito is us; we are Tito," echoes in Skoplje as in Sarajevo. The dialects differ; the words are identical.

Tito and his Politburo rule in Belgrade; they rule in Ljubljana; they rule in Cetinje; they rule in Zagreb, as in every other town and every other city. And without opposition. Regional freedom from Tito, from his Party, his Police, his Presidium, his Politburo does not exist. The Slovene state, the Croatian state, the Bosnian state, the Serbian state are, in essentials, indistinguishable sections of the all-embracing Yugoslav state.

To be sure, there is unity based on coercion, as in many sad lands. It may last some time. Similar unity lasted five hundred years there under the Turks. Even longer under the Hapsburgs. But that is not what Tito promised, nor what his agents tell the world he is giving. It is not a federation of free units. At best it is as one army with one commander and six regiments.

CHAPTER TWENTY-THREE

Tito's Regime and the Yalta Conference

TITO'S Communist-led Partisan regime in Yugoslavia is an international creation. The U.S.A. has a certain responsibility for it. Strange as it may seem, the people of Texas, Oregon, Maine, and Tennessee are back of Tito's dictatorship, according to a decision of their federal government. Tito's determination and America's diplomatic weakness forced the American nation into the deplorable situation of sponsoring tyranny.

The Yalta Agreement definitely brings us into the Yugoslav picture. Subsequent to that, we publicly recognized Tito's totalitarian state, sent him an ambassador, and received an ambassador from him. The official report on the Yalta Conference, which was issued on February 13, 1945, over the signatures of Winston S. Churchill, Franklin D. Roosevelt, and J. Stalin, devoted seven paragraphs to "Liberated Europe." The three signers pledged themselves to assist the liberated peoples to solve by democratic means their pressing political and economic problems. The liberated peoples, they said, must "create democratic institutions of their own choice." The signers insisted on "the right of all peoples to choose the form of government under which they will live."

The three governments promised to assist the people in any liberated country in forming interim governmental authorities "broadly representative of all democratic elements in the population and pledged to the earliest possible establishment, through free elections, of governments responsible to the will of the people."

The Conference also made a report specifically on Yugoslavia. It recommended that a new government be formed by Marshal Tito and Dr. Ivan Subashitch, on a previously accepted basis. In other words, the President of the United States advised Tito how to form a regime, thereby giving his blessing to the prospective regime, when formed according to the recommendations. President Roosevelt, chief of the American Democratic Party and head of the world's mightiest democratic nation, contributed toward giving our allies, the Yugoslavs, their present totalitarian state. Mr. Churchill also chipped in on this Allied gift to the Yugoslavs, but later showed regret for his part in it. Speaking in Parliament on August 16, 1945, Mr. Churchill said the following, regarding Yugoslavia and other countries: "Not many members of the new House of Commons will be content with the situation prevailing in those mountainous, turbulent, ill-organized, warlike regions.

"We must make clear where we stand in these affairs of the Balkans and Eastern Europe.

"Our idea is of the people . . . being free to express by secret ballot without intimidation their deep-seated wish as to the forms and conditions of government under which they are to live.

"At present a family might be gathered around the fireside, enjoying the fruits of their toil, when suddenly there is a knock at the door and heavily armed policemen appear. It may be that the father, son or friend sitting in the cottage is called out, taken away in the dark and no one knows whether he would ever come back again or what is his fate.

"All they know is that they had better not inquire. There are millions of homes in Europe, where this fear is the main preoccupation of family life.

". . . Freedom from fear . . . has been interpreted as if it were only freedom from fear of foreign invasions. That is the least of the fears of the common man.

"That is not the fear of ordinary families in Europe tonight. Their fear is of the policeman knocking at the door. . . . It is fear for the life and liberty of the individual, for the fundamental rights of men now menaced and precarious in so many lands where people tremble."

Four months later Mr. Churchill made a still stronger statement, regarding Tito's regime.

Mr. Churchill's description of conditions in Yugoslavia is accurate, and it is well that he at last repudiates the totalitarianism, which he did so much to create. I well recall that in the summer of 1944, Mr. Churchill's son, Randolph, sent to the world press a story about idyllic democratic conditions in Tito's Yugoslavia. Practically every aspect of the picture was false. Tyranny was lauded as freedom, repression was called tranquillity, crime was extolled as justice, and people who had been robbed, en masse, were pictured as vying with one another in contributing their sustenance to the robbers.

For years Premier Churchill's vast propaganda apparatus did everything possible to popularize such falsehoods in Yugoslavia and throughout the world, while at Yalta he helped force totalitarianism upon the Yugoslav people.

The Yalta Agreement was sad and humiliating for America, as far as it concerns Yugoslavia, because it made us accept tyranny and then try to save our face by calling it democracy. Imagine the vigorous, outspoken American Republic, even while fighting Japan, being maneuvered into emulating wily, phrase-mumbling, face-saving Hirohito!

For example, the Yalta report copiously quoted from the Atlantic Charter and emphatically insisted that the Yugoslav people should "create democratic institutions of their own choice" and should have "the right to choose the form of government under which they will live"; yet at the same moment our government assisted in setting up a regime which made the realization of these ideals impossible. What its arrangement amounted to was that America authorized a group of fanatical totalitarians to impose a dictatorship in order to introduce democracy!

The Yalta Conference recommended that a "new Yugoslav regime" be formed by Tito's taking the Subashitch group from London into his cabinet and by Tito's enlarging his revolutionary council through accepting in it, at his discretion, certain former members of the last Yugoslav Parliament. These changes involved the setting up of a regency to act for King Peter, an exile in London, and presupposed an eventual election at which the people would decide whether or not they wanted to continue the monarchy. To the superficial and uninitiated this agreement may seem not unreasonable, but actually it meant the capitulation of the United States and Great Britain to Tito. It was even worse, for it meant that as democratic America and democratic England established Tito's totalitarian dictatorship in Yugoslavia, they called it good and backed it before the world.

Of course Tito readily agreed, especially since he knew he had Russia's unlimited backing. However, he created no "new government," as Yalta required. He merely accepted a couple of unimportant Yugoslavs from London in a couple of unimportant posts at Belgrade and a couple more in imaginary posts. And even before handing out those jobs, Tito made the "Londoners" promise to pass under the yoke.

Dr. Ivan Subashitch, Premier of the Royal Yugoslav government was, naturally, not made Premier of the "new Yugoslav government." That post, along with many others, was taken by Tito. The former King's former Premier was made the titular Foreign Minister, with the theoretical right to travel about the world and say what Tito ordered him to say. Another Yugoslav "Londoner," Dr. Sava Kosanovitch, was made Tito's titular Propaganda Minister, to arrange Tito meetings, build up the Tito legend, and tell the world of Tito's democracy.

Later, Kosanovitch became Tito's Ambassador in Washington and openly attends public meetings in America directed against the policies of the United States government.

Dr. Subashitch represented neither a political party nor the crown nor a democratic group nor a newspaper nor even a table of coffeehouse cronies. He represented nothing but a few felicitous words in a Yalta face-saving formula. At Yalta, America and Britain had really said, "Dear Tito, take in Subashitch, so as to facilitate us in making speeches about democracy." So Tito did. Before long, he kicked Subashitch out and arrested him.

Young King Peter, in exile in London, had already grown very suspicious of what was going on and, shortly before the Yalta Conference, "fired" Dr. Subashitch from the "London Premiership." Then the British Prime Minister ordered the Yugoslav King strictly to refrain from meddling in Yugoslav affairs, which were to be left to Roosevelt, Churchill, Stalin, and God. Later, after a few futile protests on the part of King Peter, Churchill forced him to restore Dr. Subashitch to the fictitious premiership. Thereupon the Croatian statesman flew away to Belgrade, where he gratefully and humbly accepted any favor Tito might deem to offer.

Another Yugoslav "Londoner" accepted by Tito was Dr. Milan Grol, a Serb politician of high character and genuine democratic ideals, who had played a long and honorable role in Yugoslav and Serbian history. He was made Second Vice Premier without portfolio, receiving a title and nothing more. He not only had no power, authority, or responsibility, but was not even invited to sit at cabinet meetings. He learned about government acts from the government newspapers. He soon resigned.

Similarly, another non-Partisan from London, Dr. Juraj Shutej, a Croatian, was made Minister without portfolio, thus being left to hold an imaginary bag. The acceptance by Tito of these four "Yalta men" in nonexistent or titular posts did not affect the course or nature of Tito's government in the slightest. Even less than Hitler's accepting the collaboration of von Papen and Dr. Schacht affected Nazi policies.

Another Yalta measure was even more deceptive—if possible—than the trivial cabinet change. Tito was required to enlarge his Communist-led AVNOJ (Council of National Liberation) and place it on a broad democratic basis by adding to it suitable "non-Fascist" members of Yugoslavia's last Parliament or "Skupshtina."

This was about the same as though we had asked de Gaulle to strengthen French democracy by drawing the democrats among Laval's friends into the government. That "last Yugoslav Parliament" had been elected on December 11, 1938, under the direction of Prime Minister Milan Stoyadinovitch, one of the most out-and-out Fascists in Yugoslavia's history. Stoyadinovitch openly imitated Hitler's political methods and tried to form a party that would hail him as "Vozhd" or Fuehrer. The Parliament created under his premiership was popularly called a Police Parliament and his elections were called Police Elections. Of the 371 members, Stoyadinovitch had 304, because of a special election law. This parliament never had embodied democracy nor represented broad democratic elements; so how could it help Yugoslav democracy? In any case, Tito was free to reject every one of its members who in any way opposed him. He did pick a few of them and added them to his AVNOJ, but it was wholly a personal choice of time-servers or yes-sayers. That Yalta clause was simply the recognition before the world of Tito's self-chosen revolutionary Communist-led Partisan Council, a little group that had arrogated the right to govern Yugoslavia.

As a consequence of this Yalta arrangement, King Peter had to be given some status in Yugoslavia. Without that, Dr. Subashitch would have been no more important than any Croatian picked off the street. Whatever significance he had was due solely to Peter's kingship. The American President and Britain's Premier were sending Dr. Subashitch back to Yugoslavia as the King's mandatory;

they hoped thereby to get the King's foot into his kingdom, if only by proxy. At Yalta, America and Britain confirmed their recognition of Peter and their association with him.

And it was not only by inference. It was explicit. The Yalta Agreement confirmed an earlier agreement, according to which Tito had definitely promised that "a plebiscite would be held to determine whether King Peter should return or not, and in his absence the Royal Power should be exercised by a Regency Council." It was specifically established by the United States, at one of the most important conferences of modern times, that the Yugoslav people were to vote on Peter's return.

But in spite of that, Tito, during August, 1945, in a public speech before AVNOJ, snapped his fingers in the face of the United States and the Yugoslav people and declared that it was not compatible with Yugoslav democracy for Peter ever to return to Yugoslavia. In other words, Tito, the Croatian Communist, had determined what the Serbian people wanted. Just as Hitler, the Austrian Nazi, declared that he was the conscience of Germany. Tito proclaimed his will to be the will of the people, even in matters for which the United States had assumed a responsibility before the world. The King was officially dethroned as soon as Tito felt himself firmly in power.

I am not here making a defense of King Peter. He proved to be weak and vacillating and failed properly to lead his people during the most terrible crisis in their modern history. If he had been firm, self-sacrificing, and heroic to the end, living austerely and risking all for his nation, he might have won a place in Serbian hearts, as no sovereign since King Lazar of Kossovo. The Serbs would have sung of their heroic boy sovereign in market places and village inns, at grape gathering and wheat harvesting, for a dozen generations. They would have extolled the lad from Serbia, the scion of old Black George, the lion of the wooded hills, the eagle of the blue skies, who "alone and unsupported had defied Asiatic Stalin made of steel, the European Churchill of the ancient Marlboroughs, and mighty Roosevelt from legendary America." There would have been a candle burning before Peter's picture in half of Serbia's houses, as they burn before Saint Sava and "the Mother of God."

Peter missed that chance and personally deserves slight sympathy. However, the brusque repudiation of the dynasty by Tito actually meant the repudiation of an agreement with the United States and the humiliation of our government. But this development was foreseen by every observer of Yugoslavian events even as the Yalta Agreement was being signed.

That agreement came three months before the capitulation of Nazi Germany. The Allies and Hitler both saw that the end was near. In view of that, President Roosevelt conferred with the two other principal victors about plans for peace and democracy. He tried to find a way to give humanity the blessings he had often promised. One of the groups of people most in need of such blessings was the Yugoslavs. No one could fail to see that they were in extraordinary difficulties.

And only the United States, because of its might and democratic ideals, was in a position to help them, in any way. This does not mean that America's task was easy. It had already helped elevate Tito to a position of such power that it would have been difficult for even the greatest and best statesman to curb him, at that point. Nevertheless, something worthy, even though not very effective, might have been done. A worse fizzle than what came out of Yalta would be hard to imagine. And the saddest aspect of it is not the fact that we failed but the way in which we failed. We uttered pious words that were made ludicrous long before the year was out. We made arrangements that proved futile from the very first day.

Our government, through the President himself, officially stated that we were endeavoring to help establish, at the earliest possible moment, a Yugoslav government, representative of the people and responsible to them. However, spokesmen for our government at Belgrade, with complete unanimity, report that the regime which resulted from Yalta is not representative and not responsible to the people.

Yalta meant that we officially gave Tito a deed to the lives of all the Yugoslav men and women along with their property. And we did it with unctuous words about democracy, to the accompaniment of a Four Freedoms liturgy, as though we were doing something good. We gave America's enemies an opportunity to laugh at us not only for our temporary political impotence, but for our face-saving self-deception.

There is not one specific stipulation in the Yalta Agreement regarding Yugoslavia that actually aided self-government there. On the contrary, they all facilitated and hastened the establishment of what our own government now calls Yugoslav autocracy.

CHAPTER TWENTY-FOUR

What Is Tito Doing to the Common People?

THE supreme question in relation to Tito's regime is not how it acquired power—although that is very important—but what it is doing with that power. He said he was fighting for the common people and setting up a government of the common people. His agents have shouted "Freedom to the People" until the cry reverberates through every valley. They have plastered "Freedom to the People" over the land so profusely that the words gleam from every village. Having held power now for three years, Tito has had time to show what he can do. What has he done—for "the People"?

First, he has deprived them of freedom in practically every form. He has placed them under a Communist dictatorship.

The country is ruled by a conspiratorial party which, in turn, is run by a secret executive committee or Politburo. There are no broad, free Communist Party congresses or caucuses. There is no free election by village or town Party members, of Party representatives, who in turn elect the principal Party chiefs and the supreme Party head. On the contrary, a group of strong, daring, fanatical Communists, who were trained in conspiracy and who led the Liberation Movement during the war, have placed themselves at the head of the Party and exercise almost unrestrained control over it.

Foremost among them is Josip Broz-Tito. Though not the brightest or cleverest or most forceful, he is master. He has often been called a figurehead or front, but that opinion is erroneous. It is denied that Tito is a Croatian or even a Yugoslav. It is said he speaks Serbo-Croatian with no characteristic local accent, as though he had learned it from a book. Experts do not agree upon his history prior to 1939. But these matters are of little importance. Continuously since the summer of 1941, a self-confessed Communist, called Josip Broz-Tito, has been leading a revolutionary movement in Yugoslavia. He has been acknowledged as chief by his closest associates. He has met many sharp-witted foreigners, especially from Britain and America, and impressed them all by his self-reliance, assurance, versatility, and constancy of purpose. He has shown himself to have many qualities of leadership, has proved capable of holding his own against all odds, and plays as commanding a role in Yugoslavia as Generalissimo Stalin in Soviet Russia. I am sure he is a former Croatian worker from the town of Klanjats near Zagreb.

As Stalin has able, expert associates, so has Tito. He is surrounded by strong, hard men, who know what they want and are ready to take any measures to get it. Number one among them is Edward Kardelj, the Slovene. He is appreciably younger than Tito, narrower, deeper, more doctrinaire, better read. In some ways he is abler than Tito. As a former teacher he is better educated. From his youth he has been a devoted Communist. He tried to spread the doctrine among his fellows in little Slovenia which lies in northwest Yugoslavia. He despised the Catholic church to which most Slovenes are deeply devoted. He detested the prevailing clericalism, distrusted the little clique of intellectual Liberals, scorned the rather crude leaders of the small Peasant Party, spurned the Socialists as too soft and compromising. He wanted a sweeping reform that would uproot established society and bring in a new order. He worked untiringly for that, suffered persecution for it, went abroad, became a crusader in the world movement, followed the directions of the Third International, and prepared for "the day." When the day came he found himself in Yugoslavia and from the beginning played a leading role, soon winning general acceptance as Tito's chief adviser and associate. He largely runs Yugoslavia's foreign affairs. Far more important, he is among the half-dozen men running the party.

Yugoslav Communist number three is Moshe Piade, a Serbian Jew. He is the only Yugoslav Communist of pre-war fame in the highest party leadership. He has a classical revolutionary biography. Under the old regimes he boldly expressed his opinions in books, pamphlets, and conferences, accepting all the consequences. He urged a total overthrow in accordance with Orthodox Marxism. He excoriated the "tyrannical dynasty, the opium-giving National church, the corrupt politicians, the predatory bourgeoisie, the helpless peasant parties," and called for a revolution on the Soviet pattern. He was frequently arrested, condemned, and confined in prison. He willingly lived in poverty, finding compensation in working for the cause. When his cause triumphed, he accepted all the brutalities, terrors, and horrors associated with it and serves it both as chief ideologist and leading executive. He is one of the most powerful men in the Balkans. His favorite task is to weaken the Church and destroy private initiative.

Not far behind is Milovan Djilas of Montenegro, representative of a whole Montenegrin Communist phalanx. He is accused by his enemies of being of Albanian origin. Youthful, restless, cruel, and irrepressible, he brings fire and fury to the leadership. He took up the Communist cause as a youth, longing for power and seeking an escape from frustrations associated with his bare Black Mountains. He risked imprisonment and persecution without hesitation, helped organize the network of Communist cells, plunged unreservedly into the Resistance Movement at the outbreak of the German-Russian War, and was in the thick of much of the fighting, early becoming one of the many self-appointed generals. They made Tito Marshal; he made them generals. He was very close to the Russians, early went to Moscow on a special Partisan commission, and has shown himself to be as daring in politics as in fighting. Kardelj is smooth and informed; Djilas tempestuous and superficial, but hard and unflinching.

Somewhat similar to him is a much older man, a Serb, Sreten Zhujovitch-Cherni. The "Cherni" is a nickname, meaning black. It reminds one of the first Serbian revolutionist, Black George, who founded the Karageorge dynasty. Zhujovitch is dark, dry, sharp-visaged, suspicious. Brave as most Serbs, he took a leading part in Partisan fighting, early becoming a general. He is fanatical, intolerant, ruthless. He is the prototype of a "Great Serb," insatiable in his desire for national expansion and party domination. He is the type of man whom, through all the ages, you could imagine riding over desert and plain, smiting unbelievers, exalting the "true faith," and seizing power, wealth, and glory while doing it.

More sinister than any of the above-mentioned is Alexander Rankovitch, a former tailor, now head of the secret police. He is bitterer, slier, more Oriental, meaner than the others. He brings to the movement and to his powerful office years of frustration and envy. The world overturn, Yugoslav greatness, Russia's glory played smaller roles in his red visions than the desire to get even with more fortunate neighbors. He was lured by the words of hatred and destruction in Marxist teachings, by Communist vituperation of the bourgeoisie. And now he is in a position to crush and smash and wipe out and remove "as a cancerous growth," the "enemies of the people." He read of that in a dozen books, he heard of it in a hundred radio speeches. Those imprecations, so often uttered by eloquent comrades, became sweet to him. Now he daily and nightly searches out the Party's enemies. And eliminates them.

Such are six of the top men who run the party that runs Yugoslavia. Perhaps there are two or three others in the innermost circle. Andrija Hebrang, a Croatian partially of Jewish origin, might be among them. He has played a leading role from the beginning and is a fanatic for economic socialization. He exercises a powerful influence in driving the Party further and further toward extremes in the field of state ownership of trade and production.

Another powerful man at or near the very top is the Montenegrin, Major General Svetozar Vukmanovitch, whose conspiratorial name is Tempo. He distinguished himself by Communist activity while still a high-school student and continued when he became a law student in the Belgrade University, where he eventually got a degree. He was arrested for his activity, brought to trial, and released because of the intervention of influential bourgeois friends. After June 22, 1941, he entered the fight for Soviet Russia, choosing Macedonia as his field of operation. The lawyer soon made himself a general and became one of the small group of commanders of the Liberation Army. His fame outran his military achievements, but he won an assured place at the top. When the Liberation Front was established in power, Tempo took over the task of giving political education to the army. He became Chief Commissar. In other words, all Yugoslav youth pass through his hands and he teaches them what to think.

Such Communists set the pace and give the tone. They draw up the plans and make the decisions. But they are not isolated. They are not a group apart. They do not hold their sessions in an ivory tower. About them and closely associated with them are at least twenty other strong men of about the same caliber and equally rabid. Several are from Slovenia, even more from Montenegro, and a fairly large contingent from Macedonia. Most are fairly young. A majority entered the movement as students; only a few were known ten years ago. A large part won their places during the war. They are harder, braver, narrower, and more ruthless than ordinary Balkan politicians. They have staked their all on the continued domination of Communism and will fight for it at all costs.

To such persons is entrusted the freedom of the approximately sixteen million inhabitants of Yugoslavia. They were not chosen by the people. None had ever had an opportunity to perform peacetime service for the people. They are all revolutionists brought suddenly to power by the victory of the great Allies over the Axis. Most of them served world Communism in Spain. They are extremely, even furiously, earnest, capable hard workers. May it not be that they are using their gifts for the common good? At least, that they are accepting non-Communist cooperation?

A first glance at general appearances might give the impression that they are not monopolizing power. One cannot deny that they have preserved some of the forms and formulae of democracy. Neither house of Parliament, for example, has a large majority of formal Communist members. Nor is the Yugoslav cabinet composed exclusively of Communists. The Ministers of Education and of Justice, for instance, are not formal Communists. The original President of the National Liberation Front, Ivan Ribar, now the President of the Yugoslav Republic, may not be a Communist. Neither is Tito's Ambassador at Washington a Communist.

The political framework in which the new republic is set, namely, AVNOJ, or the National Liberation Front, is not solely Communist—in form. It is a front, a coalition. Tito's spokesmen say it is a People's Front, representing all the democratic elements. They speak of half a dozen parties participating in it. A reading of such an authoritative reference work as *The Statesman's Year Book* seems to confirm this picture; it shows the cabinet as emanating from several parties.

Before discussing whether or not this appearance is deceptive, we should do well to recall that King Alexander during his dictatorship also used men of many parties. No Yugoslav Communist tires of repeating that Alexander was a Fascist. When the Partisans shout "Death to Fascism" they have in mind—among other things—Alexander's methods and dynasty. They especially detested his former general, Peter Zhivkovitch. They loathe Alexander's son Peter. However, let it be repeated, Alexander used men from every party. Of course he picked them out himself. Many of them were stooges. He lured or inveigled political renegades into serving him. He even had two Raditches, a son and nephew of the martyred Croat Peasant leader. May it not be that Tito has followed the same practice in choosing representatives of various parties?

The answer is easy and unmistakable. There is not one vital, established political, social, or religious force in Yugoslavia behind Tito's regime. Not one authentic leader of any major Yugoslav political group supports AVNOJ and its masters. This is a sweeping statement which any student or expert may verify.

The Roman Catholic church of Yugoslavia in its entirety opposes Tito. The number of Catholic priests within the borders of pre-war Yugoslavia who voluntarily aided the Partisans can be counted on one's fingers.

The Orthodox church in Serbia was unswervingly and aggressively opposed to Tito. It still is, in spite of the fact that it lost practically all its property. The authentic leaders of the powerful old Serbian Radical and Democratic Parties have been unreservedly against Tito. Even the half-Communist leader of the extremist branch of the small Serbian Peasant Party, Dragoleub Yovanovitch, is against Tito, while the leadership of the bulk of that party is aggressively opposed to him. A few renegade members of the Serb Peasant Party serve him, as renegades served King Alexander. Most members of the small Independent Democratic Party are against Tito, though one authentic chief, Sava Kosanovitch, serves him. No non-Communist Slovene of any political or religious importance serves Tito, except Dr. Drago Marushitch, who won fame by aiding the pre-war "Fascist regimes." As for the Croat Peasant Party, long representing most of the Croatians, its authentic leaders were long in exile or in jail under Tito. They were treated by the Partisans as their chief enemies. A few Croatian Peasant renegades serve Tito, as a few served Alexander's dictatorship.

Factually, therefore, as we go down the list of every major political, social, religious organization or force in Yugoslavia we see they have not joined Tito's Front. They do not consider it a People's Front. They call it a fake and a sham.

But let us look deeper. We do not need to use the process of elimination to solve the question of who runs Yugoslavia. We can easily see what posts the Communists hold. No informed observer of Yugoslavia denies that the premiership, the army, the police in all its branches, the courts, the schools, the radio, the press, the theaters, trade, industry, finance, social security, food distribution, labor, and jobs are in Communist hands. The names of the Communists controlling each of these vital institutions are known and could be immediately given. Most of them function openly and officially as Communists. It is plain that any group of men controlling such agencies and forces in any state are in a position of absolute mastery. Outside of them there is no effective power and no moral power, except in the church and in human hearts. This can only mean that Tito's People's Front is fictitious.

The Front is a "front," designed to hide a Communist conspiracy. To this day no group in that Front officially knows the strength of the Communist Party, its budget or its expenditures or its sources of revenue. No non-Communist knows precisely the members of the Politburo. The non-Communist elements in the Front not only have no power but are not even allowed to know *exactly* who exercises power.

Continuing further with a tabulation of the institutions *officially* dominated by Communists, one may mention the Committee of Jurisdiction which serves as a Parliamentary steering committee and supreme interpreter of laws. In a word, it makes and interprets the Yugoslav laws, which a submissive legislature rubber-stamps. Of its eight members, five are known Communists, while the other three have distinguished themselves by eager service to the Communists. At least four of these five known Communists are members of the Communist Party's Central Committee and of the Politburo.

The Reparations Commission, which has charge of all funds that may be given to Yugoslavia for reconstruction purposes, contains twelve members, of which eight are Communists. The President of the Commission is the forceful Slovene Communist, Boris Kidritch, Minister of Industry, President of the Economic Council, and member of the Communist Party's Central Committee.

Of the thirty-three members of the Presidium of the Assembly (lower house of Parliament), which serves almost as President of the Republic, twenty-five are Communists, among whom are most of the members of the Politburo.

Of the twenty ministers in the Federal Cabinet thirteen are Communists, including six members of the Politburo.

Of the fifty-eight members of the Executive Committee of the Liberation Front (AVNOJ) thirty-eight are Communists, including practically the whole Politburo and the other foremost Communists.

The first thing that Tito has done to the Yugoslavs is to give them a Communist dictatorship, poorly disguised behind a Front. And an outstanding feature of that dictatorship is terror. I want to illustrate this by two moving cases of desperate fear. One was the flight of thousands of Slovenes from the Izonso Valley near the Italian city of Gorizia, into Italy, when in February, 1947, a small zone there was turned over to Tito by the American-British armed forces. This transfer came as a result of the signing of the Italian peace treaty and the migration was described by *The Christian Science Monitor* on February 18, 1947.

A fourth of the Slovene population in the area fled from Tito into the destitute, unsettled, former enemy country to escape Tito. They left homes, fields, furniture, and everything. Some of them had been Partisans. They were humble working people, peasants and artisans. For more than twenty years, prior to World War II, they had been cruelly oppressed by Italian Fascists, denationalized, and deprived of schools. They had longed for freedom, worked for it, fought for it, but they saw what Tito's "Freedom for the People" meant and when the great moment of "Liberation" came, these Slovenes preferred exile in a hostile land, among former enemies, to freedom in Slovenia and Yugoslavia. That is how they chose freedom.

Here is another case of flight into freedom. As World War II was drawing to a close, I was in Bari, Italy, which was filled with Tito's Partisans, who maintained in the vicinity a number of hospitals for their wounded. One day a girl dressed in American clothes, as were most of the Partisans, came running into a house where I was visiting. She said, through her tears, that she was a Serbian refugee from Bosnia and had been serving as a voluntary nurse's helper in the Partisan hospital. In the course of her work she had expressed doubt regarding some Communist practices and had aroused suspicion. She had been called a Chetnik and threatened with punishment. A commissar had told her, "The night will swallow you up!"

She cried a long time there in our presence before she could be quieted, yet in her tears I also saw joy, hysterical joy. She exclaimed she could hardly believe that she was "out of their clutches." She was one of many such refugees from Partisan institutions that I personally saw. The dread of a night swallowing people up hung as a specter over many Yugoslavs in Bari. It hangs over many in Tito's People's Republic.

Americans have been impressed by two convincing examples of this. One is the insistence of Tito's representatives at international conferences in Paris, London, New York, and other places that all "Displaced Yugoslavs" be forced to return home. Tito's government repudiates the right of asylum. The Partisans do not want America, Britain, the United Nations, or any other organization or country to give shelter or food to Yugoslav refugees. They want to get their hands upon them. Mrs. Eleanor Roosevelt has more than once met this Yugoslav opposition to political asylum. For at least three thousand years "places of refuge" have been accepted by the human race. Even ancient barbarians, under certain conditions, spared their bitterest enemies. But Tito's People's Regime rejects that type of mercy.

And who are these displaced Yugoslavs? Some are Serbian prisoners of war taken in April and May, 1941, as they were fighting against Hitler. They are the kind of men who brought Yugoslavia into the war on Britain's side at a time when Tito and Stalin were with Hitler. As some of them were being captured, Russian and Yugoslav Communists were helping Hitler. Yet now the People's Regime insists before all the world on having them sent back home for execution.

Likewise, in notes to the United States government Tito admitted that more than one hundred thousand persons were kept at forced labor in Yugoslav labor camps two years after the end of the fighting. Tito called them Nazis and Fascists, which is his name for every opponent.

This insistent, public refusal of asylum and this justification of slave labor illustrate the attitude of the People's Republic toward violence and terror. Tito has deprived Yugoslavs of any inalienable right to life. I have seen a carefully tabulated list, covering five hundred large typed pages, of the names of Serbs whom the Partisans were accused of having killed. Each case was described in detail. The victims were from many Yugoslav towns and villages. Some were peasants, a number were workers, most were members of the bourgeoisie. Many were teachers, small merchants, lawyers, priests, reserve officers, judges. They were champions of the established order—as are most Americans.

I would not vouch for the accuracy of every single case described in the book. It was prepared in secret under great difficulty as the war was still raging. A few of the persons listed as dead may have turned up later. But I personally know of enough individual cases that were described to convince me of the essential reliability of the report.

During a sojourn of decades in the Balkans, I learned intimately and profoundly of the violence that has long brooded over Balkan

TITO AND THE COMMON PEOPLE

homes. I have sat in Balkan valleys and pictured to myself how Romans, Greeks, Avars, sultans, Crusaders, and Nazis swept past, burning and killing. I have often seen Balkan women going to the cemeteries on All Souls' Day, and I felt that I heard them weeping for the dead of fifty generations. And now after all that, I have seen how Partisans, in the name of "Freedom for the People," stole from house to house, from market place to market place, from field to field, to eliminate their countrymen.

Such acts reached their climax when Tito's forces, following Allied victories and German withdrawal, entered Belgrade and Zagreb. I shall not attempt to fix the number of persons they killed. Many Croatians insist that one hundred thousand were killed in Zagreb and vicinity. The number of massacred Serbs is placed still higher. I think both figures are exaggerated. But it is certain that the Partisans marked their triumph by killing their fellow citizens on a large scale. The impressions of that carnage upon many Yugoslavs seem to have dwarfed the other horrors. Weeping was heard in thousands of homes. Fear swept as a storm through the land. Tito's triumph was identified in the minds of many Yugoslavs with blood. The red star on the Yugoslav flag, on the Serbian flag, on the Croatian flag, came to symbolize fratricide.

And that was only the beginning of the story. After all, there are more than fifteen million Yugoslav men and women left. Most have not been in jail or concentration camps. But no aspect of their life is free from actual or potential coercion. This is applied through many agencies.

For example, Tito and his People's Republic have maintained the largest army in Yugoslav peacetime history. Its official and real head is Marshal Tito. It is led by Communist generals and colonels and has been under close Soviet direction. After five years of fighting, its officers glow in the fervor of Communist fanaticism. Stalin's and Tito's pictures adorn barrack walls, multitudinous commissars drill all recruits in Communist doctrine, and hatred toward everything non-Communist is daily instilled. Through that school of hate must pass every mother's son, to learn that every Yugoslav who refuses to salute with uplifted fist or sing Tito's praises is "an enemy of the people."

Besides the regular army, or as a special part of it, one finds special Communist troopers belonging to the KOJ, the Communist youth organization. They are the picked and favored defenders of the regime, chosen for their physique, vigor, and devotion. They are especially well dressed, fed, housed, and trained and wear special insignia. They are as Royal Guards or as Hitler's tall, fanatical S.S. men, led by Heinrich Himmler. Their number runs into the tens of thousands.

Even more oppressive than the army is the ubiquitous secret police still popularly called OZNA, though its official name is now UDB (State Security Administration). I do not know whether its actual number is fifty thousand or one hundred and fifty thousand. No secret police secret is more secret than the number of secret policemen. However, it is ever present. It keeps a personal record, or "karakteristika," of every citizen. It tries to watch every home and office, to follow every overt act and expression of opinion. Neither letters, telephone conversations, or telegraph messages are beyond its vigilant eyes. It watches all movements of train or bus, listens to sermons and mass, notes who dares consort with foreigners, determines what must be said in speeches.

Jobs depend upon its appraisals. Food cards are distributed according to its recommendations. Rooms are rented or evacuated at its commands. Entrance to the universities and progress in the universities depend upon its secret reports. It prepares and suppresses popular demonstrations, arranges slogans which the people must shout. It sends youth off to voluntary labor service. It sits in the restaurants, imbibes at the bars, talks politics in the coffee houses, loiters in the market places, pursuing its victims. Enter the remotest village and it may ask you why you are there. Mingle with the throngs in the busiest boulevards and you may be under its eyes. When your door bell rings, or a stranger accosts you on the train, or your husband does not return at the accustomed hour, you think of Minister Rankovitch's secret police, in reality a branch of the Communist Party.

In such cases you may also think of the courts which serve it. They are People's Courts. Their official chief, the Minister of Justice, Frane Frol, is not a formal Communist, but a renegade member of the Croatian People's Party, despised by Croatian peasants, execrated by Croatian Catholics, dependent on Communist favors for his place, and faithful in serving them. The President of the Supreme Yugoslav Tribunal and the Vice-President are both Communists. The Supreme Public Prosecutor is a Communist, as is his chief assistant. The former was a political commissar. The Chief Prosecutors in at least five of the six Regional Republics are Communists.

The judges, mostly newly appointed, are Partisans, or dependent on Partisans, whose ideals of justice were acquired in the War of Liberation, where they witnessed many a drumhead procedure. They operate according to fiat-laws or laws made by a subservient parliament, containing not a single opposition member. Their aim is to strengthen the People's Regime. They gave examples of their juridical methods at the trial of Drazha Mihailovitch where the carefully selected public was hostile and where freedom of testimony was curtailed. The verdict, announced in advance by Communist leaders, was based on some testimony that was later proved false. The trial was more a political demonstration than a search for justice.

That political aspect of Partisan justice was even more strikingly demonstrated at the trial of Archbishop Louis Stepinats, the leading Roman Catholic churchman in Yugoslavia, who was accused of collaboration. Many of the men around Tito—even some members of his cabinet—were collaborators. The Chief Prosecutor at the trial had a questionable war record. And the Archbishop had been at first much in favor with Tito's Partisans. It was when he and his fellow bishops issued, over their signatures, a pastoral letter against Yugoslav Communism that Tito decided to dispose of the Archbishop. Yugoslavia's foremost Catholic churchman was sentenced to sixteen years imprisonment.

Yugoslav's People's Courts are designed to serve the People's Regime, which really means the Communist Party. From the nature of the famous trials carried on before the eyes of the world, one may conclude what happens in the thousand ordinary trials, held in little towns and villages, where Communist judges hastily try obscure anti-Communists, while well-trained Communist crowds shout "Death to the Fascists."

And the administration throughout the land is Communist-controlled. Tito laid the basis for it in 1943 at Jaice when he formed his revolutionary state to supplant the kingdom. The supreme source of power is the Politburo of the Communist Party. Under it are the six regional governments, each led by Communists, working behind a Front.

The Prime Minister of the Slovene People's Republic is Miha Marinko, Secretary of the Slovene Communist Party's Central Committee. Above him are the powerful Slovene Communists, Kardelj and Kidritch. The Croatian Prime Minister is Dr. Vladko Bakaritch, Secretary of the Croatian Communist Party's Central Committee. Over him are his Croatian Comrades, Tito and Hebrang. The Prime Minister of the Serbian People's Republic is the Communist Dr. Blagoje Neshkovitch, and about him is the whole Politburo, stationed in Belgrade. The head of the government of Free Macedonia is Lazar Kolishevski, Secretary of the Macedonian Communist Party's Central Committee. Montenegro's provincial government is headed by the Communist Blazho Jovanovitch, who is surrounded by a Montenegrin phalanx of the top Communists in Tito's regime. The Prime Minister of the sixth Republic, that of Bosnia and Herzegovina, is Rodoleub Cholakovitch, Secretary of the Central Committee of the Provincial Communist Party.

The regional governments are Communist emanations of the Communist-run federal government, and they set up the administrative apparatus in every county, township, and community. It all constitutes an unbroken network, with great Titos in Belgrade, almost as great Titos in Skoplje, Cetinje, Ljubljana, Zagreb, and little Titos in the smaller places. Everywhere one observes the same songs, slogans, placards, demonstrations, and economic system.

That economic system is state ownership and state control. Whether or not it is in accord with Marxian Communism needs no discussion. In any case, private enterprise is almost completely eliminated. One may recall that, during the war, Tito and his American apologists loudly proclaimed that the Partisans were for maintaining private enterprise. That was even written into the Yugoslav constitution of 1945. But by the end of 1946, through a law unanimously approved by the Parliament after a single day's consideration, Tito brought practically all industry and trade into the hands of the state, meaning of the Communist Party. Even before that, the Party had taken over many enterprises and controlled most of the others. At no time in any Partisan-dominated Yugoslav area has the right of private property been secure. And this applies to the country as well as to towns. The produce of the fields, even many fields themselves, is at the disposition of the state. Many Sovhozes, on the Soviet model, have been set up. No one's home or store or shop or factory or automobile or bank account is securely his own. Everything a man owns or produces may be taken at any time and has been taken in a large number of cases.

That includes one's job, whether one is a factory worker or white-collar official. All persons receiving salaries or wages must belong to the unions or syndicates, all of which are under a federation, controlled by Djuro Szalaj, a Yugoslav Communist of Hungarian origin who has come to Yugoslav direct from Russia. He brought with him the system of controlled labor. He and his office determine wages, places of work, hours of work. He prohibits strikes or public protests and arranges the speed-ups. He supervises the forced labor camps. He operates in close cooperation with the secret police and has power to hire, fire, transfer, or punish. Also to feed or to starve a worker.

The Yugoslav authorities can pronounce any man a Fascist or "enemy of the people" and thereafter deprive him of his property, business, home, or job and send him into a distant labor gang. Officially more than one hundred thousand persons are doing forced labor. Before the war there weren't one million laborers in all Yugoslavia. This means that more than one Yugoslav worker in ten has become a "slave laborer." Probably there are more than one in seven.

The Workers Syndicates or Labor Unions have been officially designated as instruments for Communist indoctrination. The Executive Committee of the Central Federation sets aside certain periods to be used for special Communist propaganda as "Schools for Communism." The Croatian Communist daily, *Viesnik*, recently wrote, "The Syndicates (Unions) must nurture the working class in the spirit of Marx-Engels-Lenin-Stalin . . . The Syndicates must be a school of Communism."

The attitude of Tito's regime toward religion and religious institutions is illustrated by the statistics reported in a Slovene Catholic paper, published in exile, according to which the 1916 parishes existing in Slovenia, Croatia, Montenegro, Bosnia, and Herzegovina in 1939 have been reduced to 401 and the number of theological students from 557 to 160, while 220 priests have been killed and 85 jailed. More than 400 have fled, the report said.

The Yugoslav Catholic bishops, in their famous pastoral that provoked the trial and condemnation of Archbishop Stepinats, said that 243 Catholic priests were killed, 169 imprisoned, and 89 disappeared, a total of 501. Many of these were executed after summary trials, without being permitted to partake of the last sacraments. All twenty-eight monks in one monastery are reported to have been massacred. Of the several hundred Catholic periodicals appearing before the war, every one was stopped. Also most Catholic seminaries were closed. Communist commissars have been sent to Catholic charitable institutions. Most land has been taken from the churches. This official, public report signed by seventeen bishops in Yugoslavia shows how Catholics appraise relations between Tito's regime and their church.

The attitude of most Orthodox priests in Yugoslavia toward the Partisan government is shown by an appeal which Irinej, the Bishop of Dalmatia, sent to his flock from exile. He said, among other things, that Yugoslavia had been turned into "a vast dungeon for all." "All are pushed toward forced atheism," he said, "and no one dares say what he thinks." "The Holy Serbian Orthodox Church," he went on, "is violently prevented from fulfilling its holy mission; its children are brutally snatched from its motherly embrace and given over to wretched 'reeducation' at the hands of the Church's barbarous persecutors." "It is plain," he almost shrieked, "that the creators of the new Yugoslav paradise are ideal servants of Satan and makers of hell on earth."

Dionisije, the Serbian Orthodox Bishop for the United States and Canada has expressed similar opinions about conditions in Yugoslavia.

Inasmuch as all the Yugoslav Catholic priests and practically all of the Orthodox priests are engaged in a bitter struggle with Tito's Communist-dominated government, their opinions cannot be accepted as entirely objective. They are the views of one side in an old and terribly furious fight. But all data from all sources show that the Yugoslav Communists are endeavoring to separate the youth from the churches, to curtail church activity, as American Protestants and Catholics understand it, to prevent the dissemination of Church publications, to deprive the churches of material support and to subject the nation to Marxist, materialistic, anti-religious teachings. American Protestants may sit back and rejoice as Tito's Communists persecute the two old "political churches," and they can easily find reasons for Tito's displeasure. But the Yugoslav Communists, in their aims and acts, are working against the Christian religion, in all its forms. A true Protestant Christian will find that an alliance, even in his heart, with Tito against non-Protestant churches is as a "pact with death and a conspiracy with hell."

The current attitude of the Yugoslav Communists toward the Church in all its forms was made clear by Dr. Vladimir Bakaritch, the Premier of the government of the Free Croatian People's Republic, who said at a public meeting in Zagreb, after Tito had been well established in power:

> "Faith is the opium of the people. This is the corner stone of every Marxist group in the world as far as religion is concerned. Marxism holds that all faiths and all contemporary churches, as all religious organizations, whatever they may be, are nothing but creations of the bourgeois reaction, which aid the exploitation of the working class and are deceptive.
>
> "It is logical that first place be given to settling the question of the attitude of the Communist Party to the Church. That is logical because, as is generally known and recognized, the Communist Party is the determinative factor in our land.
>
> "Religion will last only as long as reactionary forces rule human society."

The above, let it be repeated, is the current view of the present Premier of the main Roman Catholic "State" in Tito's Yugoslavia.

Another illustration of Tito's attitude toward spiritual values is his attempt to bring all Yugoslav cultural activity under his direction. To achieve this he has appointed a Political Commissar for Culture, Radovan Zogovitch, and this high official arranged a congress of writers in the Yugoslav capital. When the literary men and women had gathered, he said to them, "The dark spots in new Yugoslavia are the remains of the reactionary traitorous bourgeoisie, the fragments of the old colonial, predaceous state, the points of international reactionism and espionage, superficial people with feverish yearning for foreign intervention and restoration of the past."

After that, the Cultural Commissar complained about the lack of literary creation in new Yugoslavia. He told the writers that they "were behind the times" in quality and quantity. They should make up this loss and do their duty by singing the praises of the Red Army, of Yugoslav Partisans, of heroic couriers, of the Agrarian Reform, and of the present regime. "Write of the new hero," he urged, "of Mr. Nobody."

Mr. Zogovitch is the man who wrote the widely sung Partisan song, "Tito, you are us; we are you" and other devotional hymns to the Liberator. He is the faithful Communist Court Poet, but he finds other writers less active. He scolded his colleagues at the congress for not doing more along that line. "Not one single drama has been written about the War of Liberation and the building of new Yugoslavia," he said. Also he complained that there were no novels and no good criticism. He called for leaders in "political literature."

After that Tito himself mounted the platform to tell the writers what to produce. "I am against literary freedom that permits the writing of what is harmful," he said. "I don't agree with those who talk of so-called freedom of the press. Literary work must have a direction." Then he added the word of comfort. "If you don't succeed in making your writings come up to literary standards, no one will notice . . . You must get busy. Work, create, don't wait." He told them not to join international literary organizations and promised to send the worthy ones among them to study in the Soviet Union.

The seer and the bard are to be brought under Tito's control even as the prophet and the priest.

The women, in their activities, are also under Communist direction. The chief organization, swallowing up most of the others, is the National Anti-Fascist Women's Movement, and the President of its Central Committee is Mrs. Spasenija Babovitch, a leading Serbian Communist. Leaders of the Croatian Section are the Communists Matsa Gerzetitch and Kata Pejnovitch; of the Serbian Section, the Communists Ruzha Pribitchevitch and Militsa Dedier; of the Slovene Section, Angela Ocepek and Angela Mahnik, both Communists. The Macedonian, Montenegrin, and Bosnian Sections are also led by Communists.

The National Yugoslav Youth Movement or USAOJ is watched with equal care. Both the President and General Secretary are Communists, as are the leaders in each provincial branch.

The National Liberation Front of Yugoslavia for six years or more has cried, "Death to Fascism—Freedom to the People!" After exercising authority over Yugoslavia for three years, it has created a situation in which the people are deprived of freedom and has set up a system with most of the characteristics of Fascism. Neither life nor property is secure. Every phase of activity, from service in the army, through producing goods to selling them; from securing food, obtaining a dwelling, and getting a job, through studying in school, belonging to a woman's club and hiking with youth in the mountains, to composing a drama, singing a song, or worshipping God is under the supervision of Communist police, Communist administrators, Communist commissars, and Communist judges.

From the cradle to the grave there is Communist control. And even after burial, according to an official statement of the Catholic bishops, gravestones are desecrated by Communists.

CHAPTER TWENTY-FIVE

Tito Menaces Balkan Peace

TITO'S Yugoslavia, in its foreign policy, is an embodiment of National Communism. Revolutionary Communism is combined with expansive Nationalism to form the most powerful local force that has operated in the Balkans within a century. It is made still more explosive by the addition of Balkan Pan-Slavism and by a certain amount of cooperation on the part of the largely Slavic Eastern Orthodox church. So far, Tito's Yugoslavia has shown itself far more expansive than the Yugoslavia of King Alexander.

In appraising Tito's role as an international factor, one must first of all recognize his connections with Soviet Russia and world Communism. Tito's regime was placed in power largely by Russia—with appreciable Allied help—maintains the closest relations with Russia, and is a vital part of Russia's power system. This relationship between Russia and Yugoslavia is not a new development, nor is it exclusively dependent upon the nature of the regimes in the two countries. An absolutist Russian monarchy or a democratic Russian republic would also consider Yugoslav friendship vital to Russia's position as one of the Great Powers. In fact, Tsarist Russia was interested in that part of the world for more than a century.

The proximity of Yugoslavia to the Aegean Sea and to the chief Aegean port, Salonika, its long border with Greece, its Adriatic coast containing a number of excellent harbors, and its key position on the Danube have led Moscow to convert it into an integral part of Russia's vast outer bulwark of offense or defense. In theory, this relationship might be no more menacing to world peace than Britain's close relations with Holland or the United States' close relations with Cuba, but actually it is much more menacing. In any case, it is an ineradicable, international fact of major importance.

And that importance is increased by the closely related fact that Tito's Yugoslavia is a key section of the Communist World Front. Communism, in every country, is more than a local movement. It operates in more than sixty lands and in all cases is part of a world crusade. This does not mean its tactics are always and everywhere identical. In Detroit the Communists at certain times praised Roosevelt, at other times cursed him. In Rumania they parade beside the King; in Bulgaria they hate the very mention of the late King. In Czechoslovakia they are more moderate, in Albania more furious, in Belgium rather cautious, but all everywhere belong to a World Front, centering about Moscow, and all give supreme loyalty to Moscow. There is a world Party Line, and although it is not communicated daily to New York, Tokyo, and Sofia from Moscow, it is followed by all Communists everywhere, without much essential deviation or delay. The aim of World Communism is to create a World Union of Soviets centering about Moscow. And Yugoslavia is one of the most important factors in the struggle. It is the Communist pivot for the Balkans; it is a key for imperial Communist expansion in Europe, Africa, and the Near East.

Tito's government seldom acts for itself alone or for Yugoslavia alone. It usually has in mind Soviet Russia, the whole Balkans, three continents, and the world. It is one of Moscow's major fulcrums for lifting the world off its old, badly-battered foundations.

These deep, broad, intimate relations between Yugoslavia and Russia are so public that they need little comment. Tito himself and all his spokesmen proclaim them on every occasion. They have been dramatically illustrated at all the Pan-Slav congresses, especially at one held in Belgrade in December, 1946. The Yugoslav press made elaborate preparation for it. Delegates came from Russia and from all the Slav lands serving her. A permanent Slav League was set up with headquarters in Belgrade. The hero of the occasion was one of the greatest Russian military heroes, Marshal Feodor Tolbukhin. Another central figure was Russia's chief all-Slav leader, General A. C. Gunderov. The congress was proclaimed as "a new period in the history of the Slav peoples under the leadership of Russia." Copious expressions of gratitude to Russia for liberating Yugoslavia and the other Slav lands were poured out. Plans were made for continuous action among the Slavs of the world.

At the congress Slav Orthodox churchmen played a role, not comparable with that of the Marshal or General, to be sure, but far from negligible. At similar congresses in Skoplje and especially in Sofia the Orthodox church was more prominent and in all-Slav congresses at Moscow it is a major participant.

One would make a mistake in attributing decisive influence to Pan-Slavism or to Belgrade as a Pan-Slav center but he would make an equally serious mistake if he overlooked Pan-Slavism. Everyone knows the mighty role in Hitler's movement of Pan-Germanism. Centered in Stuttgart, richly subsidized, served by agents in many lands, it broadened and strengthened the world net of the Nazis. Pan-Slavism working out from Belgrade is designed to do the same for World Communism. It is active in North and South America and in many European lands.

And as Tito, with Russia's cooperation, places himself and his country at the head of the onward marching Slav world—at least symbolically—he and his associates have the feeling that they are part of an irresistible tide. Oswald Spengler has written of the Decline of the West and predicted the rise of the Slavs. We are often told of the coming "Slav century." The Slavs everywhere are celebrating their greatest victory over their ancient enemy, the Germans. With the Teutons crushed, Britain declining, the Latins in a partial eclipse, could anything seem plainer than that the Slav sun is rising over the world? Many Slavs are sure of it. And a watch tower from which the progress of that sun is proclaimed is Tito's Belgrade. That is a galvanic fact. In the hearts of Tito's comrades glows the triple vision of a grander Yugoslavia, of a Slav century, and of a Soviet world looking unto Moscow.

This exhilarating feeling of being on a cosmic band wagon finds expression in daily action. First, in establishing Yugoslavia's relations with its Balkan and Danubian neighbors, and then with the Great Powers.

Yugoslavia's attitude toward Rumania is one of official friendship, as was the case under the old regimes. Slav Yugoslavia and Latin Rumania have few conflicting claims, do not fear one another, and have never been enemies in war. They feel little mutual attraction and equally little mutual animosity. They were joined in the pre-war Little Entente and Balkan Entente and are now joined by their Russia-imposed regimes.

Yugoslavia's relations with Hungary are good, somewhat better than prior to World War II. Crushed and humiliated, Hungary is "keeping its place." Triumphant Yugoslavia seeks good relations with its repentant and helpless Magyar neighbor. Communist Tito shows a comradely attitude toward the Communist-entrapped Hungarian government. He insists on protecting the rights of small Yugoslav minorities in Hungary, as is natural, and gives not unfair treatment to a Hungarian minority in Yugoslavia. At any appearance of an independent spirit or of national restlessness in Budapest, Tito thunders out a warning about exterminating the remnants of Fascism, but that procedure isn't required very often. Communism in Hungary is the opposite of National Communism. It means the acceptance of national degradation. As long as the Communists of Budapest exercise a dominant influence and insist on national abnegation, they can count on Tito's good will. The Yugoslav Partisans treat the former Magyar enemy better than King Alexander did, because the former enemy is now obsequious.

Tito has also established cordial official relations with the former enemy Bulgaria. The Slav Bulgarians, Serbs, Croatians, and Slovenes now consider themselves brothers. This relationship may cause a radical Balkan development, namely, the unification of all the Balkan Slavs in a South Slav republic, extending from the Black to the Adriatic seas. In theory, I think this would be a good thing. If the Bulgarians want to be in the same state with the Yugoslavs and if the others want them, such unification should take place. It should not be opposed by Britain or America merely because it might happen to bring a strong Balkan state into being. The Balkan Slavs have the same moral right to unite—if they want to—as Italians, French, and Britishers had. But, as now envisaged, such a merging of Balkan Slavs would increase rather than relieve world and local tensions. It would—in effect—be an alliance against Greece, a Slav pact for acquiring an Aegean Sea coast. In effect, it would be an attempt to bring Russia to the eastern Mediterranean.

In this respect, Tito's policy, as expressed in words and acts, is aggressive and bellicose. At all-Slav congresses in Belgrade and Skoplje, claims have been raised to an outlet on the Aegean through Greece. The Bulgarian government has pressed its demands for Greek territory in official notes, as well as over the Sofia radio, in the press, at meetings. Tito's Partisans have been still more aggressive. In the Yugoslav press and over the Yugoslav radio they have repeatedly attacked the Greek government. Yugoslavs in Yugoslavia have carried on a propaganda campaign for "freeing Aegean Macedonia," that is, for partitioning Greece. Much propaganda literature has been smuggled from Yugoslavia into Greece, many revolutionists have passed from Yugoslavia into Greece and other revolutionists have sought refuge from Greece in Yugoslavia. Yugoslavia has encouraged the revolutionary, anti-government activity of Slav groups in Greece. The extent of Yugoslav aggression against Greece may be open to discussion, but the fact that Yugoslavia, by word and act, foments civil strife in Greece and encourages the movement for the partitioning of Greece is beyond question. In this anti-Greece drive

Tito is acting both as the master of Yugoslavia and the willing agent of Soviet Russia.

By all Balkan revolutionists except the Bulgarians, Tito is considered leader and champion, second only to Stalin. The Albanian Partisans consider themselves his immediate followers; the Greek Communists look upon him as an example, inspiration, and protector; many Slav Macedonians expect him to become the great unifier and liberator of Macedonia. Even the Bulgarian Communists hold him in high esteem, conceding him third place after Stalin and their own George Dimitroff. Present close relations between the Bulgarian and Yugoslav dictatorships make the Balkans more insecure than at any time between the two world wars. They are as the fuse to a bomb.

Tito's relations with Italy are of an even more explosive nature. Part of Tito's claims to Italian territory was based on sound ethnological grounds. Many of the inhabitants of Venezia Giulia, east and north of Trieste, are Slavs—predominantly Slovenes with many Croatians. They live in an area contiguous with Slovenia and had long wanted to unite with Slovenia, meaning also with Yugoslavia. From the moral, ethnological, economic, and political point of view, a unification of such Slavs with Yugoslavia was justified. Any other step would have been unjust. But in pressing his claims, Tito went so far as to demand sovereignty over almost as many Italians as the number of Yugoslavs he was freeing. His act of liberation would have been accompanied by an act of enslavement. If it was wrong for Mussolini to oppress Slovenes, much of the world thought it was equally wrong for Tito to insist on oppressing Italians. Into this dispute, also, were brought the questions of Trieste, of Russia's relations with Britain and America, and of World Communism versus capitalism. Tito fought as the champion of a fourfold cause: for Yugoslavia, Slavdom, the Soviet Union, and Communism. What he fought against was Americans, Britishers, Italians, and a large part of the United Nations. Tito himself, as well as many of his leading Comrades, repeatedly declared that it was a straight-out fight between democracy and reaction, between liberty and capitalistic slavery.

On the Trieste issue, Tito's regime showed itself a menace to world peace, fanatically expansive, bitterly hostile to the Western democracies. His Partisans carried on constant conspiratorial activity in the disputed area and were caught in several cases of brutal terrorism. His agents made violent propaganda on the spot, while his press and radio at Belgrade, Zagreb, and Ljubljana constantly portrayed Britain and America as Nazi lands. Caricatures pictured Yugoslavia's allies as Hitlers and Goerings. Tito's soldiers and agents even killed Americans, on land and in the air. And all this took place as America and the British Empire were supplying Tito with provisions worth almost as much as his whole current state budget.

No force in the Western world since V-E Day has shown itself so hostile to Britain and America as have Tito and his Partisans. Although no statesman in the world did more to place Tito in power than Winston Churchill, excepting Stalin alone, Tito has treated Britain as a mortal enemy. In 1944, the British and Americans actually saved Tito personally from the Germans. For a long period they clothed, fed, and equipped his army. They maintained scores of thousands of Yugoslav women and children in Italy and Egypt. The British protected him with their fleet on the island of Vis. Yet at that very time Tito and his Partisans defied the British. They openly offended the British in Italy, stirred up the Greek EAM against the British, encouraged the Albanian Partisans to threaten the lives of British liaison officers. I write all this from personal knowledge. As the British and Americans were maintaining and training Partisan armies in Africa and Italy, Tito surreptitiously left Vis and flew off to Moscow. His associates refused to let the British forces land on the Dalmatian coast, after the Allies had forced the Germans to evacuate it, and they seized practically all British property in Yugoslavia on the pretext that its owners had collaborated with the Germans. Rarely in its long history has Great Britain been so humiliated even by a Great Power as it was repeatedly insulted by Balkan Partisans that were incited by Tito. And that hostility continues unabated.

Toward America Tito and his regime may be even more hostile, perhaps because America is more of a world factor. America is not only treated officially as an enemy but the Yugoslav government appears to go out of its way to compromise, offend, and actually injure America. Tito acts as though he were serving as a light brigade, or an advance guard, for Soviet Russia in fighting the United States. He seems to be testing out how far he can wear America down or how much America will take. He seems to lead the shock troops of Communism and Slavdom against the United States.

For example, he kept a number of Americans as "slave laborers" and long refused to give even civil attention to United States notes about them. It is true that this dispute was two-sided, because some of those Americans may have been of German origin with unfavorable war records, but Tito treated the United States government, when protecting American citizens, as though he were dealing with an enemy, not an ally daily giving enormous aid to Yugoslavia.

Also, his government arrested a twenty-two-year-old American citizen, Roy H. Stoeckel of Kearney, New Jersey, who strayed across the border from Austria into Yugoslavia. This dispute also had two sides since Stoeckel took pictures. But that they were vital pictures seems improbable. That such picture taking, at such a point, at such a moment, by a citizen of an Allied land constituted a danger to the Yugoslav army seems difficult to believe, even preposterous. But even if we should grant that the young American had violated the code of honor among allies, he was accused of nothing more serious than taking pictures on an unimportant frontier more than a year after the close of the war. Nevertheless, he was condemned to four years in prison, which was later reduced to five months. In the whole affair Tito treated the Americans as citizens and officials of an enemy country.

Mihailovitch's trial, also, was largely directed against America. An effort was made to compromise American officers and the American army and to make us appear as collaborators with the Nazis. It was a dramatic display of hostility to the United States.

The trial of Archbishop Louis Stepinats was of a similar nature. It was not directed specifically against America, since this is not a predominantly Catholic country. But the trial was the boldest recent act of defiance on the part of any Communist-governed land against religious organizations. It is true that Tito had reason to be displeased with the Croatian Catholic clergy. Not only did they vigorously oppose Communism, but a few had committed reprehensible political acts. The bishops' pastoral admitted that. Nor does the American nation believe that any clergyman of any faith is above state courts. But the manner of the trial, the nature of the evidence, the character of some of the witnesses, the record of the state prosecutor, and the political nature of the case made the condemnation of Yugoslavia's leading Catholic prelate appear as though Tito were hurling defiance in the face of the Western world. Tito seems to delight in throwing up barricades against the West and in flouting its ideals.

More flagrant than any of these things was the shooting down of two American planes and the killing of five American soldiers. There seems to be no doubt that this was done deliberately. It is true that Tito considered himself provoked. He charged America with air-spying. But at that moment America was feeding literally millions of Yugoslavs. America was Tito's ally and we were all trying to make peace. Yet Tito's army deliberately killed Americans. It is difficult to interpret that shooting as anything but the act of a rash and irresponsible statesman, in whose hands Balkan peace is not safe. It may be that the Americans were technically at fault in touching Yugoslav air, but is there any conceivable justification of Tito's blotting out such Americans in time of peace! Tito is engaged in a kind of war with America—and a war of aggression.

After that came the closing of the American information service in Belgrade. Tito's official and unofficial agents are constantly working in the United States. His ambassador participates in meetings against the United States government. Delegates from Russia and Russian-dominated, Communist-governed lands have spoken at meetings in New York and other cities; yet at such a time Tito closed the very modest American Information Center, because an official there secretly used an apparatus of the mission to mimeograph an article from a San Francisco paper unfavorable to Tito. The act of the employee was improper, but Tito's rude reprisal showed bitter and unrestrained hostility toward America.

Even more flagrant than that was the trial and condemnation of eight Yugoslav citizens allegedly serving as "American spies." Three were executed. This was an attempt to make the Yugoslav people afraid to associate with Americans and to show the world America's impotence. Tito seemed to take pleasure in killing friends of the Americans before American eyes, thus mocking American weakness.

The trial, followed almost immediately by the execution, served as an occasion for a general radio and newspaper attack upon three Americans officially connected with the American Embassy. The Yugoslavs were repeatedly told that America was trying to get state and military secrets for the purpose of undermining Yugoslavia and threatening the independence and security of the country. America was pictured as trying to mix in Yugoslav internal affairs, find a pretext for breaking off diplomatic relations, and promote economic war or armed intervention. Americans at the trial were reported as having said that the United States was "about to liberate Belgrade." The Communists screamed of an "American plot" or "conspiracy" against Yugoslavia.

And what was it that the three Yugoslavs were shot for having disclosed? Not an atom bomb, not a Yugoslav arms factory, not the amount of UNRRA material—if any—that was being used by the Yugoslav Army, but political news. The Yugoslavs were shot for allegedly telling Americans such things regarding Yugoslavia as American Communists report daily to the Yugoslav Ambassador in Washington about America without restraint, such things as constantly appear in the *Daily Worker* and many American newspapers. At the very time those men were being shot for giving information to Americans, Tito's emissaries were holding Communist meetings in a dozen American cities and publishing in at least four American papers every kind of attack on America. According to the prosecutor, "the spies" told the Americans that "more than a hundred thousand civil servants had been dismissed, without hope of making a living in any other way. . . . A large number of concentration camps are scattered over the land. Perhaps the number of persons deprived of liberty reaches hundreds of thousands . . . Heads of families are killed at the doors of their homes by secret police agents (OZNA) who bury them at once without even providing a coffin. Merchants disappear without leaving a trace.

"Fear reigns . . . Suicides are common . . . Civil servants must take courses in Communism. Communism and atheism are taught in the schools. Communist Youth Organizations disseminate hatred of parents. The children are taught to say to their parents, 'We owe our fathers nothing because they created us as an act of pleasure, and to our mothers we are indebted for only five quarts of milk.'

"Circuit judges go from place to place condemning people almost without trial. In the Sandjak, for example, a court consisted of a Communist, a Gypsy and a Turk. The woods are full of people out of their minds, and civil war is at our doors."

One of the "spies" was condemned to death for talking to another "about murder, sabotage, Chetniks, Crusaders (against Communists), . . . tapping telephone wires and secret radio stations." The "spies" were also accused of reporting on the strength of Communist armies.

The main point of this affair is not that three Yugoslavs were shot for reporting such things as the Communists of Athens write freely every day against the Greek government, but that Tito's government almost two years after the end of the war prepared a spy case against America. However, such a Communist act was not strange. Similar arrests and trials of natives working for or with the Americans were also carried out by the Communists in Rumania and Poland, but Tito surpassed his comrades in brutality and hostility to America. And without even the pretense "that the American spies" had taken part in overt acts!

So furious has Partisan hostility to America and Americans become that Americans dare not mingle with Yugoslavs. They even hesitate to call on Yugoslav doctors when in need. The former Ambassador, Richard Patterson, reported that within a few months fourteen of his personal friends were imprisoned.

Tito's government and police have shown and show pronounced hostility to American airmen stationed in Belgrade and serving our mission there. American fliers were and are treated worse in Belgrade than many captured American bomber crews were treated in Rumania during the war, by our enemy, the Rumanians.

The Federative People's Yugoslav Republic is a source of world insecurity and disequilibrium. From its extreme northwest corner, where Tito shot down American aviators and for three years has applied extreme pressure upon Italy, to the southeast corner at Ghevgheli, where Tito's agents, officially and unofficially, are aiding the Greek Communists in their fight against the Greek government, Tito's regime is a bellicose and explosive force. From Pirot in the northeast, where Tito's Communist Yugoslavs may join with Dimitroff's Communist Bulgarians in a state of twenty million dynamic Slavs, to the little harbor of Sarande in the extreme southwest corner of Albania, which is already a political and military affiliate of Yugoslavia, Tito aggressively works for Communist expansion.

And this is directed mainly against America, through Greece, Italy, and England. Tito mans the most advanced and most bristling

Soviet outpost against what is left of freedom in the world. He is repeating a terrible ancient aggression. For centuries the Turkish sultans turned Greece and most of present-day Yugoslavia into a battle front—then into a fortress—against the Christian West. The lines of the Church eventually held and finally became strong enough gradually to win back that part of Europe. Croatia, Serbia, Herzegovina, even Macedonia, after centuries of slavery, were restored to the Western world. Now that battle has begun again. Tito and his Comrades have attacked the world of free men.

Islam in that part of the world is being replaced by another claimant to total power. The crescent has given way to the sickle. The green banner has been supplanted by the red. Armed Communist conquerors now dominate valleys and heights where despotic sultans once were lords. This new drive against the Christian West is as momentous for the future of humanity as was that of the Ottomans. The wild cry "Ti-to-ti-to-ti-to" arouses the same type of blind, cruel allegiance as did, "There-is-no-god-but-God." The radio tower has replaced the minaret; the Commissar, the Moslem Hodja. America now meets what Europe met then.

It is not advisable to make long-range, detailed predictions about Yugoslavia. However, it is useful for advocates of true democracy to get a comprehensive picture of the basic trends and forces at work in that Republic. The preceding chapters have revealed a definite social and political pattern, and everything that has happened during and since the time they were being written makes the pattern clearer.

One of the basic and vital aspects of the Yugoslav pattern was revealed in an exuberant oration broadcast from Prague, Czechoslovakia, during the month of May, 1947. The speaker, Joseph Smrkovsky, a prominent Czech Communist, shouted, "Let the world know that our [Czechoslovak] frontiers do not end behind Kosice [near the eastern border]. They extend from . . . the Adriatic and the

Bulgaro-Greek border over thousands and thousands of miles to the Pacific. These are our frontiers, the Slav frontiers! Within that territory live 250,000,000 Slavs, who would defend our frontiers if anyone were to threaten them!"

This grand and sweeping picture places Yugoslavia in a united Communist realm stretching from the Adriatic and northern Greece, across the Balkans, eastern Europe and Russia to Japan. That fact fixes Yugoslavia's place in contemporary history. In that grandiose, monolithic Slav world, Yugoslavia is a key outpost and a cornerstone.

This opinion of a leading spokesman for World Communism and for Slavdom regarding Yugoslavia's alignment confirms what Tito himself and his leading Comrades have said many times. Yugoslavia is a unit in a continent-spanning, world-threatening political system. With each passing month the cracks and seams in the Communist-dominated Slav monolith are being filled and smoothed by drastic purges and a general tightening of the Communist Party. During the month of May alone, Soviet Russia and its Communist affiliates announced "reactionary plots" in every Communist-governed Balkan land, including Yugoslavia; and all the "plots" resulted in police action against non-Communist leaders.

One of the striking signs of Yugoslavia's "Gleichschaltung" and its submergence in World Communism was the treatment by Tito of Dr. Dragoleub Yovanovitch, Serbian leader of the National Peasant Party. During the month of May, 1947, he was thrown into prison on the pretext of being a spy (one of the most serious of all Communist charges), in spite of the fact that, during his whole career, he had been very close to Communists. He worked vigorously for Yugoslav-Soviet good will. He was elected to the highest offices in "New Yugoslavia," meaning to Parliament and the Presidium. But in those posts he was not a rubber stamp for Tito. He criticized the new state budget, pointed out defects in the Five-Year Plan, protested against terror, and frankly accused the police of robbing peasants of their grain. It was for his defense of peasants that he was liquidated—politically. This is not merely the tragedy of a heroic individual, but it marks the violent elimination of the last remnant of independence in the National Liberation Front. By this and similar acts Tito has shown, within less than three years from the time he entered Belgrade as a conqueror beside the Red Army, that his state will play the role of an unrestrained autocracy.

Each new development has brought into relief the militarism of the Yugoslav People's Republic. Exaltation of military force is an outstanding mark of the regime. One cannot safely refer merely to the army; he must say, "the Glorious Army." The events of each month show that Tito's People's Republic is a military state built about its army. More and more it speaks with the sharp voices of rifles. The noted Croat leader, Dr. Vladko Machek, was quoted on May 22, 1947, as saying that Tito kept 750,000 men under arms.

Tito's regime has almost wiped out economic independence. On the last day of April, 1947, the Moscow radio joyfully announced, "Over 90 per cent of the industry in Yugoslavia has been nationalized." This means that the Communist Party has laid its hands upon practically all the commerce, factories, means of transportation, shops, and even offices of the country. This is not a charge made by Tito's enemies: it is the boast of Moscow. May Day, 1947, was devoted almost exclusively to the inaugurating of Yugoslavia's Five-Year Plan, which will make the Communist Party master of almost every economic activity in the country, except some farming. And Moscow boasts that many collective farms (*kolhozi*) are being set up in the Balkans.

It would be useless to discuss whether or not that will benefit the Yugoslav people, and it is beside the point to stress how many Yugoslavs are being ruined to advance "the cause." However, one may properly point out that Tito and all his propagandists have repeatedly assured the world, especially America, that socialization was not in his plans and that he was only a "progressive democrat." He and all his Western apologists were offended when one American or another was so wise and firm as to say that Tito was a Communist working for a Communist economy. Even as late as the spring of 1947, Senator Claude Pepper compared the Greek EAM rebels to New England revolutionaries, and scorned the thought that the "few Communist leaders" might be planning a Communist regime or economy for Greece. Well, Americans of Senator Pepper's school kept saying that Tito would not communize Yugoslavia. But Moscow says 90 per cent is so communized and Tito introduces his Five-Year Plan with as much fanfare, intimidation, and ruthlessness as Moscow celebrates its own.

A part of this social system is coercive labor, as seen in the workers' brigades. In the Communist *New York Daily Worker*, of May 29, 1947, Anton Majnaritch, one of Tito's most active disciples in the U. S. A., and "editor of the Pittsburgh Croatian Paper, 'People's Herald,' now on tour in Yugoslavia," tells of a voluntary workers' brigade building an automobile road near Zagreb. But in spite of his lyrical description of the thousands of men, women, and children, from all walks of life, working on the road, and singing, dancing, and playing mandolins to show their joy in it, the fact remains that these people are victims of compulsion. Men and women, boys and girls, are forced to live together in rough camps. The system is almost identical with Hitler's system of forced labor.

In international affairs, the pattern of Yugoslavia's provocative role has daily become clearer. During the month of May, eight of the eleven members of the U. N. Balkan Investigating Committee said that Tito's Yugoslavia was actively aiding civil war in Greece. Also, Tito-trained and Tito-sponsored delegations from Trieste are appearing in various eastern European lands to arouse enmity against all non-Communist states. Their visits are reported over many Communist radios.

On May 21, 1947, the Indonesian Republican radio announced that a Yugoslav delegation belonging to the World Federation of Democratic Youth was visiting the Indonesian Trade Union Congress in Java. Communists were there from other lands also. Tito is helping liberate Indonesia.

The Prague radio of May 15, 1947, told of a "Slav Front in Hungary." One may believe that Tito, through this Communist Front and other agencies, did what he could to help effect the Hungarian Communist coup of the last of May, 1947.

Also Tito's agents—paid and voluntary, Yugoslav citizens and American citizens—are working in many American cities. They are especially active in New York, Pittsburgh, and Detroit.

But the main role of Tito's Republic in international affairs is to serve as an extension of Russia. When Hungary, on the last of May, was brought inescapably into the Russian geographical orbit, thus enlarging the land bridge between the U.S.S.R. and Yugoslavia, Tito's Republic became a direct geographical prolongation of Russia, bringing it to the Adriatic, the border of Italy, and the vicinity of Salonika. The permanent military highways from Moscow to Trieste are open and unimpeded.

Tito's latest activity in the field of religion, closely following the line set in Moscow, is somewhat cautious. On the one hand, it seems to be influenced by the same considerations that induced Italian Communists to take steps toward pacifying Italian Roman Catholics; on the other, it aims at capturing the Serbian Orthodox church.

On May 28, 1947, the Moscow radio broadcast that "Alexius the Patriarch of Moscow and all Russia left yesterday for Rumania on a return visit to the (Rumanian) Patriarch Nicodemus. Patriarch Alexius is accompanied by the Metropolitan of Leningrad and Novgorod, Gregory, . . . and other clergymen. . . ." In other words, the Russian church sent an imposing delegation to appear before Rumanian Christians. Other delegations visited France, the United States, and Czechoslovakia. High Russian churchmen have also gone to Bulgaria. These visits have borne some fruit. The Russian church has succeeded in drawing the eyes of the Orthodox world to Moscow.

Naturally, one asks whether Patriarch Alexius has Stalin's support in his efforts. One cannot doubt it. Gregory Karpov, an active Communist, is head of the "Council for the Affairs of the Orthodox Church," and he closely watches the church's activities and endeavors to make it an instrument for helping Russia play its world role. The Russian Orthodox church is certainly trying to influence the Serbian Orthodox church, and Tito naturally is helping. He has very recently made a few concessions to the Roman Catholic church, illustrated by the restoring of a Catholic publishing house, and he has sought cooperation from Croat and Slovene Catholic peasant politicians, but has not been well received.

Meantime, Tito devotes his chief energies to undermining all religion. He seeks to do this by exalting Communism, by raising himself to the position of an idol, by turning Stalin almost into a God, and by attracting men, women, youth, and children to Communism by all the means at his disposal.

During the first week-end of June, 1947, the Belgrade radio reported that Tito received a group of visiting Bulgarian journalists and told them that "the free Balkan nations must form a strong monolithic unit." And he left no doubt as to exactly what he meant. He said in precise words that the Bulgarians and Yugoslavs would have to join against Greece, which he called a menace. He called for unity of action on the part of the Balkan Slavs. He included Albania in the Slav combination.

Thereby Tito defined the role of his Federative People's Yugoslav Republic. He is preparing it to unify and lead the "free" (meaning Communist-governed, Soviet-dominated) nations of southeast Europe against their neighbors. And he is doing this as a part of the world-wide, Moscow-directed campaign of Imperial Communism against America and America's friends.

www.ingramcontent.com/pod-product-compliance
Lightning Source LLC
Chambersburg PA
CBHW021356290426
44108CB00010B/259